# THE
# KNOWLEDGE WORK FACTORY

# THE

# KNOWLEDGE
# WORK
# FACTORY

Turning the Productivity Paradox
into Value for Your Business

## WILLIAM F. HEITMAN

New York   Chicago   San Francisco   Athens
London   Madrid   Mexico City   Milan
New Delhi   Singapore   Sydney   Toronto

1 2 3 4 5 6 7 8 9    QVS    23 22 21 20 19 18

ISBN:      978-1-260-12215-2
MHID:          1-260-12215-8

e-ISBN:  978-1-260-12216-9
e-MHID:      1-260-12216-6

**Library of Congress Cataloging-in-Publication Data**
Names: Heitman, William F., author.
Title: The knowledge work factory : turning the productivity paradox into
    value for your business / William F. Heitman.
Description: New York : McGraw-Hill, [2019]
Identifiers: LCCN 2018041807| ISBN 9781260122152 (alk. paper) |
    ISBN 1260122158
Subjects: LCSH: Knowledge workers. | Labor productivity. | Organizational
    effectiveness.
Classification: LCC HD8039.K59 H45 2019 | DDC 658.3/128—dc23
LC record available at https://lccn.loc.gov/2018041807

# CONTENTS

## PART I: **The Problem**

- What do a financial-services company and a tire manufacturer have in common?
- Why do 20 percent of earnings go missing—and unnoticed?
- Test your knowledge: three "spot the waste" stories.
- Introducing the concept of "virtuous waste."

- Buried in Babylon: the difference between tangible and intangible assets.
- Competencies: mundane work activities that are worth a fortune.
- Why your greatest assets remain unrecognized and underproductive.
- How unique is your business? Understanding the anti-standardization bias.

- Thirty thousand years of productivity improvements—in just five minutes.

- Should technology drive work activities—or the other way around?
- Why has knowledge work failed to improve when other work has wildly succeeded?
- The Industrial Revolution, "big rocks theory," and the productivity paradox.

# PART II: **The Solution**

CHAPTER 4

- Perceptive biases that trick your brain into giving you incorrect information.
- Logic biases, flawed rationalizations, and profit-robbing false trade-offs.
- The "principle of least effort": not as simple as it sounds.
- Powering past your blind spots: techniques for "seeing the unseen."

CHAPTER 5

- The immutable elements of industrial—and knowledge—work.
- Three perceptual errors that make the brain ignore these elements.
- The "better mousetrap dogma": market-based suppression of business innovation.
- Touring the anthill of knowledge work operations.

CHAPTER 6

- The rise and (mostly) fall of org charts: an unmatched masterpiece from 1855.
- How knowledge labor-cost data go missing—and where they're hiding.

- Why knowledge workers believe they're "exempt" from productivity management.
- Five lessons from a century of failed organizational theories.

- Taking inventory: the overlooked products your knowledge workers create every day.
- How "false complexity" erodes productivity—and impedes standardization.
- Lessons from the factory floor: adapting product-based management to knowledge work.
- A finance department case study: best intentions, worst outcomes.

- Beginning with basics: capacity and work products.
- The 1914 productivity death match: Frederick Taylor vs. Henry Ford.
- Separating the management of work from the performance of work.
- Reducing variance to boost productivity up to 30 percent— without technology.

# PART III: **The Turbocharge**

- "The five maybes": a simple path to business-process improvement.
- How to outachieve the overachievers to reach better-than-best-practice performance.

- Why today's knowledge work is tragically under-automated.
- Documenting and managing predictable patterns in business processes.

- Overcoming the three challenges to activity-level knowledge work improvement.
- The "periodic table of knowledge work activities."
- Which work activities are "unique"? Shattering a longstanding misperception.
- Tales of terror: real-world examples of hidden waste (with happy endings).

- Doubling and redoubling productivity, one wrench-turn at a time.
- A spreadsheet/robot smackdown.
- The Activity Cube: reconciling four "views" of operations.
- Vendor hype versus reality: how much can you actually automate?

- Counterintuitive strategy: how to win by playing "not to lose."
- Crossing the void: three strategic milestones.
- Building your knowledge work factory: a two-phased approach.
- Demons of the deep: how to avoid common implementation traps.

*For Renate*

# INTRODUCTION

# JUST ANOTHER DAY AT THE OFFICE

The following story might sound familiar. The details won't be—like all the illustrative examples in this book, it's a composite—but most of today's businesspeople will relate to the general theme.

There's a reason I want to start this journey with a simple story about good people dealing with avoidable problems. I'll explain in a minute. But for now, let's consider the story of Josh and his attempt to write something as seemingly simple as a management report for call center operations.

Josh is a smart guy. He's got an MBA from a top school. He's the very picture of the modern knowledge worker, or "white-collar worker" in somewhat older parlance. And when this story unfolds, he is an important player in the finance group of one of the world's leading consumer packaged goods producers.

It's 9 a.m. on a Friday, and the phone buzzes in Josh's office. The CFO is calling. "Morning, Josh," she says pleasantly, but Josh already knows the drill. The politeness barely masks the hair-on-fire urgency of her call.

"Morning, Jill," replies Josh, looking dolefully at the little framed photos of his wife and kids on his desk. And sure enough, the drop-everything request that Josh expected shoots forth from the other end of the line. It practically burns Josh's ear as he hears it.

"Cost of inbound call servicing . . . last six quarters . . . sorted by major cause . . . but by regional center . . . yep, yep . . . got it . . . ," he says, frantically jotting notes and forcing cheerfulness when he wants to scream, "Didn't I just do this *last month*?! And what about all the other urgent reports I needed to get done *by the end of the day today*?!"

This scenario is common among knowledge workers, and it's only going to get worse. But as this story unfolds, and the urgent requests cascade further through this organization, ask yourself, *What is the cause?*

*Why is this happening? Is it avoidable?* That's what this book is about: what goes wrong in today's knowledge work operations, why these problems occur, how much business value they squander, and—most importantly—what can be done to prevent these drains on business value from happening in the first place.

## The Data Dude

Marching orders in hand, Josh had his work cut out for him. But he did have some salvation, in the form of Alex, one of his top analysts.

Alex was sort of the anti-Josh. A physics undergrad who aced his master's degree in information technology, Alex was one of these "Chill, dude" types, with the man bun, the man cave, and his online gaming buddies. Working late on a Friday wouldn't faze him; he'd just join his pals later, since they were spread across multiple time zones all over the world. It was just a normal day for Alex.

I'd said that Alex was an "analyst." While that's technically true, it's misleading. Alex proudly identified himself as Josh's "CDW," or "chief data wrangler." He'd been with the company for four years now (he joined straight out of grad school) and didn't care about the *business*. He looked at his job from more of a hacker-gamer perspective: crazy requests like the one Josh just handed him were his specialty. They appealed to his almost innate ability to "dumpster-dive" through the company's disorganized mess of databases to tease out the information he needed. It was a challenge to him.

No one ever trained Alex. He figured it out himself, with the help of the other data wranglers at the company, who exchanged tips and tricks over coffee, like a little hacker collective.

Did they write any of this down? Did they *document* any of this vital information? Of course not. But as we'll see throughout this book, that's business as usual for today's knowledge work organizations.

## Alex on a Mission

Alex knew how to find the information that Josh desperately needed (because *Jill*, the CFO, desperately needed it . . . because *Dave*, the COO, desperately needed it . . . and because . . . well, let's not get ahead of ourselves).

What did Alex know that Josh didn't know? A lot. He'd been in these weeds before. He knew that only 20 percent of the call center's data would be recognizably labeled and useful "as is." A full 60 percent would be totally unsalvageable and unusable. That left about 20 percent—*of all the data*—for Alex to wrangle into a form that actually mattered. This was every wrangler's "sporting challenge." Alex would spend the next 12 hours writing mini apps and scripts that queried and tested the data in the company's virtual "dumpster." He'd rack his memory, recalling nooks and crannies in the various systems he'd come to know over the years. When he finally finished, he turned over a data set to Josh (with the caveat "I'd say this is about 70 percent accurate") and head home to his Xbox.

During the drive home, Alex waxed philosophical. "What's the point?" he wondered. Sure, he was paid well. But why spend his best years on a corporate hamster wheel? The irony, he knew, was that just a few months of firmwide data *cleaning*, in lieu of *wrangling*, could eliminate these problems at the source. That kind of standardization work could even be outsourced to the company's low-cost offshore centers.

But that wouldn't happen. After four years with the company, Alex had seen it all before. Lots of times. All the senior suits would blow a fortune on some shiny, new technology that made big promises, which *he knew* it couldn't deliver. And he was just an analyst. But sure enough, like clockwork, he'd see the droves of bright-eyed college grads from the tech vendor's company swarming all over the offices, installing their ingenious new "solution." He could see through this stuff like the emperor's new clothes. *All they were doing was transferring the same shoddy data from the old system to the new one.* There was no process to actually man-

*age the data in the first place.* Talk about job security: he could stay "chief data wrangler" for life.

But that wasn't to be the case. When Alex got home, he found an intriguing letter in his mailbox. It was a job offer and onboarding package from a hot, new tech start-up in Seattle he'd recently applied to. He'd give his two weeks' notice on Monday—and take all of his hard-learned tribal knowledge out the door with him when he left.

## Meet Dave, the COO

The following Monday morning, bleary-eyed Josh turned in his report—replete with Alex's wrangled data—to Jill, who had requested the report in the first place.

But Jill can't be blamed for all of this. She'd gotten a drop-everything request from Dave, the COO. And before you heap blame on *him* . . .

Dave's got an impressive background in manufacturing operations. He's one of these logical thinkers who's always trying to get to the root of a problem. "We can't do that! That's just a Band-Aid!" is one of his signature complaints. But Dave had gotten word of an urgent brainstorming session that was called by the divisional CEO. *The objective:* Generate ingenious, breakthrough ideas to improve operational performance, slash costs, and boost customer satisfaction. And do it quickly. Both the board and the competition were breathing down their necks.

That's why Dave originally had asked Jill for the call center report. Now he paged through its findings; he jotted down a laundry list of ideas he'd suggest in the upcoming meeting. To him, each seemed like a no-brainer.

For example, he'd propose closer coordination between the call center and marketing. That's because the people in marketing never included call center managers in their planning process. The result was that poorly worded promotions flooded the market, and the call center staff, in turn, were flooded by queries from confused—and angry—customers. Where was this new "lower pricing" they were promised? Why wasn't that coupon accepted? Where was the "free gift" they were supposed to get? Blindsided by marketing, the call center managers had no time to prepare proper scripts for their reps—who were just as confused as the customers. The current backlog of complaints topped 50,000. For the class-action attorneys who represented customers, it was blood in the water, and they were circling like sharks.

Next on Dave's laundry list came suggestions for the company's billing group. Invoices were so confusingly formatted that customers called the contact center with questions all the time. The company's "self-service" website was anything but, which drove even *more* customers to the call center. There, on hold, they'd be infuriated to hear a recording suggest that they hang up and visit the company website.

At the retail store level, the company's sales reps were equally confused. In an attempt to surmount the problem, Dave's operations group had installed quick-reference instructions at each point-of-sale terminal; retail reps simply needed to pull up a screen for help. But they didn't. When walk-in customers had questions, *the retail reps simply speed-dialed the contact center for help*. It was easier. Dave bristled at the thought. It was an insane waste of margin. But only one of hundreds.

## A Happy Ending?

The big brainstorming session didn't go the way Dave wanted it to. In reality, it went the way CDW Alex had predicted. Rather than roll up their sleeves and tackle the mundane mess of junk that was clogging the company's operational arteries like so much bad cholesterol, the CEO and chief marketing officer—surprise—decided to make a big push with new technology. Brand-new, costly systems. Sexy, new mobile apps. (These would replace the last generation of "sexy, new mobile apps," which had failed to reduce the same errors in new account setups just three years prior.) It would all work miracles. Why were they convinced? Because the vendor promised it—and those demos were so cool. And there would be a slick, new "management dashboard" that would provide a magical view of all these promised improvements. Jill, the embattled CFO, was the lucky recipient who would have to make the dashboard work (wranglers wanted). "Gee," thought Dave, trudging out of the meeting afterward, "I'm sure that all this shiny, new technology will solve everything . . . Yeah, right. It's just another Band-Aid."

## An Old Solution to Modern Problems

That's enough storytelling for now. I think you get the point. Although the problems they faced were as big as they were disparate, all the players in this story have one thing in common: *they all lack a low-tech approach to their challenges.* In other words, they need *industrialization*—standardization, specialization, and division of labor.

The following chapters explain, step by step, how to do just that. All these examples are based on real-world challenges that my firm, The Lab Consulting, has helped Fortune 500 leaders overcome, using techniques successfully honed over the course of 25-plus years. And get this: *none of the techniques in this book requires new technology.* Improving knowledge work operations is about finding, and eradicating, the impediments that are hiding in plain sight.

To begin with, it's necessary to see problems from a new perspective—albeit one that's been practiced, in various degrees, for a very long time. We'll take a whirlwind journey from the hunter-gatherer economy through modern business, tracing these trends to their roots. We'll see how the most valuable assets in today's businesses have migrated and how to capitalize on this massive shift. We'll delve into the brain's predictable biases and blind spots to understand how to avoid false trade-offs, such as "Should we cut costs *or* improve the customer experience?"

Because this is a book about improving the productivity of knowledge workers, it's also necessarily a book about *people.* It's about their perceptions. Their habits. Their all-too-human foibles. And ultimately, it's about the stunning business value that can be unlocked by understanding and addressing the root causes of avoidable work that plagues knowledge work operations today.

# THE

# KNOWLEDGE WORK FACTORY

# PART I

# THE PROBLEM

# CHAPTER 1

# WHERE IS WHITE-COLLAR WASTE HIDING? IN PLAIN SIGHT!

The numbers are shocking. Today's knowledge workers waste *a third of their day, every day,* on activities that could be reduced, consolidated, or eliminated altogether. These efforts are misperceived as customer service, creative problem solving, or simply the unavoidable cost of doing business. But nothing could be further from the truth. This is "virtuous waste," a catchall phrase for the types of well-intentioned error correction, review, rework, overservice, and needless variance that permeate virtually every aspect of knowledge work operations today.

Among the Fortune 500 alone, this virtuous waste squanders over *$3 trillion* in shareholder value each year. Currently, that's roughly equal to the *combined* market value of Facebook, Apple, Amazon, Netflix, and Google (collectively known as FAANG), or figured another way, 11 percent of the value of the S&P 500.[1]

## Virtuous Waste Squanders $3 Trillion in Shareholder Value

- 10 million total knowledge workers are employed in the Fortune 500.[2]
- 30 percent of their work activities are avoidable virtuous waste.[3]
- 3 million full-time equivalent workers perform avoidable virtuous waste activities.[4]
- $180 billion is spent on compensation to these virtuous waste workers.[5]
- 20% of earnings[6] are diverted to this virtuous waste compensation.
- $3 trillion in value[7] to shareholders is lost to virtuous waste.

But that's merely the *direct* cost. The *indirect* costs—and strategic risks—are immeasurable. While knowledge workers are furiously busy performing these avoidable tasks, they fail to spend enough time—and thought—on the truly important parts of the business. They're not innovating. They're not investigating ways to make their work more effective. And they're certainly not measuring their own productivity. This is important because their work is the most valuable in the business: converting prospects into sales, transforming unmet customer needs into new products, and understanding where margin is made—and lost—throughout the enterprise.

If you ask people, at any company, about their efforts to find and eliminate this waste, they'll tell you, "Sure, we do that already." True—but not well enough. Typically, a company's *office furniture* is more rigorously documented and managed than its knowledge work operations.

So that's the status quo, and it's astonishingly persistent. All companies are doing the same thing. It's just business as usual. What, then, is the big deal?

Aside from the squandered value and massive opportunity cost, strategic pressures are mounting from the outside. Barbarians are massing at the gates. Activist and private equity investors are hassling companies to get productive, downsize their overhead, or otherwise reduce this waste. Most dangerous of all are the digital hijackers. They want to steal your knowledge work, digitize it, and possibly abscond with the rest of your business. Amazon and Uber are the most high-profile examples, first stealing the critical knowledge work activities of retailers and cab companies and then co-opting the rest of these value chains. Smaller companies, like Kabbage and Jobber, are digitizing the knowledge work activities of everything from small business lenders to plumbers and housecleaners.

This chapter provides three stories, all composites of real-world scenarios. Each story outlines precisely how knowledge work waste manifests itself in the frantic pressure of day-to-day operations and describes the competing priorities, deadlines, and obstacles typical of life in today's knowledge work organizations. It can be somewhat challenging to simply identify the waste. And from the individual employee's vantage point, removing this waste can seem like an insurmountable task. These stories illustrate the subtle characteristics of this waste. And if you detect a distinct feeling of *discomfort* as you read these tales, it's probably because you'll recognize characteristics of these scenarios in your business.

But before we talk about all this knowledge work waste, let's get our terms straight. Just what is a "knowledge worker," anyway?

## A Definition of "Knowledge Worker"

The term "knowledge worker" is attributed to management writer Peter Drucker in 1959. And while you can find varying, conflicting, and certainly *confusing* definitions of "knowledge worker" online (see the sidebar),

### A Knowledge Worker Is *What*?

If you search online for a definition of "knowledge worker," prepare to be confused. Wikipedia says that "knowledge workers are workers whose main capital is knowledge."[8] *What the heck?* It doesn't get more elliptical than that.

Then it adds that knowledge work differs from other work because its primary task is to perform "nonroutine problem solving" that requires "creative thinking." But what help is that? That could define *all* work.

Note that the original definition perpetuates a dangerous misperception. It says that the workers' knowledge is *their capital*. Really? Do they—or should the business—own the details of knowledge work? The *know-how*? Are knowledge workers really the best candidates to design their own work methods and improve their own productivity?

And is their work truly nonroutine? Do you really believe that it can't be standardized?

Spoiler alert: *Of course it can.* We'll be tackling these costly misperceptions, and others, in Chapter 4.

for our purposes, think of a knowledge worker as a traditional white-collar, or office, worker.

In the typical business, this includes all the employees who are not directly involved in making or moving tangible "things." They work in organizations such as sales, research, accounting, order management, customer service, engineering, human resources, and many more.

Note that this definition of "knowledge worker" *excludes* manual workers, blue-collar workers, and the armies of frontline service workers that populate industries such as retail, food service, transportation, and hospitality. Yet in some industries—such as financial services or healthcare—*everyone* is a knowledge worker.

By the way, some estimates claim that knowledge workers now account for over half of the workforce in the world's advanced countries. This book will use a more conservative figure of roughly 30 percent. Regardless, their productivity, or lack thereof, holds vast implications for a business—or even an entire economy.

## "Spot the Waste" Story 1: The Invisible Rework Factory

As vice president of operations for a top-10 U.S. property and casualty insurer, Bob was widely regarded as an operations "hero." It was part of his personality. Bob was an enthusiastic, collaborative, hands-on leader. He would never complain, never give up, and never ask his teams to do anything he wouldn't do himself.

Bob joined the company right out of college, after earning his undergrad degree with a double major in finance and accounting. When his kids got older, he went back to grad school for an executive MBA. Now Bob was sitting in his office at the company's headquarters campus (the "home office"), pondering what seemed to be an intractable operational challenge.

Like any other insurer, Bob's company had multiple operating groups. Some were responsible for marketing, sales, and product development.

Bob was responsible for virtually all of the operations "downstream" from these—from processing new business applications through final resolution of claims. There was a factory-like, end-to-end flow to his operations. His new business team received policy applications submitted from the company's sprawling network of insurance agents. This group would review each "app" and prep it for submission to his underwriting group, which, in turn, would either generate a quote for the agent or reject the prospect. If and when the customer purchased the policy, another of Bob's teams would shepherd it through the issuing process. An executed policy would be sent, or "issued," to the policyholder and the agent. And if those policyholders filed insurance claims, the claims processing group in Bob's organization processed and paid these.

So Bob was the leader of a crack team of end-to-end processing operations managers whose pragmatic, can-do attitude always managed to get the job done—whatever it took. But it was steadily becoming harder, each year, for all of his managers to keep up: their nights were gradually getting longer; their vending-machine "dinners" more frequent. And now the challenges were about to get tougher.

The new CEO wanted to grow revenue but keep costs flat, particularly employee headcount—a strategy she called "increasing operating leverage." The goal was to retain existing customers, but permanently price the company's policies more aggressively to attract new, high-quality policyholders—in the same markets, with the same high-value products and the same superior service. It was a conservative strategy, compared with the conventional growth strategy that targeted new markets with new lower-value products and deep, temporary "teaser" discounts.

This strategy didn't feel "conservative" to Bob. To meet these goals, his teams would have to process at least 15 percent more volume, yet still maintain their top-quartile service levels. No new hires would be allowed. Even a steady diet of late-night, vending-machine dinners would not give Bob and his managers enough hours in the day to pull this off.

Now the sales period was rapidly drawing to a close, and Bob was pushing his operations leaders to clear out a massive backlog of unprocessed work. Naturally, he didn't want his organization to be responsible for any delays in booking new sales to meet targets. While he could have gone home earlier and simply delegated this after-hours fire drill to his leadership team, that wasn't his management style.

Everyone across Bob's organization, from top to bottom, was busy. Slammed, in fact. So, clearly, there were no more worker-hours to be had. And the staff efforts required were quickly exceeding the definition of "heroic." That's because a full 40 percent of new business applications arrived "not in good order," or NIGO, in industry parlance. That meant that these applications required substantial remediation by Bob's people, with multiple e-mails and phone calls to the agent or the customer, or both.

As Bob was pondering his capacity problem, he got a call from Jane, the enthusiastic new head of IT. A vendor had just shown her team an exciting, new, cloud-based application for the field agent sales force. Jane saw this as a chance to help Bob and his new business team. NIGO applications would be a thing of the past. The new technology would require agents to complete their electronic applications correctly before the system would accept them. "Everyone in the industry is adopting this," she claimed. "This technology will do the standardization work for you."

Bob thanked Jane for the news. He asked her for a link to the technology demo and promised to look it over soon. After he hung up, he groaned to himself at the idea of yet another tech solution—too slow, too costly, and these had never met the vendors' promises in the past. And then Bob briefly flirted with the possibility of transferring some of his group's work to Jane's IT organization. After all, the company was establishing a shared services center within IT. Maybe if he called it "insourcing," it wouldn't count as an increase in anyone's headcount?

Nope. That maneuver would never get past the CEO, or Jane.

## "Spot the Waste" Story 2:
## The (Re)Scheduling Experts

Raylene had worked at the tire plant for 12 years when she was offered her latest promotion to join the scheduling team. Raylene was excited. It sounded like a vital position.

Raylene was always good at math. After high school, she got her associate degree in engineering technology at the local community college. And while working at the plant, she easily mastered a half-dozen company-sponsored courses in inventory control, supply-chain management, lean manufacturing methods, and several others. Raylene particularly enjoyed the material she was currently studying to complete her Six Sigma Black Belt certification.

Raylene was eager to put her newly acquired knowledge to work finding and implementing improvements for the company. She was encouraged at the recent news that the company had appointed its first female plant manager. This was big news for Raylene. She felt that her career options were promising and feasible.

The plant scheduling team that Raylene joined was small, consisting of just seven engineers. But their purview was huge. They oversaw a plant that employed more than 2,000 workers and operated 24/7 throughout the entire year.

For her new position, Raylene's training was entirely learn-as-you-go (everyone was far too busy to write anything down). The first—and most important—thing that Raylene learned was that the plant needed to "make its ticket" every day. This was defined as achieving the daily production quota that was issued by the corporate office. Achieving zero variation from this target was the central focus of everyone on the plant scheduling team.

Raylene soon learned that her plant enjoyed a top-quartile ranking within the company for schedule compliance. But from day one, she obsessed over the production target. *How was this set? How could she help increase it?* She asked others on the team about this topic, but their responses were vague. Shrugging this off as just a quirk of the team's culture, Raylene settled in to learn more about her new job.

Her first assignment was to act as a roaming assistant for the entire team. This would provide her with an overview of the plant, prior to earning the responsibility for scheduling one of its eight subareas. Raylene was excited at what seemed to be a great, hands-on opportunity!

The plant's daily "ticket," or production quota, was prepared each day by the industrial engineering (IE) team at the firm's corporate campus. To generate each plant's ticket, the IE group kept a database of rigorous scheduling standards for every work activity on the plant floor and the distribution centers. For each standard activity, the company had developed precise estimates of the time required to perform it. These were detailed data. Activities were typically measured in increments of minutes (or even *seconds*). And just like each item in the materials or supplies inventory, each activity included a bar-code number. These standards, in turn, were arranged into a daily production schedule comprising roughly 100 subcomponents, or subschedules, for various machine stations and materials-handling processes—even the power plant that generated steam and electricity. A critical path model considered the sequence of activities and made certain that irrational combinations couldn't be planned into the schedules.

Wow! As Raylene learned about all this planning and precision that was already baked into the process, she began to wonder what, if *anything*, she would do with her time all day. Everything about the process appeared precisely documented and fully automated. Would she be forced to simply sit back and *watch* as this well-oiled machine hummed along?

No. Raylene got her wake-up call at 7 a.m., only two hours into the first shift. The news came fast and hard: Materials produced in the belting room couldn't be moved to the plant floor. Why not? All of the transit carts were full.

This had cascading consequences. Without the materials coming in from the belting room, the tire machines would soon go down. What was that adage? "For want of a nail, the battle was lost"? Something like that.

Raylene watched as the schedulers quickly huddled with the area foremen. And just like that, *they solved the problem.* The solution was ingeniously simple: they manually changed the product mix from the original schedule, keeping the tire machines "fed" and producing—and preserving the integrity of the all-important daily ticket. Raylene watched in fascination as scheduling engineers and plant technicians pulled out calculators and went to work to add single "override" line-item adjustments to the plant schedule. Everything calmed down.

But that was just the calm before the next storm. Barely a few minutes later, the plant manager received an urgent call from the corporate office. The head of corporate sales needed a schedule change—now. A major automaker—one of the company's oldest and largest customers—needed to accelerate a delivery or its assembly line would go down.

"Why was this an emergency?" Raylene wondered. After all, the plant was supposed to maintain a "safety stock" of those exact tires for that customer. But as it turned out, most of this emergency inventory had been depleted to fill a shortfall caused by internal scheduling changes earlier that week. Quickly, the scheduling team sent Raylene out to visit the plant warehouse to take a physical inventory of the remaining tires. This way, the team members could more accurately recalculate the new schedule overrides. Raylene nearly broke into a run. They needed those inventory numbers now!

By the end of the day, Raylene was exhausted. She'd discovered that this dawn-to-dusk reworking of the schedule was business as usual. "I guess this well-oiled machine has more human glue holding it together than I'd imagined," she thought to herself. Viewed in this light, Raylene realized that her new job wasn't about scheduling. It was about full-time rescheduling. That's because, in addition to the plant manager and the head of corporate sales, more than *100 plant foremen and production team supervisors* were able to request schedule modifications. Their requests came whenever machines failed, raw materials were unavailable, or maintenance crews finished late. Each change was well intentioned, even heroic. All the people in the plant shared a common goal: they all wanted to "make the ticket."

Raylene adapted quickly. She soon developed a pocket crib sheet that she used to adjust the schedule and improve the daily compliance score. Like her coworkers, she didn't think much about improving productivity anymore.

## "Spot the Waste" Story 3: The Case of the Conflicting Customer

Tom had worked for nearly two decades at one of the world's largest and most renowned media companies. He was currently the COO of the Americas division, managing operations for both print and digital media properties that included newspapers, books, and television broadcasting.

Now Tom sat in his home office, late one Sunday evening, with a pad of sticky notes, poring over a thick, internal document of market research findings. He'd already tagged more than a dozen pages as he wondered to himself, "Why isn't anyone else familiar with this document or its findings?" The report was an extensive, annual survey of customers' purchase-related needs, based on interviews conducted by a well-known market research firm.

Now, on a Sunday night, the report felt like a mystery file. Fully three years ago, when Tom was named COO of the division, no one had ever mentioned it. It was like it never existed. Yet here it was, packed with relevant information that kept Tom up late and turning pages.

Tom resolved to quietly solve this mystery. He'd begin asking around, discreetly, starting at tomorrow's meeting with the division's marketing/sales executive team (MSET) to review the team's new strategy to increase advertising profitability for the company's many newspapers.

Tom was well suited for this task. His early career was in aerospace engineering. And despite his low-key manner, he had a Sherlock Holmes–

like ability with facts and analytical reasoning. That's what helped him sail through his MBA program, change careers, and move into executive management.

Lately, however, Tom found that his rational style was at odds with the more intuitive approach he encountered in the media business. Tom wasn't fazed. He could be as persistent as he was mild mannered.

Still, the challenges facing Tom were formidable. Newspaper sales had been declining steadily for years. How could Tom and his team possibly grow revenue and margin, which were concentrated in what's known as "display ads"? These are the artwork and photos for everything from local car dealerships and furniture retailers to national, even global, makers of computers, mobile phones, and perfumes. These display ads ran in both the print and digital editions of the newspapers. They were the lifeblood of the revenue stream.

Tom pondered this challenge as he stepped into the MSET meeting. It was the grand unveiling of the team's new strategy for addressing customers' top, purchase-related priorities. The first three objectives for achieving these goals, as detailed in the new MSET strategy report, were clear:

1. Expand the "one-stop shop"—offer more ad products to customers.
2. Increase customers' "ease of doing business" with the company.
3. Introduce techniques enabling ad reps to act as "consultants" to customers.

These top objectives, Tom soon discovered, were offered by the MSET as justification for a massive new technology request.

Tom paused to discreetly pull out his dog-eared, sticky-noted copy of the market research report. As suspected, the "top needs" being discussed in this MSET strategy meeting were far down on the priorities list outlined in the "mystery report." In fact, the mystery report noted that the newspapers' existing customers were already well served—even *over*served—for these exact priorities. Why, then, was the MSET strategy targeting these lower-priority needs? More disconcerting than that: Why was it failing to target the mystery report's top three? Or even the top *five?* These needs were currently *under*served.

Tom investigated in his low-key manner. Rather than put people on the spot during the meeting, he approached them individually afterward. He asked them, simply, if they were familiar with this mysterious market research document that had captured his attention.

"Of course!" was the universal response. "We review it every time it's published." Then came the interesting qualifier: "But that's easy, because the thing hardly ever changes. And we've already satisfied the top customer priorities."

But as Tom gently probed the executives, he made an intriguing discovery. There was no consensus regarding who "the customer" was. The definitions he got were all over the map:

- Some said it was the reader of the ads.
- Others claimed it was the producer of the products or services being advertised.
- Still others said that "the customer" was the external media buyer who chose which media to use for each ad campaign.
- And one even said that the customer was the ad agency for the advertiser.

Even more troubling, when Tom asked any given executive whether he or she believed that the others shared his or her perception, the answer was always a confident "yes."

No one on the MSET seemed to consider that each ad sale would span multiple "customers," with varying—and sometimes conflicting—priorities, forming a complex value hierarchy and decision network. Instead, as team members individually read the report, they found their own personal perceptions confirmed somewhere within its hundreds of pages. And once they did, they seized on it and pursued it with passionate, well-intentioned focus. Now it suddenly made sense why the MSET members argued so stubbornly with one another whenever Tom tried to broach the subject of customers and their priorities.

## Quiz Answers: How Obvious Was the Waste?

The ensuing chapters will provide lots more detail about how to spot, and eradicate, the waste that's hiding—in plain sight—throughout all knowledge work operations. But first let's get back to the three stories at hand.

As you read these, bear in mind two important points: (1) This kind of waste is ubiquitous. It pervades knowledge work throughout all industries, functions, and verticals—worldwide. And (2) the lion's share of the improvements (75 percent) that eliminate this waste and deliver the vast majority of the benefits *don't require any new technology, product changes, or capital investment.*

Initially that sounds amazingly simple—unbelievable, in fact. However, this initial impression will change as you become more familiar with the perceptual changes and challenges involved. "Simple" is not necessarily "easy."

### 1. Bob and the Invisible Rework Factory

As you recall, Bob's organization was stretched to its limit. There was no way he could meet the CEO's new demands without more headcount—or by miraculously adding more hours to the day.

But Bob was mistaken. What he couldn't see was that his organization already possessed *more than twice the capacity* it needed to meet the CEO's new productivity goals. The reason could be summarized in a single word: variance. Bob's organization, like every other at his company, failed to consistently and quantitatively measure productivity. No such metrics existed at the individual-employee level. Instead, Bob's organization managed its productivity with summary-level averages. And many subgroups managed operations with line-item spending budgets designed by the accounting department. Consequently, Bob couldn't see that the best employees on his new business team—the top quartile—performed *three times as much work as the bottom quartile.* Nor could he see that the bottom quartile was also less effective in each of his subgroups. The new business team's low performers issued policies that had the highest level of customer rejections. Similarly, the claims processing team's low performers consistently overpaid more claims than the high performers did. But none of this valuable variance was visible.

Meanwhile, conventional knowledge work management methods limited the productivity improvement potential in Bob's organization. More variance. That's because few instructions existed for any work. Employees were free to design their own inconsistent work routines. Many of these included built-in, redundant checkpoints and review steps. These costly additions rarely changed the end product in any meaningful way.

And while each activity was performed with the best of intentions, many could simply be eliminated. Clear instructions for completing new business applications would cut the NIGO remediation work activity by *two-thirds.* Documenting work routines among employees who perform similar tasks would identify the best practices to transfer to the low performers. These could also provide the first wave of near-term standardization eliminating unnecessary work steps. This would allow virtually all of the remaining activities to be streamlined. And installing quantitative performance measures would document the improvement progress and reduce the threefold variance within weeks.

And what about that latest "IT breakthrough"? That was one story that Bob had seen before. He recalled, all too clearly, the time that new workflow technology was purchased and deployed for the field agents. The technology was installed according to spec, *but nobody ever standardized the work.* Variance won again. The promised highly structured "workflow assembly line" was never realized. Instead, the state-of-the-art technology merely served as a repository, essentially a glorified share drive, for work in process.

## 2. Raylene and the (Re)Scheduling Experts

Perhaps it was easier to spot "hidden waste" in Raylene's conventional factory than in Bob's "knowledge work factory." All of those adjustments to the schedule were taking their toll. On average, the daily plant schedule was manually modified more than 2,000 times every 24 hours. That's *730,000* schedule changes annually, or one for every 15 tires the plant produced.

What's worse, these manual adjustments were hiding, even encouraging, plantwide underproductivity. The belting-room episode is a perfect example. On the surface, it looked like a simple logistics problem that could be solved with the addition of more transit carts. But *why* were those carts full in the first place? It was because half of the materials filling them had passed their expiration date. And *that's* because the materials handlers didn't understand the guidelines for positioning the carts on the plant floor. Why didn't they understand? Because they were low-cost, undertrained external contractors. It's just one of a series of "for-want-of-a-nail" stories that replay every day.

The irony is that if the daily plant schedule had been evaluated like a tangible product (such as a *tire*), it would be subject to numerous quality checks. Periodic analysis would quantify the costs of its defects. But because the company viewed the scheduling team as a knowledge work/support organization, the group's intangible work product—the schedule—was not subject to similar rigorous quality checks. The costs of its defects were not quantified.

The scheduling team's routine adjustments technically kept the plant "on schedule." But this schedule was effectively a diary of daily changes rather than a management tool. This well-intentioned practice conspired to hide hundreds of small daily operating snafus that added up to a significant plantwide productivity shortfall of 13 percent.

Raylene and her colleagues couldn't see the stunning financial impact of this hidden waste. But *you* can. Given the robust demand for its products, the tire company's 13 percent capacity underutilization could have been filled—and monetized. The capacity shortfall cost about $46 million annually in lost gross margin—dollars that could drop directly to the bottom line. At recent price-to-earnings ratios for the company, this translated to *$435 million in squandered shareholder value,* or roughly $1.2 million per daily plant schedule. Put another way, each of the 100 plant-floor employees who visited the office to make their daily one-off adjustments to the schedule was costing the business and its shareholders over $4 million in lost market value.

### 3. Tom and the Case of the Conflicting Customer

When we last left Tom, at the world-famous media company, he'd detected a complex customer-priority matrix that wasn't fully or consistently perceived by the other members of the marketing/sales executive team (MSET). What's worse, these customer perceptions weren't centrally documented, defined, or reconciled. That's ironic. The company's newspapers did a better job of managing their ink and newsprint. Colors, digital code, display formats . . . all were centrally managed to ensure a consistent user experience and manage the company's august worldwide brand image. Clearly, the company knew it must invest to manage its readers' perception, an inarguably valuable intangible asset.

Yet this insight did not uniformly extend to its knowledge work assets. There, variance reigned unnoticed. In Tom's case, the diverse definitions of such basics as "display-ad customer" and "purchase influencer" didn't even merit a discussion, let alone a sticky note's worth of documentation. Figuring out how to meet these customer needs most effectively could transform this invaluable intangible asset into a competitive weapon, if the know-how were only documented within the company. But it wasn't. Unfortunately, that's not unusual.

The waste that all of this kept hidden is far bigger than you might think. Consider the issue of quality. As Tom queried the executives on the team, he found that everyone agreed that "quality" was a top priority for purchasers of display ads. Fantastic! A perception that everyone agreed on. But what exactly *was* "quality"? Again, the answers Tom got were refreshingly consistent. Everyone used terms like "image resolution," "paper fiber density," and "pixel quantity."

But this was the internal consensus. The following week, Tom attended a conference of advertisers. When he tested this definition of "quality" on them, they grinned. "Are you kidding?" they quipped. "You're a *news-paper*. We *expect* all those things at a *minimum*. When *we* say 'quality' we mean: Did you run the ad when you promised to? Did you run it in the right location? At the right time? On the right media? Did you bill us the correct amount?" As Tom made mental notes, the gloves came off: "And by the way, compared to your peers, you're *way* behind. You guys are the worst for pre-campaign commitment. It messes up our whole ad place-ment schedule."

"Pre-campaign commitment?" Tom repeated to himself. He wasn't expecting this one. He resolved to dig deeper when he got back to his office.

The media company's well-intentioned, yet misdirected actions are a classic example of waste that's hiding in plain sight. And the costs were massive. For example, the MSET's focus on the wrong definition of "qual-ity" resulted in an error rate that was more than triple the industry aver-age. The company's publications continually had to run free ads (known as "make-goods") to compensate for the ads they'd incorrectly run at the wrong times, in the wrong locations. Given that a single ad could easily cost $60,000 or more, this translated to tens of millions of dollars of avoid-able waste—and squandered margin.

At the same time, there was a gaping disconnect between the papers' publishing operations and the advertising team. While the newsprint edi-tion's operating execs relentlessly optimized pressroom operations and reduced printing costs, their lean printing schedules created unintended adverse consequences. Their efforts hindered the advertising team's abil-ity to "lock down" ad placement positions at the early dates offered by competitors. This annoyed advertisers to no end, as they struggled to plan consistently timed campaigns and lock in ad space in a once-and-done manner. Meanwhile, the accounting staff wasted countless hours reconciling discrepancies in billings and quotations. Customer service and sales staff spent untold hours performing rework tasks while trying to soothe advertisers' frayed nerves.

## How "Virtuous Waste" Gets Its Name

Tangible waste—the kind you might find, say, on a factory floor—is obvious. Things like scrap, returned goods, and downtime rarely provoke a philosophical discussion about whether or not they're waste. Perception is straightforward. No interpretation is required. And the opportunities for reducing waste are widely perceived as valuable.

Make the transition to knowledge work, however, and you might quickly find yourself ensnared in a philosophical debate about whether waste is waste. The scrap piles that exist in knowledge work are intangible—virtual. They consist of the same keystrokes, mouse clicks, and screen views that constitute value-added activity. Perception is not straightforward. Interpretation is required. And when this interpretation is not managed, variance creeps in and the costly misinterpretation begins.

If you visited Bob's organization and interviewed any of the knowledge workers who were furiously busy correcting the NIGO errors on the inbound new business applications, you might hear an explanation like this: "No, no. This isn't waste. The applications always come in this way from the agents. I am preserving revenue; I'm helping the agents become more productive; I'm helping the customers get service . . ." They perceive, or perhaps rationalize, that their corrective activities are essential and valuable—virtuous.

> DEFINITION: **Virtuous Waste**
> Corrective work activities misperceived to be unavoidable, valuable effort.

You'd get a similar explanation from Raylene's schedulers or the accountants issuing credits for advertising errors at Tom's media company. Knowledge workers everywhere rationalize waste as virtuous activity— that's just one of the many reasons that it's able to hide in plain sight. The ensuing chapters provide many more, and we'll use the term "virtuous waste" throughout.

Virtuous waste is rooted in misperceptions that are rarely noticed or challenged:

- The root causes are "unavoidable."
- Remediation is valuable, even "heroic."
- The corrective work is "unique."

But then knowledge workers will always say (as will that Wikipedia definition) that their work is unique. Remember the "nonroutine problems" that require "creative thinking"? Few people would voluntarily describe their work activity as similar and repetitive.

The reality is far more mundane. As it turns out—and as we'll learn, in detail, in this book—two-thirds of knowledge workers' tasks are actually similar and repetitive. In other words, they're ripe for industrialization. Hence the title of this book, *The Knowledge Work Factory*.

What about that "unavoidable" claim? It's another misperception that serves as an excuse not to analyze and investigate—a handy shortcut to inaction and maintenance of the status quo. In reality, one-third of these "heroic" rework activities can be avoided or eliminated altogether, without the need for any new technology, thanks to the time-tested principles of industrialization: standardization, specialization, and division of labor.

But all this still begets the (fair) question: *If virtuous waste is so widespread, then how come no one sees it?*

One major reason is that the landscape of business value has shifted beneath our feet . . . as Chapter 2 will explain.

## CHAPTER 1: **TAKEAWAYS**

1. White-collar, office, or knowledge work is vaguely defined as *nonroutine problem solving that requires creative thinking.* Wasted effort in knowledge work receives scant attention.

2. Knowledge workers waste *a third of their day, every day,* on activities that could be streamlined, consolidated, or avoided altogether. For the Fortune 500 in 2017, the overlooked costs are stunning:
   - 20 percent of earnings
   - $3 trillion in shareholder value
   - Almost equal to the combined value of Facebook, Apple, Amazon, Netflix, and Google, or FAANG

3. Knowledge work waste has characteristics that help it pass virtually unnoticed:
   - The root causes are misperceived as "unavoidable."
   - Remediation is rationalized as valuable, even heroic: "virtuous waste."
   - Work activities are misperceived as unique, thwarting investment in standardization.

4. Knowledge work is ripe for application of the time-tested principles of industrialization:
   - Standardization
   - Specialization
   - Division of labor

# CHAPTER 2

# DID YOU NOTICE THAT YOUR MOST VALUABLE ASSETS HAVE SHIFTED?

You may notice that this book uses the word "hidden" a lot. It talks about hidden value, hidden waste, and hidden assets. But to businesspeople, it doesn't seem possible that something, anything of value, can "hide" in today's competitive environment. This counterintuitive notion of "hidden" is much easier to dismiss than to ponder. Why can't you find it? Why can't a competitor find it? A start-up? If true, what on earth could be going on?

These are reasonable questions. And they have reasonable, but counterintuitive, answers. This book provides the luxury of fully explaining, in comfortable detail, how all this "hiding" got started—and how it morphed into the "unchallengeable," underproductive status quo. That's good, because once you trace today's hidden business value to its painfully mundane destinations, you begin to notice examples everywhere throughout knowledge work. That new noticing makes it much easier to accept this counterintuitive notion of "hidden." And then it finally becomes much easier to embrace the simple, but unconventional, management steps required to unlock this value in your business.

In this chapter, we're going to talk about a tectonic shift in business assets. We'll explore the seemingly mundane work activities that are worth a fortune. And that will help you to recognize the intangible assets that represent massively valuable low-hanging fruit for near-term standardization improvement.

We're going to talk a lot about intangible assets. But first, let's ask what may seem to be an incredibly basic question: *What are they?* The answer isn't easy, for several reasons.

First, there's not much discussion of the topic in management circles. For example, pick up one of the world's most popular finance textbooks.[1] Since 1981, it has served as the "bible" in the world's top-ranked graduate business schools. The latest edition is almost 900 pages long, but only 7 of these pages discuss intangible assets, which make up the bulk (85 percent) of business value today.

Economists have also overlooked this tectonic shift in asset value. In fact, until the early 1980s, it's hard to find *any* mention of intangibles in scholarly journals. Even today, the literature is woefully thin given the significance of the topic. See Figure 2-1.

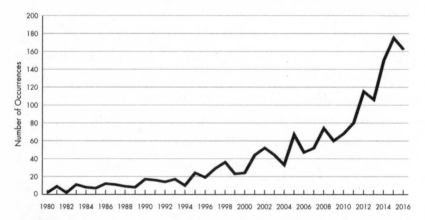

**FIGURE 2-1**    References to intangible assets in scientific journals remain woefully thin.

Republished with permission of Princeton University Press, from Jonathan Haskel and Stian Westlake, *Capitalism Without Capital, the Rise of the Intangible Economy* (Princeton, NJ: Princeton University Press, 2018), 6; permission conveyed through Copyright Clearance Center, Inc.

Second, even the experts struggle to define intangible assets. Most definitions are negative, describing what these assets are not, just like the definitions of "knowledge worker" in Chapter 1. (Spoiler: That's quite a coincidence, and it might help to explain the perceptual challenge—why these assets, which are knowledge work activities, are "hidden.") These negative definitions simply state the characteristics that intangible assets lack: physical substance and simple evaluation criteria. That's not very helpful. Economists at the United Nations labored for nearly two decades before finally agreeing on how to measure macroeconomic investment in intangible assets. And intangibles remain a perennial topic of debate among scholars, regulators, and investors.

So it's not surprising that businesspeople struggle to perceive or define them. It's understandable that they believe they know the definition when they really don't. But most execs simply shrug off the question as irrelevant to their daily work. They leave it to the accountants and the stock market to think about. That's a big mistake that overlooks a bigger opportunity.

The easiest way to learn about *intangible* assets is to start by understanding *tangible* assets.

## Take Two Clay Tablets and Call Me in the Morning: Insights from Ancient Babylon

"Tangible" means "able to be touched." Therefore, tangible assets have physical form. They are *things*. They're real. You can see them, you can touch them, and it's hard to mistake them for anything else. But it's easy to confuse them with the *source* of wealth.

Travel back in time 7,000 years. That's the age of the Babylonian clay tablets that archaeologists have unearthed. And what's on them? Accounting ledgers. They reveal (at least to the archaeologists who can read this stuff) merchants' inventories of things like grain, wine, and cloth. *Tangible assets.*

"Fine," you say. "How does that help me today?" With a little patient pondering, it can provide more insights than you might think.

At first glance, a Babylonian merchant's business that was represented on the clay tablets would appear to be a simple operation, based solely and unquestionably on tangible assets. Add to the inventories of grain, wine, and cloth other tangible *things* like warehouses, millstones, and fleets of carts and donkeys for distribution. Today, businesspeople would call that a "value chain." And accountants would categorize all of these tangible assets under the headings of "Inventories" and "Property, Plant, and Equipment." Simple enough.

These are some of the oldest and most easily perceived assets in business. Thus, it doesn't take a great leap of imagination to assume that the first written management method—accounting—would naturally develop to document assets with physical form, or "things." Physical assets grew in scope and complexity, creating the need for accounting. So, naturally it was invented—simple. And over the ensuing millennia, accounting improved, rules and standards evolved—a logical progression of continuous improvement. But this is hindsight's dull, dry, historical march-of-progress view. Although it doesn't explicitly say so, this retrospective view implies that business back then was rudimentary, not complex and nuanced like it is today. It's easy to look at some old clay tablets and smugly presume that there wasn't much challenging knowledge work going on back then. Babylonian execs weren't required to generate and manage a lot of complicated insights. Nothing like today's complex world.

This simplistic view implies that accounting arose primarily as a management tool for *tangible assets*. We could accept that. But let's not. Instead, let's ponder *intangible assets* in Babylon.

We'll need our imagination. Why was accounting suddenly invented then? Small merchants didn't need it. They could conveniently keep track of their limited assets (e.g., several carts, a dozen baskets) in their heads. More likely, some merchants grew so successful and large that it was much more difficult for them to keep tabs on their growing base of tangible assets—their accumulating wealth—in their heads. But why did some merchants grow? What might explain the source of the outsized variance in their tangible wealth?

These large, successful merchants might have more closely resembled today's commodities traders than small shopkeepers. They speculated on weather trends, harvest yields, and the successful return of trade caravans. But they did much more. They posted spotters at the ports to identify the arrival of ships with goods that might affect the market price of their existing inventories—that's market research and business intelligence. They borrowed money, exchanged currency, and extended credit—that's banking and capital management. They were effectively ancient white-collar, or knowledge work, executives running early forms of investment banks. In relative terms, they likely faced a trading, information, and capital management environment no less challenging and rewarding than today's stock exchanges. They built their fortune with trading know-how, or work methods—their competitive edge—just like it's done today. And just like today's traders, they kept some of those valuable work methods, *intangible assets,* in their heads. But as they succeeded and grew, the traders transferred other, more mundane knowledge work activities to others in their organization. The traders retained and guarded their personal activities. Their know-how was the *source* of the wealth that manifested itself as commodities inventories, carts, and donkeys—tangible assets. But who constituted the knowledge worker organizations back then? Some were slaves.

For the larger Babylonian merchants, keeping track of their portfolios of tangible assets was as tedious, time-consuming, and essential as it is today. They solved this by inventing clay-tablet accounting. Slaves recorded and tabulated the data. They were ancient clerical knowledge workers—the back office. Perhaps they even had their own hierarchy of middle management—ship spotters, credit managers, and accounts payable processors. Regardless, the slaves' back-office know-how and work methods enabled successful Babylonian traders to devote their time to applying their more valuable trading and capital management know-how at a scale larger than the constraints imposed by their personal memories. Think of their know-how as the ancient version of modern-day trading algorithms or front office operations, and the clay tablet recordkeeping as back office operations. Under this alternative view of history, the ancient Babylonian execs suddenly look pretty clever indeed. They invented accounting as a way to make their know-how (i.e., the *intangible assets* that comprised the source of their business wealth) much more productive. They turbocharged it!

This ancient know-how and all the supporting work methods, including the tablets, are forms of *intangible assets* that today are broadly termed "economic competencies" (more about this shortly). But there's really no widely used, popular term to describe these conceptually elusive assets. Today, just as in ancient Babylon, these assets still consist of the numerous mundane tasks of knowledge workers. And that's where the source of business wealth—know-how—*still* resides.

Most businesses today would say, "So what? We've got this covered. No need to waste time looking here for improvement. We've long since automated everything possible. All that's left is what's in people's heads. And even if we've overlooked something, our competitors will find it and we'll respond." This is a comforting but costly misperception. It is an oversight that hides trillions of dollars in squandered value. Executives today would be wise to reconsider where they go hunting for improvement opportunities. They might want to take a page from the ancient Babylonian merchants' playbook and concentrate on making their intangible, knowledge work know-how more productive—turbocharge it. Because, even after 7,000 years, that's still the source of business wealth.

## Intangible Assets, Not Intellectual Capital

If *tangible* assets are things that can be touched, then *intangible* assets must be those that can't. Seems logical enough—straightforward.

But here's where it gets thorny. When most businesspeople hear the term "intangible assets," they immediately think of what might more appropriately be called *intellectual property*: patents, franchises, copyrights, trademarks, and others. Some might even argue that conventional accounting methods (rooted in those Babylonian clay tablets) currently accommodate these intangible assets on the balance sheet, and that managers possess ample experience in managing them. This might be true for intellectual property, no argument there. But these are only part of the intangible story. And here's the killer blind spot that concentrating on intellectual property creates for executives: *these typically represent a minority of total intangible assets—usually about 25 percent—so the rest get overlooked.*

## Modern Accounting Rules: The Enemy of "Competencies"

This naturally leads to the question, *What constitutes the remaining 75 percent?* Think of the clay tablets, the work methods of the record-keeping slaves, and, of course, those Babylonian-era "trading algorithms." As mentioned above, these intangible assets of knowledge work know-how are what economists today broadly describe as "economic competencies" (we'll use "competencies" for short). Today they are growing rapidly. They are valuable. They merit investment and management attention. Prosperous Babylonian merchants understood that. They designed their clay tablets to be helpful. However, modern accounting and finance have since evolved to focus ever more precisely on tangible assets—like grain and donkeys. (Recall: Intangible assets are covered on only 7 of 900 total pages in that finance textbook.) Today intangible assets must be booked as "expenses." That's unhelpful. It's where much of the perception problem begins.

Today's accounting rules make it hard to perceive the importance and value of competencies. In turn, this makes it difficult for modern-day managers and their (non-slave) accountants to keep tabs on their growing base of knowledge work know-how—and turbocharge its productivity. The result: after 7,000 years, accounting is now delivering the exact opposite of its original, intended purpose. It is helping to *suppress* the productivity of intangible assets. Over the course of the last 70 years, its explanatory power for valuing businesses entering stock markets has all but evaporated, declining from 85 percent in 1950 to 20 percent in 2013. During this period, spending on intangibles grew dramatically. For example, two critically valuable knowledge work expense categories—research and development (R&D) and selling, general, and administrative (SG&A)—measured as a percentage of company sales, grew by 50 percent. See Figure 2-2.

Why aren't competencies managed, or even *noticed?* It's partly because they don't show up on the balance sheet with all of the other assets. Simple as that. These "people assets"—leaving on the elevator every night—appear as "operating expenses," as continuing costs, on the income state-

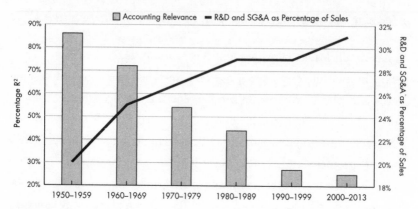

**FIGURE 2-2**  Modern accounting rules obscure the value of intangible assets.

Republished with permission of Wiley Books, from Baruch Lev and Feng Gu, *The End of Accounting and the Path Forward for Investors and Managers* (Hoboken, NJ: John Wiley & Sons, Inc., 2016), 89; permission conveyed through Copyright Clearance Center, Inc.

ment. This not only mislabels them, but it also puts intangible assets at a severe perceptual disadvantage. The reason is that when executives see "operating cost," they respond instinctively: reduce these costs, increase income—now!

Assets are perceived more favorably. They attract attention that's focused on investment and productivity. The very definition of "asset" includes terms like "useful" and "valuable." That sounds fun. Contrast that to "expense." It's defined with words like "necessary" and "required." That's not fun. As a result, when competencies appear on the books as "operating expenses," these won't be instinctively viewed as valuable. After all, *why would anyone invest in an expense?* It's counterintuitive. Making matters worse is the fact that operating expenses are recurring. This creates the perception that reductions will deliver annual savings and increased income indefinitely. That's ironic and counterproductive, because competencies are the source of income and wealth. This anti-investment bias resulting from accounting rules is another major perceptual impediment for the business value bottled up in competencies.

But let's say you overcome your own anti-investment bias. You resolve to actively manage these expenses as intangible assets. It won't be easy. That's because in modern-day businesses, these expenses are also fragmented. They appear as innumerable accounting line items, such as indirect labor, office expense, third-party services, and more. Even within these categories, expenses are defined for the convenience of accountants. Management will struggle to decipher them—but only after they can locate them. The line items are scattered, often inconsistently, across the enterprise accounts from R&D, through sales, HR, marketing, and customer service.

This "scattering" is another revealing insight. For *tangible* assets, such as a building or machine, accountants meticulously and logically group relevant line items together—installation, maintenance, and upgrades. They want to be sure that the line-item costs closely reflect the characteristics of the asset. After all, some of these costs might be summarized and depreciated along with the asset. It's less convenient and requires more work for the accountants, but it makes it easier to visualize and comprehensively manage tangible assets. There's that Babylonian strategy again: invest more in accounting—clay tablets—to boost the effectiveness of asset management. The point is, accountants already have the tools and skills to vastly improve perception and management of competencies and help claw back the earnings squandered inside the enterprise on virtuous waste. Unfortunately for shareholders today, accountants, like managers, can easily overlook the intent of the original Babylonian clay tablet strategy. Accounting was developed to leverage know-how and competencies in order to generate more business wealth—not just to track grain and donkeys.

## *Digging Deeper to Uncover Competitive Opportunity*

It's only when you dig deeper into these competencies that you begin to see what's hiding there. Economists define two categories of competencies. The first is called "general competencies." This includes things like databases, R&D, and general business methods. These general competencies are intangible assets, but they are relatively large, conventionally defined, and easy to visualize.

Ah, but the *second* category of smaller, more granular intangible assets is the one that concerns us. These are known as "firm-specific competencies" and present more challenges. They are ill-defined and difficult to visualize. These include the know-how and practices, down to the detailed activities, of both workers and management. Many are specific to individual firms.

These are work activities—the minutiae of a company's tasks, know-how, and practices—and that's why they're so easily overlooked. Viewed individually, these activity-level intangible assets probably seem irrelevantly small. Managing them seems tedious and uneconomical. But collectively, these are anything but small. Today, these activities provide a large share of a company's competitive advantage and its source of wealth, just as they did for Babylonian execs. They recognized that "tedious" can be valuable. See Figure 2-3.

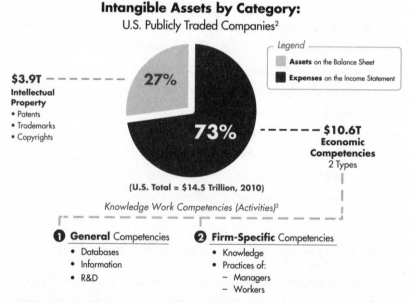

**Intangible Assets by Category:**
U.S. Publicly Traded Companies[2]

**$3.9T** Intellectual Property
• Patents
• Trademarks
• Copyrights

27%

73%

Legend
■ **Assets** on the Balance Sheet
■ **Expenses** on the Income Statement

$10.6T
**Economic Competencies**
2 Types

(U.S. Total = $14.5 Trillion, 2010)

*Knowledge Work Competencies (Activities)*[3]

❶ **General** Competencies
• Databases
• Information
• R&D

❷ **Firm-Specific** Competencies
• Knowledge
• Practices of:
  – Managers
  – Workers

**FIGURE 2-3**   "Economic competencies" constitute nearly three-quarters of intangible assets and are routinely overlooked as sources of both business value and competitive advantage.

In fact, most day-to-day competitive battles are waged not on the fields of intellectual property, but in the tedious trenches of knowledge work competencies—the neglected segment. And, of course, this notion at first sounds counterintuitive.

## Parity Versus Disparity: Where's the Edge?

Managers invest heavily to develop and protect the intellectual property listed as intangible assets on the balance sheet, such as patents, trademarks, and copyrights. They know how to do this. It involves well-known procedures, business processes, and widely available expertise—technical and legal. But most businesses face competitors that are similarly endowed with—and equally invested in—their own comparable intellectual property assets: brand names, secret formulas, proprietary technologies, and unique manufacturing methods. Sure, there are the rare, lucrative monopolistic exceptions, but most businesses are constantly challenged by numerous competitive substitutes and alternatives for their intellectual property. That means that competition is often a strategically cramped game of inches. Breakout opportunities are scarce. Stalemates are frequent. Welcome to competitive parity.

So, where's the *dis*parity? The edge? The breakout opportunity? It's hiding in plain sight. The beauty of the widespread misperception of knowledge work is that it offers a massive overlooked breakout opportunity. Competencies represent vast, uncontested competitive spaces, the ultimate goal of strategic theorists. Imagine an unexplored gold field of strategic possibility. And, at least for now, competencies offer lots of flexibility for experimental trial and error—unlimited "degrees of strategic freedom." Incumbents could not be more favorably positioned. Whether they recognize it or not, their claim in this gold field has already been staked in the form of their existing knowledge work operations. Now, all they have to do is recognize it, go prospecting, and begin mining.

The industrialization lessons from the past century of manufacturing provide a "how to" guide, a prospector's map, for exploiting this opportunity. And the staggering, historical gains in manufacturing productivity provide precedents for setting aggressive goals for mining the knowledge work opportunity.

For business and technology strategists, knowledge work competencies represent the modern-day equivalent of the Comstock Lode, the storied vein of gold and silver discovered in Nevada in 1850. Competencies offer opportunities to mine immense, immediate business wealth while simultaneously advancing their competitive "mining" technologies: robotics, artificial intelligence, data science, and business intelligence. But unlike those nineteenth century bonanzas, no heavy equipment is involved. The initial "drilling" is conceptual and introspective—perceptual.

Day-to-day knowledge work improvement efforts bear uncanny parallels to conventional mining operations. Work activities (the ore) are "excavated," and documented. Waste activities are "extracted." The value-added activities that remain are reprocessed with industrialization methods: standardization, specialization, and division of labor (including automation). The knowledge work factory can be as methodical and predictably profitable as any conventional mining operation. But there's one fundamental difference: knowledge work "mining" does not deplete these assets—it turbocharges their productivity!

That's the premise of this book. And later chapters will show precisely how operations that rarely draw a second glance—things like claims payment processing (Bob), advertising billing operations (Tom), and plant schedule changes (Raylene)—squander breathtaking amounts of earnings and business value. At best, these competencies are typically managed informally or intuitively. At worst, they're managed by exception—that is, correcting errors or firefighting. Most frequently, it is a combination of the two. Sound familiar?

The longstanding failure to industrialize these *firm-specific competencies* provides the opportunity addressed by *The Knowledge Work Factory*. It's an opportunity as old as Babylon. However, since 1970, it's grown in value more than fivefold.

## Where Have All the Assets Gone?

As Figure 2-4 shows, intangible assets now account for *85 percent of the S&P market value.* That's downright astonishing. The change was swift.

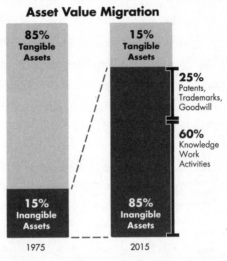

### Asset Value Migration

**85%**
Tangible
Assets

**15%**
Tangible
Assets

**25%**
Patents,
Trademarks,
Goodwill

**60%**
Knowledge
Work
Activities

**15%**
Inangible
Assets

**85%**
Inangible
Assets

1975            2015

**FIGURE 2-4**   Intangible assets now constitute 85 percent of asset value.

For the distribution of tangible and intangible assets, see "Intangible Asset Market Value Study," Ocean Tomo Investment Group, accessed January 1, 2018, www.oceantomo.com/intangible-asset-market-value-study/. The Lab's experience and analysis confirm these figures.

People assume that businesses are rational, productive, and Darwinian. Rules are clear and simple. Waste is relentlessly tracked and purged. Operations are continually automated with the latest technology. Underproductive businesses, practices, and executives quickly adjust to the pressures from competitors and shareholders. The marketplace notices everything.

During the generations when tangible assets were king and accounting accurately reflected value, these assumptions were pretty much true. But then things changed. Radically. Starting around 1970, a 50-year golden age of productivity growth ended for the United States and most other developed economies. This golden age began around 1920, when businesses first applied the principles of industrialization—standardization, specialization, and division of labor—on a large scale. The result was an increase of factory-floor worker productivity that helped deliver a broad, sustained productivity growth rate of 3 percent annually for *five decades*— a growth rate roughly double that of the preceding 50 years.

But then, during the 40-year period from 1975 to 2015, business value shifted dramatically, as the majority of U.S. workers migrated from the plant to the office. Business value moved out of the familiar realm of tangible assets, such as property, plant, and equipment. It left the plant floor and moved "upstairs" into the offices where white-collar workers toil with their minds in areas like finance, engineering, sales, and customer service. See the "Fast Facts" in Figure 2-5.

### FAST FACTS: Knowledge Workers

Knowledge workers are the world's best-educated, most highly paid, and most under-standardized human resources. Consider these statistics:

Growth of knowledge work jobs vs. total jobs (Since 1920)

# 6 to 1

Knowledge workers in the Fortune 500

# 9 million

Knowledge worker time wasted: under-standardized tasks

# 35%

Cost of "under-standardization" in the Fortune 500

# 20% of Earnings

 **3 million**

Of 9 million knowledge workers in the Fortune 500, the full-time equivalent (FTE) of 3 million are wasted by "under-standardization."

**FTEs**

**FIGURE 2-5**  Under-standardized knowledge work squanders roughly 20 percent of earnings. Analysis excludes service workers (e.g., food, retail, transportation, hospitality) and is based on a Fortune 500 price-to-earnings ratio of 16 from *Fortune* magazine and The Lab's experience, analysis, and benchmarks.

The world of business management was not prepared to deal with this massive shift. Knowledge workers have always existed, but they were never so numerous, their activities never so valuable. In the past, knowledge workers (and accountants) were charged with improving the productivity of tangible assets: factories. And they succeeded wildly. During the last century, manufacturing worker productivity skyrocketed fiftyfold, delivering history's greatest increase in economic wealth.[4] But the productivity gains didn't follow the asset migration "upstairs." The next chapter will explain why. But for now, let's continue on that "hidden" theme. Let's see why your business's intangible assets remain *unrecognized* and *underproductive*.

## Why Intangible Assets Are Underproductive: The "Anti-Standardization Bias"

"Our business is unique, so our (knowledge) work can't be standardized."

This is a widely held misperception. It's almost never supported by documentation or analysis. And fortunately, it is virtually never true. So that means it's still a source of untapped value. This is the "anti-standardization bias." It perpetuates the status quo, while obscuring the business-improvement opportunity of our time: industrializing knowledge work. See Figure 2-6.

Analyze knowledge work closely. You will discover that most of it is similar and repetitive. Remember that definition of "knowledge worker" we found, back in Chapter 1, that mentioned nonroutine problems and creative thinking? It's simply not supported by facts. Sure, it's partly true. But in reality, fully two-thirds of knowledge workers' tasks are similar and repetitive—the exact opposite of nonroutine. And a *third* of knowledge work activities are avoidable waste. Only about 10 percent of all knowledge workers are dedicated full-time to work that fits the nonroutine, creative problem-solving definition. In other words, the vast majority of knowledge work activity is ideal for industrialization.

## THE ANTI-STANDARDIZATION BIAS

"Our business is unique, so our knowledge work can't be standardized."

**Perception: Nonroutine Work**

Common perception holds that knowledge workers "solve nonroutine problems... that require creative thinking."[5]

**Reality: Repetitive Work**

However, observations show that *two-thirds of knowledge workers'* tasks are similar and repetitive— ideal for "industrialization."[6]

**Penalty: Virtuous Waste**

Without industrialization, knowledge workers spend 25–40% of their time on avoidable activity—*virtuous waste.*

**Knowledge Work Tasks**

33% nonroutine

67% similar, repetitive

**FIGURE 2-6**   The anti-standardization bias is a powerful perceptual impediment to industrializing knowledge work.

## "But Our Business Really *Is* Unique . . . Isn't It?"

Knowledge workers and their managers will typically concede that their operations waste time throughout the day. But they will just as quickly point out that it's unavoidable. Their business is unique. Their jobs are unique, and even the work activities are unique. They will pay lip service to the industrialization idea: "Why, of course, we'd *love* to standardize and make our lives simpler. Maybe even automate more." But then they'll throw up their hands. "It just isn't possible, because the work here is so different." In other words, it's not *obviously similar.*

Of course it's not. It never is. If it were, it would already be standardized. Standardization is a strategy—a chosen course of action. The very definition of "standardize" is "to *cause* something to conform to a standard." Standardization is not a particularly sexy topic. Few are aware of the long-term historical struggles required to standardize anything. For example, it took a century just to standardize the threads on nuts and bolts. And after firehose-compatibility problems hindered efforts to contain the Great Baltimore Fire of 1904, there was a move to standardize hose fittings in the United States. Despite progress, that firehose standard-ization task continues to this day.

Yes, every business is unique. But businesses are unique in the same way that every city skyline is unique. Once you zoom in on the buildings, you start to notice similarities: the doors, ceiling tiles, wallboard, lighting fixtures, and more are standardized. But drill deeper and you'll see that the systems—heating, cooling, and electrical—are all similar and built from standard components. Business can learn from this.

## In Hindsight, Everything Always Seems Clear . . .

Assets moved swiftly from the tangible—like the factory and its equip-ment—to the intangible—like its knowledge workforce. Yet those work-ers and their competencies (assets) have been classified for years as "expenses," perpetuating their ability to hide in plain sight and underper-form. The resulting value drain and improvement opportunity are massive and overlooked.

But over the same period, the industrialization of *tangible* assets has succeeded wildly. So why haven't *intangible* assets been similarly industri-alized all this time? Why the disparity?

That's a story 30,000 years in the making. Get set for a whirlwind tour of business productivity history—starting with the hunter-gatherer econ-omy and concluding with high tech and the "productivity paradox"—in Chapter 3.

## CHAPTER 2: **TAKEAWAYS**

1. The 40-year period from 1975 to 2015 saw the vast majority (70 percent) of business value migrate rapidly:
   - From tangible assets, mostly property, plant, and equipment
   - To intangible assets, mostly "economic competencies," or knowledge work methods
2. Newly emergent intangible assets are neither well defined nor widely understood:
   - Definitions are negative, describing "what they are not."
   - Accounting rules require most intangible assets to be classified as "expenses," i.e., costs.
   - Most assume intangible assets are limited to patents, trademarks, etc.
3. The largest category (>70 percent) of intangible assets, "economic competencies," is made up of loosely standardized knowledge work operations and methods:
   - Databases and information
   - Knowledge and know-how
   - Practices of managers and workers
4. The "anti-standardization bias" obscures perception of valuable opportunities to "industrialize" knowledge work competencies: two-thirds of knowledge work activities are similar and repetitive, ideally suited for standardization, specialization, and division of labor.

# CHAPTER 3

# HOW WE GOT HERE:
# THE LONG JOURNEY TO MYOPIA

What's the best way to improve performance of knowledge work competencies? The only way: industrialization.

This chapter makes a bold assertion. It argues that since time immemorial, there has only been one improvement in business, and that improvement is *industrialization*: standardization, specialization, and division of labor.

Skeptics, which include almost everyone, will say, "What about steam? Electricity? Computers? The *wheel,* for crying out loud?"

All of that will be addressed. But just know, right now, that the big takeaway from this chapter is this: *industrialization is the only improvement.*

This argument is carved into three sections. In the first, we're going to talk about the Industrial Revolution, "big rocks," and the infamous "productivity paradox." In the second, we'll see why senior executives and experts—along with just about everyone else—are blinded to industrialization opportunities by what can be called the "fat-tail perceptual bias." The third part provides a whirlwind tour of productivity history, showing how the basic principles of industrialization have existed since the days of the hunter-gatherer. At the end of the chapter, we'll discuss the three "pillars" of industrialization—none of which, as we'll see, are new developments.

Let's dive in!

## The Industrial Revolution, "Big Rocks," and the Productivity Paradox

Do you remember learning about the Industrial Revolution in school? There's no denying that it was responsible for history's greatest increase in human productivity and economic wealth.

Today's businesspeople often refer to major opportunities for achieving breakthrough improvement benefits as "big rocks," so I'll use that term here. The Industrial Revolution, we're taught, was composed of three "big rocks." But is that true? Let's look at them:

The first big rock was steam power. This freed humans and animals from the primal duty of delivering physical effort. From the power loom to the locomotive, steam delivered astonishing gains in economic productivity. Application of steam technology helped advance the most modern industries of the day: textile production, iron making, and coal mining. Over the century spanning 1760–1860, annual output productivity growth[1] increased fourfold in Britain, the cradle of the Industrial Revolution.[2] This enabled the nation's economy to accommodate a threefold increase in population over that period—with no reduction in the standard of living. Impressive.

The second big rock was electricity. Widespread electrification enabled more efficient plant layouts, moving assembly lines, and new tools for increased manufacturing productivity. Arguably as important, small appliances—from washing machines to telephones—increased productivity in the home. Vast new markets were opened. By any measure, the electrification period from 1920 to 1970 was another golden age of productivity growth. During this period in the United States, total factor productivity (TFP) grew at an annual rate that was four times greater than that of the preceding 30 years, from 1890 to 1920.[3] TFP is a more modern way that economists measure the productivity contribution of long-term technological change. They estimate that TFP can explain 60 percent of the average growth in output per worker.[4]

Then the third big rock appeared on the scene: digital technology. It was amazing. Productivity continued to soar upward, relentlessly.

No. It didn't.

In fact, it *flatlined* compared with steam and electricity. With the exception of a modest uptick between 1994 and 2004, economic productivity growth has stagnated at levels more representative of the nineteenth century.

Think about that. Since 1970, productivity growth seems trapped in a time warp. We're surrounded by the latest technology: apps, social media, and numerous free services. Yet the growth of today's office worker productivity hovers stubbornly at Dickensian levels—even less, according to some sources.

This is not a new, twenty-first-century problem for office work. Its roots can be easily traced back to the early 1900s; read about that in the sidebar. And back in 1987, Nobel laureate Robert Solow quipped, "You can see the computer age everywhere but in the productivity statistics."[5] Computing capacity in the United States increased a hundredfold in the 1970s and 1980s amid billions of dollars in investment, while annual worker productivity growth slowed from roughly 3 percent throughout the 1960s to about 1 percent throughout the 1990s.[6] By now, this persistent phenomenon has its own name: the "productivity paradox."

So what gives?

## Explaining Away the Productivity Paradox

This glaring gap between IT gains and knowledge work productivity stagnation seems almost impossible to believe. And many don't—it is easier to deny. The recent explanations for the productivity paradox broadly fall into three categories:

1. **You need to wait.** Many point out that it takes a long time—decades—to wring productivity gains out of new "big rocks." That's because everything else downstream of the big rocks must also change. Steam

## The Punch Card Paradox

Early office technology predated computers by decades. In the 1920s, solutions such as the Rand Visible-Card System and Acme Visible Records promised a revolution in office worker productivity, using tech, such as filing systems and punch cards. They would (gently) "force their owners to use the facts," as their sales pitches proclaimed.[7] The appealing implication was that office management would be relieved of the same type of wholesale overhaul of operations required by previous big-rock revolutions: steam and electricity. They would not have to streamline office workflows, standardize one-off methods, or specialize the activities of employees. Nor (it was claimed) would they need to continually measure the effectiveness of their industrialization efforts with productivity reporting.

The technology was sold and installed, and then it languished, with few of the promised productivity gains being realized. Sound familiar? In the office, business leadership sidestepped the difficult yet necessary steps to industrialize office work to make the most of the new technology. The tech vendors, starting in the early 1900s, "industrialized" their sales efforts to focus on management's aversion to knowledge work industrialization. It worked, but their products were "abandoned as soon as the spell of the brilliant salesman wore off," according to William Henry Leffingwell, author of *Scientific Office Management*, way back in 1917.[8]

In other words, the more things change . . .

power had a stubborn productivity paradox problem. It was a costly, inefficient new technology that required roughly 60 years of refinement and capital investment to displace low-cost water-powered manufacturing and canal-based transit.[9] Electricity also endured its own well-documented productivity paradox when it was first introduced into manufacturing. But manufacturing adapted, and that paradox was gone in a couple of decades.[10] Most researchers set the birth of the digital age in the 1960s, when mainframes entered the workplace. By the time of Solow's 1987 quote, mainframes had given way to the ubiquitous world of personal computers. Today we have mobile phones, cloud computing, and artificial intelligence. In other words, we're closing in on *six decades* for this "lag" to catch up. Really? We've already had technology adoption lessons from two big-rock productivity revolutions. Didn't we learn anything? How complicated can it be?

2. **You're measuring it wrong.** This explanation contends that we simply don't know how to measure the benefits of today's new technologies. Those in Silicon Valley argue that many of the technological benefits are free and thus aren't captured via conventional measures. Yet another prominent economist, Alan Blinder, uses simple reverse engineering of the "implied value" of this new technology to prove the financial futility of this explanation. As he stated in the *Wall Street Journal* in 2015, "To account for a 1.6 percentage-point decline in the productivity growth rate for 10 years, all those new apps, social media and free services would now have to be worth almost $2.5 trillion more per year than in 2005. That's not believable."[11]

3. **You're mismanaging.** Conventional wisdom would seem to render this explanation impossible. After all, markets are efficient, right? That means that someone would surely figure out how to make businesses more efficient via IT and reap the benefits thereof. Heck, just look at Amazon: it's doing it for retail. Google did it for advertising. These are good, fact-based examples. But consider some other, far more persistent and troubling facts, based on The Lab's own research and database: (1) Current, well-proven technology can easily automate roughly half of current knowledge work activities. (2) Knowledge workers spend roughly a third of their day performing avoidable tasks. (3) Three-quarters of these can be eliminated with *no* technology. All that's needed is the application of the "forgotten" fundamental enabling principles of the Industrial Revolution: standardization, specialization, and division of labor.

## An Alternative "One-Rock" Theory

Now let's return to this chapter's opening: namely, the bold assertion that there is only a single, unchanging "big rock" of improvement that has successfully and reliably improved the work efforts of humans since the dawn of civilization: industrialization. And the only thing that changes is the enabling technology for this industrialization. If we tentatively accept this theory, then we have to revise our conventional view of the Industrial Revolution and its multiple big rocks. For the sake of discussion, let's see where this one-rock assumption takes us. It will cause us to rename, more prosaically, each of history's waves of productivity gains. These new, less-sexy names also provide helpful insights.

First, the Steam Age becomes "the industrialization of the tangible work efforts of humans (and draft animals) powered by steam technology." After a long, 60-year period of adjustment, businesses finally solved the industrialization puzzle, and productivity soared. Next, the Electric Age would be renamed "the industrialization of the tangible work efforts of humans using electrical technology." This required industrialization activities similar to those for steam, but with a different energy source. Businesses required a much shorter period of adjustment, and productivity gains vastly exceeded those of steam.

This brings us to the Digital Age. Following the same descriptive protocol, it should be renamed "the industrialization of (and here's the catch) the *intangible* work efforts of humans," or thinking tasks. But for office work, why should it be misleadingly named for that particular (digital) technology? Office technology-based efforts have been under way now for a century. They preceded the office computer by at least 50 years and involved punch cards, filing systems, and conveyors.

Whoops! This doesn't work so well. It appears that office work productivity remained stalled in its tracks, both before and after the digital computer. It should've gone much faster than steam and electricity. After all, those industrializations depended on standardizing boilers, railroad tracks, wrenches, metallurgical specs, and a host of other complexities like tunneling through mountains. But in the office, for two generations before the computer arrived, there was nothing to standardize except data, filing systems, and work tasks. And now, after the computer, we're another 60 years into it with still no productivity gains to show. That's at least a *century* of no productivity growth in office, or knowledge, work—the intangible assets that now constitute 85 percent of business value.

This unconventional, one-rock view delivers a different set of embarrassingly simple and practical explanations for the productivity paradox:

- Business leaders aren't good at noticing intangible work; they haven't given enough thought to its productivity and value.
- They *notice* intangible work but are convinced that it cannot be industrialized and thus have never tried.
- They notice intangible work and appreciate the value of industrializing it. And they've tried—but stopped because they were not successful.

## The "Fat-Tail Perceptual Bias"

The productivity paradox is lastly a technology problem. Secondarily, it's a management problem. But first and foremost, it's a *perception* problem. Solving the paradox means changing the time-honored, traditional way of looking for improvements. It means searching beyond the big rocks. It means overcoming the "fat-tail perceptual bias"—focused on a few major breakthrough innovations—and zeroing in on the "long tail" of small rocks that management and workers alike routinely overlook. It also means—and there's no polite way to put this—avoiding the shortcuts promised by technology providers.

This is a bitter pill. It's an oversight so embarrassingly and outrageously obvious that almost everyone refuses to believe it: "Impossible! I would have noticed these improvements if they were that valuable." As I said, it's not about technology or management; it's about perception—more specifically, the systemic biases in business perception. And while Chapter 4 will cover this in more detail, suffice it to say that most executives don't exactly begin their quest for knowledge work improvements by pondering the human cognitive flaws that generate oversights and permeate business organizations.

In fact, only 10 percent of CEOs and senior business executives even turn to their own CIOs when it comes to sources for IT-related business innovation. Most turn first to industry publications and newsletters—packed with articles by technology vendors.[12] Better yet, do they invest in rigorous observation of their own operations? Establish an internal industrialization team, like Henry Ford and other early pioneers did? Nope.

Solving the productivity paradox in a business is a humbling experience for management. It starts with recognizing and recalibrating your "overconfidence bias." That's the inherent, laughably large disconnect between every human's subjective confidence and the real world of objective facts. *Example:* Ninety-three percent of U.S. automobile drivers rank their abilities as above average![13]

Only after you've cracked this counterintuitive perceptual nut can you begin to industrialize. And only *then* can you move into the realm of effective technology-driven automation.

## Is "Boring" Unimportant?

Take a look at Figure 3-1. It represents the pervasive view of technology. It shows that almost all of history is flat, uneventful, and boring, right up to 1775 and the invention of Watt's steam engine.

The graph in the figure, by the way, is taken from a 2014 book by prominent experts from MIT—professors widely considered to be among the leading thinkers on technology, the productivity paradox, and the future of the digital world. Although they're not the original creators of this graph, the way they *labeled* it is telling.[14] When they first introduced this graph, two pages earlier in their book, without the steam engine date, they included the following caption: "Numerically speaking, most of human history is boring."[15] In terms of productivity, the statement may be factually correct. But it seems to devalue everything that happened before

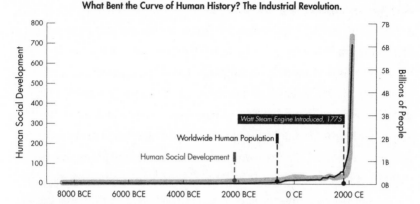

**FIGURE 3-1**    The focus on technological innovation downplays nontechnology industrialization techniques: standardization, specialization, and division of labor.

This graph appears as Figure 1.2 in *The Second Machine Age: Work, Progress, and Prosperity in a Time of Brilliant Technologies* by Erik Brynjolfsson and Andrew McAfee. Copyright © 2014 by Erik Brynjolfsson and Andrew McAfee. Used by permission of W. W. Norton & Company, Inc.

the steam engine—like the water-powered, industrialized textile mills that steam technology struggled to supersede for 60 years. The "long tail" that precedes the world's greatest increase in wealth and productivity is under-appreciated and overlooked. Its lessons for office work improvement are, presumably, as obsolete as a flip phone.

(Incidentally, Watt's wasn't the first steam engine. An engineer named Hero of Alexandria described one way back in the first century AD! Chapter 5 will provide more detail about it and other historical oversights.)

These MIT professors are insightful people. But they are, after all, people. And that means that they are subject to the same, very human biases of perception as the rest of us. They, along with their book, are reinforcing a widespread bias that technology—and technology alone—drives industrialization. That's what's known as a "confirmation bias": the tendency to search for, interpret, favor, and recall information in a way that confirms one's preexisting beliefs.[16]

## *But What About the Long Tail?*

These "hindsight histories" of the Industrial Revolution focus solely on the big-rock introductions of "breakthrough" technology: the wheel, the steam engine, etc. Viewed from our present-day vantage point, it's easy to imagine that these were as swiftly disruptive as the rise of the World Wide Web. After the wheel appears in the history of civilization, that job is over and done. Not much else there. Time to move on. That's the "fat-tail perceptual bias."

Sweeping pronouncements like that steam engine caption on the graph cause minimal attention to be paid to the long tail that precedes the big rocks. Consequently, people regard this period as the tedious, inefficient development of the technologies that eventually enabled the big rocks: wheels, tools, gears, thermodynamic science, and so on. Once the big rocks arrive, they incorporate and carry forward the worthy, critical few technologies (or so it's commonly accepted). Think of Apple or Microsoft acquiring a small application and folding it into its operating system. All else that's left behind is either obsolete and discarded or relegated to a nominal supporting role.

Think of the Babylonian merchants in the last chapter. For them, accounting and clay tablets represented cutting-edge financial technology: their big rock, or the fat tail of improvement. And by the way, the wheel arrived 3,000 years *after* the Babylonians had standardized the knowledge work of accounting.[17] For today's businesspeople, computers and algorithms now represent the cutting-edge, big-rock technologies— the fat tail. And accounting has now drifted into the long tail. It receives scant attention. This critical, intangible knowledge work has lost its status as an asset worthy of investing time to review, simplify, and industrialize. It has become "boring." Maybe so, but that doesn't mean it ever becomes any less important to us than those clay tablets were to the Babylonians. Whenever something becomes boring to pundits, watch out, because that's probably a danger sign.

Henry Ford, by contrast, was passionate about accounting. As he implemented the world's most advanced manufacturing technologies to create the moving assembly line, he had costs for every decision and operation calculated to the penny. It took about a year to launch the first end-to-end final assembly line. As Ford and his managers searched daily for automation ideas, they did not consult trade journals, like today's executives. Ford went straight to the plant—and his CFO. By then, 1913, accounting was long since relegated to the "boring" long tail. *But Ford did not find it boring.* He treated accounting as an asset and a tool, just like his plant equipment and engineers. He invested in improving cost accounting far beyond what was typical, insisting that graphs be created showing trends and cost curves. Statistical visualization graphics were relatively new then. Scholarly research has shown that few companies in history have so thoroughly documented the relationships between production decisions and financial implications.[18] In the five-year period ending in 1916, Ford increased production fifteenfold.

But visit the world's largest companies today, and it's hard to see what they've learned from Ford. The businesspeople mentioned above are focused on their websites and their algorithms. Their accounting is an explanatory disaster. Finance employees must hold reconciliation meetings prior to critical executive meetings. They have to make certain that everyone has the same figures for revenues, margins, and inventories. They consult trade journals and attend conferences to learn of the latest automation technologies. They are looking for ideas. They don't begin by reviewing their own operations, where useless complexity and a lack of clear instructions cause vendors to generate a 30 percent error rate on inbound order billings.

"Boring" is a dangerously misleading presumption. If we *neglect* the long tail, the consequences for value can be costly and easily overlooked. Henry Ford didn't find accounting boring. And executives today shouldn't either.

And when they get frustrated scouring the long tail for improvement ideas, they should also take heart. Even Henry and his team overlooked the moving assembly line hiding in plain sight—*right in the long tail of his existing factory operations.* The Ford foundry—like most foundries, flour mills, and breweries since the age of water and then steam power—included a moving assembly line in the form of conveyor systems. In the Ford foundry, electricity powered the conveyors, bringing the work to the workers. But nobody noticed. It was only when William Klann of Ford visited the Swift Company's meat-packing operations that the idea occurred to him to adapt conveyors for assembly in the auto plant.[19]

# A Whirlwind Tour of Productivity History

Remember that promised whirlwind tour of productivity history? It fits in nicely with today's obsession over big rocks. And there's no better context for discussing big rocks than the Stone Age.

## Stone Age Industrialization

The argument that industrialization is the only form of improvement is based on the long tail of human history. Standardization, specialization, and the division of labor are fundamental to the way humans have organized work since at least the Stone Age. Industrialization is pervasive:

- **Olduvai Gorge.** Flint and stone artifacts unearthed at this famous archaeological dig in Tanzania reveal that our ancestors were creating tools as far back as 2.5 million years ago.[20]
- **Boxgrove, United Kingdom.** This village in West Sussex has yielded a treasure trove of 800 flint hand axes, crafted some half a million years ago. All were made in the same location, and yet some are better than others, suggesting that there were mentors sitting right beside apprentices. Even today, the flint-knapped tools are impressive. When one was given to a professional butcher, he marveled at the ease with which it let him do his work, with long, smooth, fatigue-saving motions.[21] And why were all these hand axes found in one location? Simple: The place was a meat-processing site. That's industrialization for you.

- **The English Lake District.** Toward the end of the Stone Age, a quarry for carving axes was established at this site; you can still see the shards of chipped stone here today. Yet here's the thing: this quarry is situated *on the side of a mountain, 2,000 feet above the valley floor.* This was no casual place to find rocks. It was a virtual "production line," requiring specialization and division of labor. A small shelter is carved into the rock nearby, suggesting that the toolmakers actually lived here.[22] It's an industrial site.

- **Lascaux, France.** Cave paintings here, dating back 17,000 years, are so beautifully rendered that they've been described as "professional."[23] But how can you create beautiful artwork if you need to spend your days, say, hunting animals? The answer: you *can't.* You need to be released from your duties—division of labor—to devote your time to this *specialized* work—and art is knowledge work.

- **From Ancient Egypt to Renaissance Italy.** There were multiple levels of craftsmen and artisans in ancient Egypt, from apprentices to masters, who divided and specialized their work activities. Just look at the decorations within those ancient tombs. Thousands of years later, skilled craftsmen continued to rely on a similar tiered training structure: Leonardo da Vinci began as an apprentice. Leonardo also contemplated pin and needle manufacturing. His sketchbooks document his plan to become wealthy via a Ford-like conveyor device that would greatly increase productivity. Leonardo did not become a wealthy pin maker. He was undermined, not only by his legendary procrastination, but also by his faulty and overstated financial projections—accounting forecasting errors.[24]

## Adam Smith to Henry Ford and Beyond

Now fast-forward to 1776. That's when the economist Adam Smith published his seminal book, *An Inquiry into the Nature and Causes of the Wealth of Nations*, commonly referred to simply as *The Wealth of Nations.* Although he borrowed from other sources (such as Diderot), he's the one who formally set down in writing the fundamental, eons-old principles of industrialization: standardization, specialization, and division of labor.

Right in the first chapter of his book, Smith tells a famous story. He describes an English pin factory—perhaps apocryphal—in which one worker could effectively produce 4,800 pins a day, compared with one worker under the old method, who could only craft about *20* per day. The trick was the industrialization:

> One man draws out the wire, another straights it, a third cuts it, a fourth points it, a fifth grinds it at the top for receiving . . . the important business of making a pin is, in this manner, divided into about eighteen distinct operations . . . all performed by distinct hand.[25]

There's a good chance you learned about this story in school. But here's something that school didn't teach you: *pins had been made for thousands of years.* Why did it take so long for them to become industrialized?

Smith points out things like economic pressures, and we can mention other factors, such as available workforce and so on. But the bigger point—the one that really matters for your knowledge workforce right this minute—is that these industrializations don't simply happen on their own. They require hard thinking about overlooked activities that are similar and repetitive. Everything about this thinking is managerially inconvenient. That's part of the reason why it wasn't until the eighteenth century that pin making was industrialized.

Don't believe that improvement opportunities hide in plain sight? Read about the breakthrough in bricklaying in the sidebar. Or consider new applications of ancient ideas. *Quick:* What's one of the oldest inventions you can think of? (Besides accounting.) The wheel, right? It's ancient and relegated to the boring long tail. Every possible use for it has already been devised, right?

Wrong. Somebody, just a few years ago, got the smart idea of attaching wheels to a piece of luggage. Somebody else made a fortune by inserting them into kids' shoes, hence the "wheelie." What's next?

Of course, the industrial legend you most likely think of first is Henry Ford. But the idea of the "industrialized" knowledge work factory was most famously articulated by Frederick Winslow Taylor in his legendary treatise, *Principles of Scientific Management*, back in 1911—right around the same time that Ford was gearing up his production resources. Taylor, like Adam Smith, was a theorist and codifier. And although his work is often perceived as solely focusing on manual labor, it applies equally well to knowledge work.

So the principles are timeless. But they must be *applied*. That's the crux of the productivity paradox. Think that computers are going to magi-

## A Bricklaying Revolution

Bricks are *really* ancient. Since we've been using them for thousands of years, you'd think that we'd automatically wrung every last ounce of productivity out of the bricklaying process. Nope.

In the early 1900s, Frank and Lillian Gilbreth filmed bricklayers and analyzed the results frame by frame. They saw that the bricklayers were certainly busy, but hardly efficient. They weren't wasting bricks or mortar; they were wasting *effort*.

The Gilbreths realized that little changes—such as shifting the supply pile of bricks from the ground up to waist level, reducing the worker's reach, and optimizing the amount of mortar on the trowel— could yield amazing results. Using the Gilbreths' improvements, bricklayers went from 300 bricks a day to 300 bricks an *hour*.

The takeaway for your white-collar workforce: just because it's been done the same way forever doesn't mean it can't be improved, radically. The same principles of industrialization that apply to construction apply, equally, to your knowledge workers.

cally transform your knowledge workforce? Think again. You need to first industrialize the processes the knowledge workers employ to take advantage of the technology.

Flintknappers and Babylonian accountants used the same standardization and division-of-labor techniques that Amazon uses today digitally. So remember: just as the passing of time alone doesn't ensure progress and automation, neither does it render obsolete all those ancient (and proven) ideas, techniques, and inventions—the ones hiding in plain sight, in the long tail. In fact, in the sidebar you can read about some early low-tech knowledge work factories that were tragically decades before their time.

## *Fighting for Efficiency*

In case you don't think standardization is as important as I'm describing it, consider two sides of the story. In the first—back in 1917—there were 994,840 varieties of *ax* available for sale in the United States. Nearly a *million* different varieties. In the second side of this story, standardization gets mandated, and the results are astonishing.

While most people remember Herbert Hoover as the face of the Great Depression, he can be thanked for the creation of the National Bureau of Standards, whose mandate was to eliminate things like, oh, *a million types of ax*.[26] Thus an enormous part of industrial efficiency was gained by the standardization of such mundane "long-tail" items as nuts, bolts, and the wrenches to turn them.

Fast-forward to World War II. This is when industrial magnate Henry Kaiser ran two shipyards—one in California and the other in Oregon—to build freighters known as Liberty ships. Sure, they were using by-then standardized nuts and bolts. But it still was projected, at inception, that each location would require eight months to build a ship.

That was in 1942. By the next year, the time to build a ship was slashed to a matter of *weeks*. Ultimately, the turnaround was reduced to just four *days*.

## Early Knowledge Work Factories

By 1917, advocates of industrialization methods for office work first came on the scene. L. W. Ellis successfully industrialized a large advertising organization, achieving a fourfold increase in total productivity. His improvements included a specialized office workflow and standardized forms, ads, and job activities. These were disruptive changes—they were mandated. Notably, office machinery was brought in *afterward*. But office managers everywhere rejected this successful, disruptive industrialization approach. Disheartening? Consider this next story.

As early as 1920, other prominent management innovators—such as "office management engineers" W. H. Leffingwell and C. C. Parsons—demonstrated to business executives that white-collar, or knowledge, work operations could be simplified and standardized for massive productivity gains.

Without technology, these innovators created "knowledge work factories" that capitalized on the ideas that were then enabling mass production in manufacturing: standardization, specialization, and division of labor. They streamlined office workflows, standardized procedures, and simplified activities for workers and even customers. Free-form business processes were standardized into virtual, well-documented assembly lines. In such unlikely organizations as marketing and advertising, this delivered breakthrough gains in productivity and effectiveness.

So what happened? Why are names like Ellis, Leffingwell, and Parsons all but forgotten today?

By this point in the book, you can probably guess the answer. Management simply rejected the idea of mandating standardization in office work. Perhaps because knowledge workers previously constituted an insignificant share of total employees and business value. Back then, *tangible* assets were king. Increasing the productivity of property, plant, and equipment was the most valuable improvement available. In 1920, the idea of knowledge work factories was too far ahead of its time. Today, it's too far behind.

How was this done? Yes, they used big-rock technology-investment improvements to create prefabricated parts. And yes, there was a healthy internal organizational competition between the California and Oregon facilities. But the pressures of wartime yielded a powerful and often-overlooked resource: the long tail of smaller, nontechnology improvements, identified by the employees themselves. More than 250 of them wrote letters with valuable, overlooked opportunities for increasing production efficiency.[27]

Just who owns these kinds of "decision rights" is a hotly contested issue, even today. We'll discuss that a lot more in this book.

## The Three Pillars of Industrialization

"Standardization," "specialization," and "division of labor" have been mentioned a lot. It's not because I'm a Smith (or Taylor or Ford) acolyte. It's because these principles are ubiquitous, underutilized, and timelessly valuable:

- **Standardization.** This exists at multiple levels. There's the interchangeability aspect we've mentioned with the Bureau of Standards and all those nuts and bolts. But there are also reference standards (think of BluRay, Bluetooth, etc.). There are interoperability standards, such as communications for emergency workers and air traffic control. At a large insurer, by contrast, call center workers used no standards for recording the reasons for inbound calls. Of course, this caused chaos. But this chaos went unnoticed because that's just business as usual in the world of knowledge work.

- **Specialization.** Specialization applies equally to machines and workers—and that includes all workers, especially knowledge workers and their intangible tasks. The easiest way to think about it is to imagine the number and diversity of tasks performed by a worker or a machine. For handmade shoes, for example, a single cobbler might perform all or most of the tasks. As shoemaking is specialized, different machines might perform a single task, alongside workers doing the same. The fewer tasks performed by a single worker, the more productivity rises. And interestingly, the largest gains are often the first. When assembly lines were first introduced in manufacturing, it was not unusual to see a 50 percent increase in productivity on the very first day![28]

Most people are surprised to learn that knowledge work, and mathematics in particular, was one of the first areas to adopt Smith's doctrine and benefit from specialization. Around 15 years after publication of *The Wealth of Nations*, Gaspard de Prony was busy with a team of mathematicians developing a set of logarithmic tables for publication by the French government. Anxious to finish quickly and economically, he hired a wide range of mathematicians of varying skills and wage rates. He assigned the most skilled to oversee entire calculations while more economical, lower-skilled workers toiled with simpler, underlying math work. Four decades later, Charles Babbage cited this work specialization by Prony as helping to inspire his vision for the first mechanical computers, which he designed in the 1830s.[29] And yet today, almost two centuries later, knowledge workers confidently continue to insist that their simplest tasks cannot be standardized and similarly specialized. And their management executives defer to this misperception.

- **Division of labor.** Smith talked about the people drawing out wire to make pins. But the division of labor can be further subdivided: There's . . .

  1. **Division of work.** Think of the ancient Egyptians dividing work on the pyramids among skilled craftsmen, artisans, stonecutters, and porters. That's the same way today's general contractors and subcontractors divide work. Next there's . . .

  2. **Division of job positions.** Think of a factory where the work is divided by job—like a machine shop. Each machinist performs groups of activities and is responsible for the quality of the output. Even the cavemen's flint-tool lines are examples; it's really a workroom with craft or artisanal workers who design their own "bun-

dles" of activities and methods (like knowledge workers today). And then there's . . .

3. **Division of work management.** This is what can be called the "specialization of specialization." It occurs when the design of production is removed from the workers and transferred to a "specializer." In factories, the task of specializing labor became industrial engineering (i.e., a specialty). But knowledge workers, like the cavemen toolmakers above, generally retain the "decision rights" to design their own production methods. That's because of . . .

4. **Division of perception.** This has not been widely adopted within businesses. The perception of what work can be feasibly standardized is still as uncontrolled and autonomous as a century ago, when the U.S. market was crowded with a million ax models. The same is true today: no one is taking inventory of countless one-off perceptions in the business. But just like Herbert Hoover, executives could mandate that the perception of knowledge work activities be standardized and documented. And then industrial engineers could go to work industrializing the million unnecessarily different ways that knowledge workers perform tasks as simple as chopping wood: reconciliation, reporting, reviewing, and more.

As hinted earlier, there's still that big hot-button issue of autonomy, or decision rights. Who owns what? This is about how work is designed and done. And it's always been hotly contested. In fact, in the early days of the U.S. Armory at Harpers Ferry, West Virginia, when the productivity-driven plant manager insisted on introducing division of labor, one of his craftsman gunsmiths murdered him.[30]

In today's conventional factory, autonomy is as tightly managed as the inventory. Yet in the office, it's a free-for-all, and a source of continual complaints. People are perennially confused over precisely who's responsible and accountable for various work activities, such as checking for errors—thus, you get checkers checking the checkers.

So the trillion-dollar question for management is this: Will your business decide to actively manage according to these timeless principles, or will it simply let knowledge workers continue operating randomly on rules of thumb? Of course, in the long run, there are timeless remedies for those who ignore timeless principles. Upstarts will ultimately arrive and apply these industrialization principles to existing business models. Everyone might snicker, but eventually one will walk away with the entire value chain of an industry. Sears did it to the general store, Walmart did it to Sears, and Amazon is now doing it to Walmart. See Figure 3-2.

**FIGURE 3-2**    Amazon's willingness to embrace the timeless principles of industrialization is reflected in its profit margin compared with Walmart's. Walmart data reflect profits before interest and taxes. Amazon data are for developed markets and exclude Prime video and international investments.

This graph is based on data from Inflection Capital Management, "A Deeper Look into the Culpability for the 'Retail Apocalypse,'" accessed June 8, 2018, www.inflectioncapital.co/insights.

## Nothing New Under the Sun

Oh, and one more thing, as long as we're in timeless mode: all of the ideas discussed above are very old news—well over two centuries old for Prony's application of them in knowledge work. Almost nobody knows about how these can be applied to knowledge work because they were first published in that context by Charles Babbage, hidden in the wake of Watt's steam engine, only 50 years after that first big rock, but about 150 years before the dawn of business computing—the Digital Age. They fell into the most boring segment of the boring long tail of history, in between two big rocks—steam and electricity. During this period, Babbage, along with his collaborator, Ada Lovelace, was designing the first mechanical computer and the algorithms that would enable its operation. In fact, Babbage, a fan of both Smith and Prony, concisely summarized two of the central ideas that form the core of this book. First, he recognized that knowledge work, which he termed "mental operations," can benefit from division of labor just as easily as manual work, or what he termed "mechanical work." And second, he noted a type of "virtuous waste" prevalent then, as today, throughout knowledge work: performing tasks below your pay grade. The following quote is drawn from his "notebooks."

> We have seen, then, that *the effect of the division of labour, both in mechanical and in mental operations*, is, that it enables us to purchase and apply to each process precisely that quantity of skill and knowledge which is required for it:
>
> We avoid employing any part of the time of a man who can get eight or ten shillings a day by his skill in tempering needles, in turning a wheel, which can be done for sixpence a day;
>
> *And we equally avoid the loss arising from the employment of an accomplished mathematician in performing the lowest processes of arithmetic.*[31] (Emphasis added.)

This chapter has helped to explain the infamous productivity paradox and highlighted the fact that investment in office technology has failed to produce comparable productivity gains—in stark contrast with the other "big rocks" of the Industrial Revolution. And even if the overlooked "long tail" of timeless improvements has not contributed to the paradox, one might reasonably wonder: Why don't businesspeople look at the long tail?

Why don't executives first turn to their CIOs, their CFOs, their operations, or their employees for improvement insights? Why do businesses believe that you must choose between goals, such as improving productivity *or* improving the customer experience? Why do almost all U.S. auto drivers think their skills are above average?

The answers are sometimes wired deep in your brain. In fact, there are three discrete types of biases. Chapter 4 will shine a much-needed light on these.

---

## CHAPTER 3: **TAKEAWAYS**

1. Breakthrough productivity gains are conventionally perceived as the adoption of breakthrough technologies—the multiple, big-rock theory of improvement.
   - The Steam Age
   - The Electric Age
   - The Digital Age
2. The Digital Age has failed to produce meaningful, measurable productivity gains in knowledge work despite the adoption of office technology—from the 1960s on.
   - The causes of this phenomenon have defied detection since at least the 1980s.
   - In recent decades it has been known as the "productivity paradox."
   - However, the same paradox is documented in the early 1900s, when offices adopted precomputer technology.
3. An alternative, one-rock theory argues that industrialization is the single, timeless method for improvement—only the enabling technologies change. Implications:
   - The productivity paradox is lastly a technology problem.
   - Secondarily, it is a management problem.
   - First and foremost, it is a *perception* problem.

---

# PART II

# THE SOLUTION

# FINDING—AND FIXING—YOUR BUSINESS'S BIGGEST BLIND SPOTS

Imagine yourself spending a typical day in the life of today's knowledge worker: You take your morning commute, head toward the Starbucks in your office building, and tap the app on your phone to order. Strolling inside to collect your order, you scroll Facebook and the news feeds. The music playing in the store is catchy . . . what's that song? Your phone tells you. You purchase it instantly and file it in your cloud library. You pick up your coffee and ride the elevator upstairs, while checking the status of your latest Amazon order. Good news! That Roomba shipped. Soon you won't have to vacuum the apartment.

As soon as you reach the office, however, you're transported back in time. Sure, the workstations have the latest technology. But all of these technology upgrades have done little to improve the *work activities.* Reconciling numbers. Correcting errors. Manually gathering missing data. Roughly 40 percent of the documents that arrive in the office—even though they're electronic—can be classified as "not in good order," or NIGO.

And so the work begins. Remediating files. Hunting down and filling in missing data. Phoning others to correct all those errors. Why can't things get done right the first time? It's the antithesis of the Starbucks/Amazon/Spotify world you just left behind.

Over the course of the day, you spend a couple of fragmented hours on the phone correcting the NIGO and fruitlessly attempting to prevent its recurrence. You explain the same instructions to seemingly indifferent coworkers, over and over again.

But they're not indifferent. They're furiously busy correcting the NIGO that arrived at *their* workstations.

Next, you start extracting data to create the report that your manager requested yesterday. The prospect is depressing: experience indicates that you'll be forced to spend hours cleaning, reconciling, and reorganizing the data—more rework. You wonder, almost aloud: "Why doesn't somebody clean up the data in the data warehouse? Whose job is that anyway? Better yet, why wasn't it better organized in the first place? We've got brand-new technology, yet it's just loaded up with the same old junk data from the old system."

## Does Anyone Actually Notice?

If people kept track of these activities and timed them, they'd see that at least a third of the day is sucked into a sinkhole of rework, remediation, and countless other avoidable tasks.

But in knowledge work, *nobody keeps track.* Nobody even thinks twice about these minutiae. Nobody perceives this as a vast, costly ocean of counterproductive, avoidable waste. It's just business as usual.

To the knowledge workers on the front line, it seems patently obvious that all this could be improved. With even some simple fixes, most of the wasted effort could be removed or reduced.

But they are not confident. In the larger scheme of things, they assume everything must be working according to plan. There *must* be some economically rational explanation. There's no way the company would ignore or violate such a basic rule of commonsense economic logic. Somebody would notice such valuable waste. But nobody *does* seem to notice.

## The Miswired Brain

This chapter will explore the *reasons* that all this waste continues, unchecked, in knowledge work organizations everywhere. The reasons may be surprising, empowering, and ultimately fascinating, because they're hardwired into our brains as *Homo sapiens.* That's precisely what makes them so stubbornly difficult to recognize and surmount. But it can be done. Importantly, overcoming these cognitive barriers is the crucial prerequisite to all the nuts-and-bolts/how-to chapters in Part II of this book.

This chapter provides an overview of the cognitive biases that derail the best intentions in business. It will zero in on the seemingly simple (but deceptively nuanced) *principle of least effort.* And it will conclude with a story of a well-meaning CFO who gets his conventional perceptions of productivity improvement shredded—in a good way.

## Cognitive Bias, or What You Think You Think

Remember, in the last chapter, that 93 percent of U.S. automobile drivers rank their skills as above average? That's no outlier. Consider some of these other painful examples:

- Eighty-seven percent of Stanford MBA students believe that their academic performance falls above the median.[1]
- Perhaps they did their undergrad work at the University of Nebraska . . . where 68 percent of the faculty once rated themselves in the top 25 percent for teaching ability.[2]
- High school students are not immune. More than 70 percent of SAT test takers rank their leadership capabilities above the median.[3]
- Roughly 85 percent of these students consider their ability to get along with others to be above average.[4]
- A full 25 percent of SAT test takers believe that they fall in the top 1 percent.[5]
- And here's the capper: test subjects in similar experiments routinely rank themselves "less susceptible to these biases than the average American."[6]

Biases are everywhere. Scientists have studied and cataloged a diverse range of nearly universal errors that evade detection and hide in plain sight. The one noted multiple times above has a name: it's called the "overconfidence effect."

These kinds of ingrained perceptual quirks pervade business, passing unnoticed, while costing trillions in squandered opportunity. Overcoming them is what can be described as "cognitive business improvement."

## Don't Trust Your Brain (or Your Eyes)

Look at Figure 4-1. Square A is much darker than Square B, right? Wrong. They're the exact same shade.

**FIGURE 4-1**   Think A and B are different shades? Think again.

This is a classic optical illusion, so powerful at tricking the brain that many people still refuse to believe it even when they see proof. Figure 4-2 provides that proof. The gray person on the left is the exact same shade as *both* Squares A and B.

It's called the "same-shade" illusion, and it's one of dozens. It's also the easiest way to understand cognitive business improvements. They're like illusions or mirages that fool our most basic thought processes—particularly judgments that everyone takes for granted. Consumers perceive identical cola samples to taste different. Eyewitnesses recall events that never happened. Distractions cause movie audiences to overlook glaringly obvious editing errors.

**FIGURE 4-2**  As the lighter gray person shows, both A and B are actually the same shade.

The same thing happens in business. Consumers call a contact center with easily preventable problems, and executives think of it as customer service—not glaringly obvious errors. Executive teams will ponder "trade-offs" where none exist: cost versus quality, operational versus strategic, and so on. And if analysis unexpectedly reveals certain products to be unprofitable, executives will rationalize that these money-losers are indispensable to the customers who purchase the profitable ones.

Cognitive biases share many features that ideally suit them as opportunities for near-term business improvements:

- They're widespread.
- Their causes and effects are often highly predictable.
- Similar biases frequently occur in predictable operational areas.
- Rewiring your perception requires no new technology.

These features are annoying but valuable. If they're widespread and predictable, then their solutions are rarely unique and can be reused, like blueprints or templates. If they're commonly found in identical organizations or functions, then discovery efforts can proceed reliably, often with pinpoint accuracy. It's like following a map. And the findings from small analytical samples can be extrapolated to large populations.

Perhaps most appealing of all, *cognitive business improvements are extremely economical and low risk*. Because most cognitive improvement consists of adjusting existing *perception*, most of the related business improvements involve similar adjustments to existing strategies and operations. Consequently, the vast majority of cognitive business improvements, roughly 75 percent on average, require no fundamental change to existing technology, products, or infrastructure. This is an insight that can be put to profitable use.

## But If It's That Easy . . .

Why isn't everyone doing it? Why isn't it easy to discover and decode?

It all sounds deceptively simple. But cognitive business improvement is actually difficult for the very reason described above: it requires the brain to be essentially rewired. Ingrained thinking habits need to change. It may be comforting to know that even professional researchers of cognitive biases—and some are Nobel laureates—readily admit that they still fall victim to the phenomenon, despite their deep awareness of it!

Not only do cognitive biases undermine individual executives' decisions, but they often become officially institutionalized throughout the organization in the form of business processes and operating policies. More insidiously, they can easily pervade the undocumented "tribal knowledge" of the organization. In a diabolically perverse irony, it turns out that the organizations within the enterprise with the greatest potential to shape the company's perception of the value of cognitive business improvement are also the ones that most favor tribal knowledge for their operations: knowledge workers.

By shunning the "foolish" drudgery of standardization and documentation, the "wisest" organizations in the enterprise become the most vulnerable to cognitive biases—especially the "overconfidence effect," aka "illusory superiority" (see some painful examples in the sidebar). It's nothing new. Shakespeare summed it up: "The fool doth think he is wise, but the wise man knows himself to be a fool."

## Where's the Rigor?

Cognitive biases—such as the overconfidence effect—hide in plain sight every day.

*The finance group* can locate an inventory of office chairs pretty easily. But let them try to find an inventory of management reports. It's often impossible. There may be thousands, tens of thousands . . . no one knows. There's no central repository, no rules for naming them, no catalog of unified descriptions. So when you find and compare a few, don't be surprised when the numbers don't reconcile. This is tragic and costly, because *these are the reports required for measuring productivity, profitability, and the company's ability to produce value.*

*In the marketing department,* executives would consider it inexcusable to deliver even the simplest products—shampoo, toothpaste, toasters—without rigorously consistent, multilingual operating instructions and parts descriptions. And they might even face a lawsuit or regulatory complaint if they don't. Internally however, marketing executives from around the world will routinely be expected to comprehend and operationalize abstract concepts relating to brand image, customer characteristics, and purchase preferences without any instructions at all. The fonts and colors for the company logo are consistent and well defined, but customers' purchase-related priorities often exist as tribal knowledge.

## The Three Flavors of Cognitive Bias—and Improvement

Broadly, cognitive business improvements fall into three categories:

1. **Perceptual improvements** focus on the way we perceive reality— or perhaps more accurately, the way in which we *mis*perceive it. This includes everything from the false notion that employee-to-employee performance variance "really isn't that much," to the seemingly trivial impact of operational errors, to misperceptions of randomness or complexity where none really exists, to good old-fashioned virtuous waste.

2. **Logical improvements** cover problems of mental processing. They deal with the organization of ideas and connections between those ideas that can generate false conclusions. Examples include false precision (the insistence on additional detail, even when there's no economic benefit), selective comparability (unintentionally favoring comparisons that support the status quo), and the all-too-rich category of false trade-offs: things like "operational *or* strategic," "cost improvement *or* service improvement," and "cost reduction (save) *or* revenue increase (grow)."

3. **Methodology improvements** deal with the application of cognitive errors and their manifestation in daily activities—the institutionalization of misperception. Examples include unclear decision rights (who determines work design, priorities, and service levels?), confusing, often contradictory definitions (e.g., costs, customers, channels), and undocumented "tribal knowledge."

## The Principle of Least Effort: Not as Simple as It Sounds

Yes, the "principle of least effort" (also known as the "principle of least work effort") is a genuine scientific theory—and not some fancy way of explaining away shortcuts. It's based on straightforward, rational economic logic. And businesses of all types and sizes violate it every day—while (over) confidently believing that they don't. Although it was discussed and published as early as 1894, the principle is generally attributed to the linguist George Kingsley Zipf, who wrote *Human Behaviour and the Principle of Least Effort: An Introduction to Human Ecology*, first published in 1949.

Most people who hear the words "principle of least effort" immediately presume that they understand the concept. It appears self-explanatory. The name of the principle seems to articulate its inherent logic. Some will call it "the path of least resistance," suggesting an electric circuit. Others will think of a travel analogy, "the shortest distance from Point A to Point B." All these characterizations are ostensibly correct. And all imply a logical obviousness that only a fool could overlook. It's a no-brainer. Ask senior business executives if they believe they're successfully following the principle of least effort and they'll smirk. Of course! That question doesn't even merit an answer.

It seems to go without saying that businesses and their workers instinctively adhere to this operating principle as consistently as they obey the law of gravity. But they don't. And the devil is in the subtly nuanced details. Throughout business, particularly in knowledge work operations, this unquestioned principle is systemically overlooked, violated, and misapplied. It costs a fortune in waste and lost opportunity. But just like in the NIGO story that opened this chapter, nobody notices. It's just business as usual.

But how can successful businesses violate such a fundamental error in logic? It seems impossible, but it's actually easy—and pervasive.

## A World Without Detours?

Let's take the analogy of the journey from Point A to Point B. If everything about this journey is obvious, simple, and easily perceived, then there is only one shortest distance—one economically sensible alternative. This single, obvious route will clearly avoid waste. There will be no planning errors (NIGO), no missed turns (operating errors), and no backtracking (rework). Any alternative routes can confidently be discarded at face value. No documentation and analysis will be required to make comparisons. And when an obvious, no-brainer, A-to-B travel situation exists, it's true that only a fool would overlook or misapply the principle of least effort.

But in business, these "ideal travel conditions" rarely apply. And if they do, executives don't expect much profitability unless they have a monopoly. "Blazing the trail for the best route" seems to epitomize successful competition. This is the job of executive management. Capitalizing on opportunities to practice the principle of least effort seems like a no-brainer, unworthy of even mentioning. Overlooking it seems impossible.

Yet the problem is particularly acute in the intangible operations of knowledge work. Here, minimal investment is made to analyze the best route from A to B. Precious little effort is expended to document and analyze the "competencies" that constitute daily work routines *so that those requiring the least work effort can be selected.* In the travel analogy, this would be like the driver who prefers to trust his instincts rather than ask for directions or find a map. That's how businesses routinely violate the principle of least effort. They are vastly and absurdly overconfident in their power of perception, just like the 93 percent of U.S. auto drivers who rank themselves above average.

## Breaking It Down

A close reading of George Zipf's original definition of the principle is helpful for understanding the knowledge work oversight. In his 1949 text, he summarizes it this way: "In simple terms, the Principle of Least Effort means, for example, that a person in solving his immediate problems will view these against the background of his probable future problems, *as estimated by himself.*"[7] (Emphasis added.)

This sounds so naturally logical and reasonable that it hardly seems worth the effort of writing it down. Business managers reading this will nod their heads knowingly. "Sure, that's exactly what I do." In terms of perception, manufacturing execs should be on the same page as knowledge work execs. After all, every manager has to anticipate and solve problems. They all have to perform the mental calculus associated with their decisions, *"as estimated by himself"* or herself. And they have to live with the consequences. But if we are talking about work effort, then the term "probable future problems" seems vague and overly broad.

Fortunately, Zipf provides more detail. He states that people will "strive to minimize the probable *average rate* of work-expenditure over time."[8] (Again, emphasis added.) By the way, this principle doesn't just apply to businesses. Zipf was a linguist, so he was interested in word usage. But others have applied it to hunter-gatherers and even computers. To some *manufacturing* execs, this language—"minimize the probable average rate of work-expenditure over time"—now begins to sound more familiar. And it should:

- They keep track of workers' activities. They time these.
- They calculate the work hours and associated costs.
- They even record and reduce the rates of inbound NIGO.

In short, *they demand hard data that quantify their "average rate of work-expenditure over time."* They track their progress toward complying with this fundamental law of logic. These data shape these executives' fundamental perceptions. Manufacturing management methods bolster the prevailing perception among business executives that the principle of least effort is alive, well, and pervasive throughout all business operations. Surely, the market forces of competition demand nothing less.

But it isn't true. Most executives involved in *knowledge work* have no such comparable data. For them, "average rate of work-expenditure" is a qualitative or aspirational notion—a gut feel. It will shape their perception. It will influence their estimates of "probable future problems." But it's business as usual. They will not notice that their operational decisions are largely unmoored from operational facts such as *average rate of work-expenditure over time.*

Zipf concludes with a straightforward observation: "Moreover, he will strive to solve his problems in such a way as to minimize the *total work* that he must expend in solving both his immediate problems and his probable future problems."[9] (Again, emphasis added.)

Now it's getting more complicated. This is no longer a no-brainer; it's an algorithm. *Manufacturing* execs will read "total work" and think of concepts like "total cost of quality" or "total cost of ownership." These include maintenance and the rework arising from inbound errors. Like Henry Ford, they maintain detailed cost and performance charts. To them, the words "probable future problems" imply an actual trend line, or a Six Sigma statistical forecast, derived from operating data. In other words, this involves mathematical probabilities, minimization tools, and algorithms that optimize productivity.

*Knowledge work* executives, by contrast, will have virtually no comparable data. They will give up easily, surrendering with cognitive rationalizations, such as, "Our work is unique," "Collecting data is uneconomical," or "New technology will fix it." For them, *this* is their "least work effort" alternative. It's how they solve both their immediate problems and their probable future problems. Done!

## Overconfident Perception: The 800-Pound Gorilla

Senior knowledge work executives, by acting on intuition alone, overlook opportunities within their operations to rigorously apply the principle of least effort. This isn't surprising. As humans, we are hardwired to vastly overestimate our capabilities of perception. If you thought those 93 percent of drivers who are "above average" were bad, consider the following oversight. It's often called the "invisible gorilla," and it's directly relevant to helping you recognize your business's biggest blind spots.

In a now-famous 1999 experiment, two Harvard psychology professors performed a simple test of what they term "the powerful and pervasive influence of the illusion of attention. We experience far less of our visual world than we think we do."[10] They asked their test subjects to watch a brief video of basketball players on two teams, one dressed in black shirts and the other in white. The subjects were asked to count the number of ball passes between the white-shirted players as the two teams moved around in a small circle. Simple enough. However, during the video, with no prior warning, a person dressed in a gorilla costume walks into the players' circle, thumps both fists on its chest, and leaves. The basketball players do not seem to notice the gorilla; they continue uninterrupted throughout the video.

After the video concludes, the subjects were asked if they noticed anything unusual while they were counting passes. *Half of the subjects did not notice the gorilla.* And when shown a replay, many reacted with disbelief, even anger. A significant number of them offered denials and rationalizations, insisting, for example, that the videos were switched or otherwise rigged. They resisted acceptance of their observational shortcomings, even when faced with conclusive proof. Despite numerous replications of the experiment over nearly two decades, the results are always the same: overconfidence is highly resistant to fact-based evidence.

Separately, the "gorilla" psychologists used large-scale surveys to determine whether people believe that they would notice an unexpected event even when they were focused on another task. A large majority, 75 percent, were confident that they would.[11]

## Are You Blind to Your Own Blindness?

Other research has shown that the vast majority of us believe that our own perception is less subject to bias than that of others. In a sample of more than 600 U.S. residents, more than 85 percent believed they were less biased than the average American. Only one out of this group of 600 conceded that he might be more biased than average.[12] This phenomenon is called the "blind-spot bias." In business, it insulates against managerial self-doubt—but it also discourages valuable introspection and scrutiny of operations.

In other words, our perception and judgment are significantly blinded by our numerous personal cognitive biases. And this deficiency is topped off by another. As if our "blindness" isn't bad enough, we're also blind to our own blindness.

> We're blind to our blindness. We have very little idea of how little we know. We're not designed to know how little we know.
> —*Daniel Kahneman*[13]

---

# A Silver Lining

We've just run down an agonizingly long list of fundamental, hardwired blind spots that prove the staggeringly consistent unreliability of human (and executive) perception. How, then, can you ever trust yourself—or others—when it comes to decision making? Better still, how can your business benefit from these predictable misperceptions?

The first step toward capitalizing on this overconfidence opportunity is to embrace ignorance. Ignorance is not a void. While it's traditionally been shunned as a weakness among businesspeople, it's the clay that scientists use to mold their theories every day. Modern researchers have proved that admitting ignorance is a high-level cognitive function. As the writer Kathryn Schulz observed, we're not bad at saying "I don't know," we're bad at *knowing* we don't know.[14]

This is not a new insight. The value of ignorance has been noted repeatedly by thinkers since the eras of Confucius and Socrates. But with the rise of intangible assets, there's never been a more valuable time than now to profit from it in business.

# A Story That Will Scorch Your Eyeballs

What would life—business life, at least—look like in a bias-free world? Is it even possible?

It is. The following story provides an example. Remember Raylene, the beleaguered scheduler in the tire factory from Chapter 1? Well this story takes place at the same company.

And I've created a new character here, for illustrative purposes, named Nick Clearsight. He's the one who has been able to work past his biases.

Nick is a founding partner at a private equity (PE) firm. His company has invested heavily in a large, publicly held, underperforming business— Raylene's company—that competes in a stodgy industry: tires. Nick's PE firm is an activist investor, attempting to stimulate major change in the tire company. And Nick has been personally assigned to quickly increase the value of the PE investment, along with the share price, by improving operating performance, without waiting for new technology, outsourcing, or capital investment.

## *The Irresistible Force Meets the Immovable Object*

This story begins as Nick flies into town to have lunch with the tire company CFO, Toby Surefoot, a man who has yet to ponder the possibilities and promises of predictable business misperceptions.

After some small talk, Nick focused the conversation. He told Toby, "You already know that you guys do a fantastic job of manufacturing tires. The company has accumulated and refined more than a century's worth of technical data and practical know-how for designing and manufacturing them. We didn't invest to tell you how to make tires."

Toby nodded cautiously. Where was this headed?

Nick smiled. "What would you say," he asked, "are the most valuable improvement opportunities for the company? When I say 'improvement,' I'm talking about something, anything, that will increase margins, earnings, and the share price. Near-term, long-term, it doesn't matter—anything and everything. What comes to mind for you? Assume you owned the business."

Toby had given this lots of thought before. He replied with confidence, "I think my list would be the same as what we have on our plate right now.

We need to upgrade the plants. There's a new generation of tire-making machines coming out soon. These could reduce our shop-floor labor in the fabrication room by at least 15 percent. But they're expensive and will also require some plant layout changes and technology upgrades."

Nick: "Anything else?"

Toby continued, "We need to upgrade our enterprise resource planning, or ERP, system. Our IT group has already requested funding. Also, we could automate many of the workers' activities in our distribution centers. Robotics in distribution is unbelievably cool."

Nick paused, and then he replied, "So, all the improvements depend on technology? Most involve capital investment for production? And the goal of each is to reduce the hourly labor in your plants and distribution warehouses?"

Toby was suddenly self-conscious. What had he overlooked? "No, no, of course not," he offered, recovering. "We have lots of other improvements. We still have our stock buyback program under way. That will boost earnings per share. Personally, if I owned the business, I'd also increase debt, leverage the balance sheet a bit more to boost return on equity for shareholders. But the board would never go for it. They're highly risk-averse."

Nick chuckled. "Financial engineering then? That's a switch. Usually, we outside investors are the ones who get slammed for our interest in this topic."

Toby paused. Nick reassured him. "Look Toby, I'm not trying to give you a hard time. I'm simply trying to illustrate my point. The areas of the business where you instinctively hunt for value—manufacturing, distribution, and the hourly workforce—are already close to fully optimized.

"What we know from our investing experience is that the conventional productivity hunt is way too narrow. Businesses repeatedly cover the same ground, missing the forest for the trees. They overlook massive improvement value—and massive strategic vulnerabilities. These hide in plain sight, just below the surface of conventional observation. Think of a stolen, priceless work of art that's hidden underneath a velvet painting of Elvis."

Toby snickered but resolved to be diplomatic. "Well, Nick, I think I can tell you pretty confidently that we don't have any velvet Elvis paintings, or priceless artwork hiding beneath them. We would notice those."

Toby continued, "There simply aren't any 'massive, overlooked improvement opportunities' hiding in our company. I would've seen them. Or any of a thousand other people would have. This might disappoint you, but *making tires is our core competence.* It's what we know how to do best. We are incumbents in a very mature industry. It's not glamorous. I don't see any Silicon Valley start-ups targeting the tire industry. If you and your investors want a big score, maybe we could do an acquisition. Otherwise, our improvement gains are bound to be incremental. All the breakthroughs in tire manufacturing are probably behind us."

Toby didn't expect Nick to agree, but he did. "Exactly!" Nick said. "So then why are all your improvement efforts focused on the already optimized activities of *making tires*? These are a *minority* of total activities—and total employees. Why aren't you looking for productivity improvements everywhere *else* in your business? Why not examine all those other activities in the business as minutely as tire making? Could there be breakthroughs there?"

Toby squinted skeptically.

Nick continued, "You don't look very hard there. You assume that it can't be improved like your plants—industrialized. You're confident that you would notice the value if it were there. And even if you overlooked it, you're certain that someone else would surely notice.

"But what if that 'someone else' was outside your business? Obviously, my PE firm noticed. That's why we're here. But what about someone even more disruptive—Amazon, maybe? This overconfidence hides massive improvements. They hide in plain sight. Overconfidence is the velvet Elvis that hides the priceless masterpiece. And from what I've seen, Toby, this company, like most industry incumbents, is *full* of velvet Elvis paintings."

Toby tried not to sound sarcastic. "OK Nick. Tell me about these improvements that 100,000 employees and millions of our other shareholders—not to mention competitors—manage to overlook every day."

Nick was unfazed. "Where to begin? Overlooked opportunities fall outside the expected range on both ends of the spectrum: Some are too big to notice. Others seem too small to matter."

Toby: "Start with the big ones."

Nick began his list. "How about employee populations? When you mentioned 'productivity improvements' just now, you were targeting the employees who work in the plants and distribution networks. But these 'direct' labor employees are only about 40 percent of the company's 100,000 employees—and their activities have been scrutinized for a century. What about the other 60 percent? Why not study those 60,000 'indirect' employees at the same level of detail?"

Toby replied, "Because those 40,000 directs are the ones our business managers chose as most valuable for productivity improvement."

Nick scowled. "Wait. Aren't *you* a business manager? Isn't the CFO supposed to be the ultimate arbiter of value? How can you allow 60 percent of the workforce to go virtually unexamined?"

Toby was ready with his reply. "Given the high volume of tires we produce, the economics are more favorable."

Nick pounced again. "The 40 percent is more favorable than the 60 percent?"

Toby nodded.

Nick: "Who ever forced you to *choose*? This isn't an either-or situation. That's a false trade-off—another velvet Elvis."

Nick was on a roll. "I don't see why you can't pursue both. And I don't buy the 'favorable economics' argument, either. We don't even need a cocktail napkin to do this math. Look at it like this:

"For every $1 of revenue that comes in the door, the direct labor today consumes 9 cents of it. You said that your tire automation is going to save 15 percent of the labor in the fabrication room. The fab room is a minuscule portion of the plant total, but no matter. I'll apply this reduction to companywide direct labor. The economics are still inferior.

"I'll multiply the 9 cents by 15 percent, round up, and give you 1.5 cents of labor savings. But that doesn't drop straight to the bottom line. It has to run the gauntlet of overhead, or selling, general, and administrative expense—SG&A."

Nick continued, "The company has to spend on engineering and managing this new equipment. Your finance group has to create reports for this project. This SG&A burden is *28 percent* companywide. So now, after SG&A, your savings of 1.5 cents is down to about 1.1 cents."

Toby saw his opening. "Well, Nick, that single penny, or 1 percent, is worth $350 million in stock value to our shareholders. We'd be negligent if we didn't do it."

Nick: "I totally agree. But why stop there? I'm saying that you should also be scrutinizing the productivity of the other 60 percent of employees using the same 'factory' approach.

"Let's say that you saved 15 percent of the labor in the SG&A, or indirect operations. Even if we plug these SG&A people in at the same low labor cost as the factory workers, this generates a savings that's 50 percent greater than your 1.5 cents because there are 50 percent more of them. That takes us to an indirect savings of 2.25 cents, on top of your direct savings. But as you know, the average cost of the SG&A employees is more than *double* that of the plant workers. So that doubles the 2.25 to 4.50. That means that we can multiply the value of your 1 penny of net direct labor savings, that's worth $350 million to shareholders, by 4.5 for this SG&A labor savings. And SG&A savings drop straight to the bottom line. That translates to about *$1.5 billion* in shareholder value, or more than four times the value of your plant-floor productivity improvements. But why not do them both? That way you'll add over *$1.8 billion* in market value."

It all sounded good. And looked great on paper, cocktail napkin or no. But Toby had heard this SG&A argument before. He was ready with the rebuttal: "We've tried to reduce SG&A labor before. We invest in technology to keep these workers productive. We've cut headcount through mandates, but it just comes back. Most of SG&A is just the unavoidable cost of doing business. It's like the old saying, 'You can't cost-cut your way to greatness.' It's counterproductive."

Nick took a deep breath. Ah, the familiar incumbent defenses: false trade-offs, selective comparisons, and the old "We've already tried that." It was frustrating. Management wouldn't tolerate these same arguments from their plant-floor employees.

He decided to approach the topic from a different, more disruptive, angle. "Toby, a few minutes earlier, you said that Silicon Valley wasn't interested in the tire industry. You said it wasn't glamorous enough to attract any start-ups' attention, right?"

Toby nodded. "That's true. I mean, Amazon sells some of our competitors' tires. There are also a few other smaller, web-based resellers. But we don't think the web is a profitable channel for us, and we don't sell through it. But I can't think that Amazon wants to make tires."

"No," Nick agreed, "but it didn't want to publish books either. It didn't have to. And look at the damage to the incumbents in *that* industry. You're expecting them to attack your front lines, to make tires. But Amazon is actually in the SG&A business. It'll attack you from the *rear,* where you don't expect it. It'll attack your SG&A. It doesn't have to make tires to seriously damage your business. It's already selling tires, so it's already outperforming many of your company's existing SG&A groups, like your finance department.

Toby raised his brows. "How do you know Amazon is better at SG&A than we are?"

Nick: "Because you just told me that it's already selling your competitors' tires. That means that it's buying these from your competitors. Those competitors are making a profit. Amazon is not selling at a premium; it generally sells at market parity, but often less. So that means that Amazon's SG&A includes your competitors' profit, Amazon's profit, plus the cost of all those SG&A processing activities that Amazon performs: order management, payment, warehousing, advertising, delivery, and so on. Let me put it to you differently: If your SG&A is lower, then why aren't you underselling Amazon? Why aren't you guys selling elsewhere through the web?"

"Because," replied Toby, "it would reduce our average margin and aggravate our existing brick-and-mortar distribution channels."

"Okay, then," shrugged Nick. "Then just wait until Amazon aggravates them—and you. Think about the strategic vulnerability of your high-cost SG&A. It's an Achilles' heel. Today, for every dollar that comes in the door, 60 cents goes to producing tires and 12 cents goes ultimately to earnings. So that adds up to 72 cents total. The remaining 28 cents goes to SG&A at your company.

"Today, that figure represents massive, underrecognized improvement value for your business and our PE investors. But for Amazon, your 28-cent SG&A is another big juicy target market. Your new tire-machine improvement plan will target the usual suspects: plant labor and technology. And after a big capital investment, if everything goes well, it could perhaps add another penny to your 12 cents of earnings. *But it ignores your SG&A exposure.* I just showed you how to take almost a nickel out of SG&A, with *no* technology. And my experience shows that there's typically *double* that amount available. But you have to get your industrial engineers scrutinizing every activity throughout the company—not just the plant and warehouses. You need to industrialize your SG&A 'factory,' just like Amazon has already industrialized its business."

Toby slumped back in his seat as Nick wrapped up his argument. "One day, not long from now," Nick predicted, "Amazon will convince one of your competitors to sell tires to them for close to your direct cost: 72 cents. And Amazon will find some low-cost offshore manufacturer who will purchase the same new tire-making technology that you are considering. Maybe the manufacturer is installing it as we speak. The moment this happens, your 28 cent SG&A becomes a massive competitive disadvantage. Amazon will load up its automated warehouses with the competitor's tires and slam away at your cost structure.

"Maybe it won't even be Amazon. Walmart and Costco already have retail stores with automotive centers. They could sell tires on their websites and also provide installation in their auto centers. The fact is, Silicon Valley start-ups and digital start-ups everywhere are looking for operations to standardize, simplify, eliminate, and automate—to 'industrialize.'

SG&A is a juicy target. They don't have to manufacture tires to create a massive strategic liability for you."

---

## CHAPTER 4: **TAKEAWAYS**

1.  Layers of cognitive biases and misperceptions are hardwired into the human brain, posing two types of costly problems for business:
    *   They upend simple, painfully obvious notions, such as the principle of least effort.
    *   They persist because humans are biased to believe they are less biased than others.

2.  Within knowledge work, cognitive bias offers valuable, predictable improvement opportunity in three categories:
    *   Fundamental perception and observation, e.g., of operations, markets
    *   Logic and reasoning, e.g., avoiding false trade-offs
    *   Methodologies and tools, e.g., documentation errors, tribal knowledge

3.  Manufacturers have overcome these biases by industrializing their production and distribution operations. However, all "unindustrialized" knowledge work operations represent a major competitive vulnerability—for manufacturers as well as service providers.

---

## CHAPTER 5

# TRANSFORMING YOUR BUSINESS INTO A KNOWLEDGE WORK FACTORY

The earliest days of launching or leading a knowledge work transformation can be downright daunting. How do you begin to organize your thinking? This chapter lays the foundation for the knowledge work factory: the four elements of industrial (and knowledge) work. To do it, we're going to take a closer look at a real factory and see how it compares—and contrasts—with a knowledge work organization. We'll reveal the three errors that conspire to hide the knowledge work industrialization opportunity. We'll draw some intriguing parallels with a successful organization 50 million years in the making. And finally, we'll provide an effective two-pronged, first-stage approach for successful knowledge work industrialization.

## Your Organization Isn't a "Factory." But How Might You *See* It That Way?

Overwhelming. Initially it feels hopelessly intimidating to even *imagine* launching an industrialization effort in a knowledge work organization. You may be Raylene on a seven-person scheduling team. You might be Bob, managing several thousand employees in insurance operations. Size won't matter. Whether your organization is large or small, the prospect of industrializing its knowledge work is a perceptual challenge that arrives like a punch in the gut.

Where do you even start? As you survey the offices full of knowledge workers, the sheer number of tasks being performed appears infinite. Unmanageable. And before any industrialization opportunities can even be identified, it appears that someone must first document, catalog, measure, and model *each one of those tasks*. It's enough to boggle the mind and coax it into overconfidently using the "least effort" bias as an escape—"too complex!"

Push back against first impressions. Withhold judgment. Don't start by considering the initiative's work plan or activities. Instead, as uncomfortably Zen-like as it may sound, *start by considering your own mind and how to overcome its twin traps of misperception and overconfidence.*

Sharpen your perception to recognize the four major elements of industrial work that can help organize knowledge work into a virtual factory. They're hiding in plain sight. But with just a little unconventional perception, they will become apparent. And subsequent chapters will show how to use them to formalize your knowledge work factory and supercharge productivity.

## Go It Alone . . . at First

Here's an important guideline for your initial efforts: *resist the urge to consult others,* especially knowledge workers.

Why? Because "nobody knows anything." (More about this in Chapter 6.)

They have no industrialization experience. Facts are scarce. But like 93 percent of U.S. drivers, they will overconfidently weigh in with their "expertise."

Ask them if they think it's feasible to "industrialize" or standardize any portion of their work. With rock-jawed certainty, they'll confirm the status quo: "Standardization is impossible." "Our work is unique." And they will quickly provide excruciatingly detailed anecdotes supporting their anti-standardization bias.

Without gathering any data, or laying preemptive perceptual groundwork, you may feel ready to quit before you start. "It's too costly," you'll find yourself thinking. "Too slow. Too risky. It's not worth the effort. And besides, industrialization principles have been around for centuries. If these could be applied to knowledge work, then surely somebody, some business, or some expert would've already done it by now. It seems absurd for us to be pioneering it in our business."

Of course it seems absurd, but that's just overconfident perception talking. Paradoxically, as the notion of industrializing knowledge work is contemplated, *over*confident perception responds with a sudden attack of organization-wide *under*confidence. "Can do" becomes "No can do."

Overconfidence bias never hesitates. It responds with carved-in-stone certainty. And overconfidence never invests. It doesn't pause to consider that a little bit of near-term standardization inconvenience can deliver a competitive productivity gain that lasts forever. Industrialization helps the entire organization conform properly to the principle of least effort—not use it as a shortcut. But overconfidence is not a big-picture thinker. So recognize overconfidence and put it on pause. And initially avoid accepting knowledge workers' opinions on industrialization.

## A Mental Tour of a Conventional Factory

Begin by picturing a conventional factory in your mind. We're going to take an imaginary video tour of it, visualizing the elements of its industrial operations as we go.

The tour begins outdoors. The camera pans across the exterior of factory walls, warehouses, and other peripheral buildings. It zooms over the delivery trucks, each filled with raw materials, and enters the plant floor. Here, a wide-angle shot reveals rows of interconnected production lines. As the camera tracks alongside a moving conveyor, it shows a hive of tightly choreographed activity as workers and materials move about.

Now we cut to a fast series of close-ups:

- Individual workers perform single, repetitive activities.
- The workers then hand off parts to robots, working right beside them.
- The workers use their hands; the robots use their surprisingly dexterous pincers.

As our video tour concludes, we see perfect finished products pouring off the production line. Potato chips or cars, it doesn't matter; our perception is entranced by the speed, volume, and consistency delivered by continuous-flow mass production—the miracle of industrialization.

Well, that was interesting, but was it *useful?* Perception will leap to say no. Overconfidence offers a simple, circular explanation for this miracle of industrialization: "Oh, that's *factory* work. Of *course* it's standard, because it all consists of *standard activities.* How obvious."

Conventional perception never contemplates the fact that *these factory activities were not always standard.* And it was *not* always obvious. At some point in time, people confronted the "hopelessly overwhelming" task of making them standard. It was massively inconvenient, just like always. A painfully long tail of activities preceded an industrialization miracle. The breakthrough seems embarrassingly obvious only in hindsight.

So how did they do that? Where is the industrialization instruction manual? Unfortunately, the long tail of activities that precede any industrialization miracle is rarely the subject of video tours or even history books. These amateurish, trial-and-error industrialization efforts are almost never well documented. After all, what entrepreneurs have the time to innovate furiously while *also* documenting the tedious history of their effort? Consequently, the histories of industrialization efforts, the "instruction manuals," are written by the marketplace victors. Most are memoirs, reconstructed with, and subject to, the benefits of hindsight bias, decades later. The long tails of activity end up as footnotes. If we're lucky, there might be the odd, surviving photo that provides a contextual glimpse of the "amateurs" before their trials and errors finally succeeded (see Figure 5-1).

In Chapter 9, we'll dig into some of these memoirs to identify detailed insights on the methods for our industrialization efforts. And now, as promised . . .

**FIGURE 5-1**    This image shows the entire Microsoft workforce in 1978. Who could have expected what Microsoft would become?

Photo by Kevin P. Casey/Bloomberg via Getty Images.

## The Four Elements of Industrial (and Knowledge) Work

Let's replay the video from our imaginary plant tour. If we look closely, we see that it has recorded four essential elements of industrial work. These are the building blocks that enable the standardization of knowledge work. Fortunately, each of these elements currently exists within knowledge work operations. The first challenge is to perceive them. Then, with documentation and a bit of trial and error, we can refine and rigorously manage these elements to bring the miracle of industrialization to knowledge work operations.

## Element 1. Capacity

In an industrial factory, "nameplate capacity" is the term used to describe the intended, full-load, sustained *output* of the facility. It is measured in units, or throughput. Think of tonnage from a steel plant. This throughput is perceived as the product of buildings and machines. It's a function of the obvious "things"—tangible assets—that visitors invariably recall from their plant tour. Throughput figures are adjusted downward to reflect expected capacity constraints or reductions. For example, it is reduced for machine maintenance downtime. For our purposes, nameplate capacity is a net figure.

By comparison, in knowledge work, not everyone today thinks in terms of units of output. Thus throughput is not our first choice as a good measure for the capacity of a knowledge work factory. Employees are its assets. And these employees' available work time is a simple way to quantify capacity. Just like in a conventional factory, we can adjust it downward to reflect expected constraints or reductions: vacations, sick time, lunch breaks, and similar deductions. This will yield the nameplate capacity of our knowledge work factory in "net available hours."

### Spoiler Alerts

Later on, in Chapter 8, we will combine nameplate capacity with work-product volumes (element #4, "Products," below) to calculate through-put—and then, just as in a conventional factory, we will begin to use productivity-based performance management. This will represent completion of the first of two phases for the development of our knowledge work factory.

Still later, in Chapter 11, we'll use business-process maps to further divide organizational capacity into detailed work activities (element #3, "Work Activities," below). This provides a more granular view that delivers an activity-based management capability. That will complete the second phase of our knowledge work factory development project.

## Element 2. Processes

Assembly lines represent the most classic, most tangible, and most fun-to-observe production processes to recognize in a manufacturing plant. For knowledge work, we must use the more ambiguous—and less tangible—business processes. Several of these are widely known already. For example, those involved in accounting operations might mention the "record-to-report" process. They are referring to the business process that begins with the initial recording of general-ledger entries (debits and credits), includes the financial close, and ends with the issuance of a report—we will term this report a "work product." This could include anything from an informal internal operating report to an external, highly regulated financial disclosure report. You might recognize the widely used terms for other common end-to-end business processes, such as the "order-to-cash" or "procure-to-pay" processes. These represent only the big, well-known processes. There are thousands of smaller ones.

As we conceive our knowledge work factory, it's helpful to start to think of business processes as summaries—or data tables—of work activities. Documenting business processes defines the quantities, sequences, and dependencies of work activities.

## Element 3. Work Activities

These have characteristics that are surprisingly similar for both conventional and knowledge work factories. Yet knowledge workers struggle mightily to visualize their work as "activities." There's a simple, one-word explanation: duration. In a conventional factory, activities are typically measured down to fractions of minutes, often to two decimal places. Activity durations will be relatively uniform and consistent. If any single duration becomes too long, it will be subdivided to reflect what is likely a process, or a sequence of smaller activities.

Why do that? It's because conventional factory management thinks about optimizing work activities as pieces, or portions, of total nameplate capacity and production processes. In a conventional factory, activities are perceived as merely predictable and manageable portions of the total available capacity. This is not an open question. It's not debatable. Everyone understands that the sum of all activities must reconcile precisely with the total capacity figure—even if some activities are avoidable waste. This is the job of management. This is what Raylene, our plant scheduler from Chapter 1, is charged with planning. If the plan is under capacity, then there will be "lost," or wasted, time. If it's over capacity, then overtime will be required, or the work will be delayed.

By comparison, knowledge workers will define "activities" vaguely if at all. They will describe indefinite durations of days or weeks. These are too long to be useful; long-duration activities begin to resemble processes and cause confusion. These activities need to be broken down into smaller, more manageable pieces. In the same breath, however, knowledge workers will also define activities with durations of only a few seconds. They don't think of activities as standard-duration, predictable portions of the total available capacity. Often, they will fiercely debate the feasibility of applying this notion to knowledge work—it is highly feasible.

Once you commit to enter the world of brief-duration knowledge work activities, their similarities become more obvious. Activities begin to resemble each other more closely. Processes are no longer confused with activities. And standardization no longer seems impossible. Try to think of knowledge work activities as generic, short-duration tasks, just like in a conventional factory. For example, knowledge workers "receive" a work product: via e-mail, electronic files (systems), hard copy, etc. These activities can be assembled to describe more complex subprocesses, such as "filling out a form on a computer" or "fulfilling a request for a brochure." Yes, this initially seems impossibly tedious—overwhelming. But in practice it quickly becomes very easy because activities are similar and repetitive.

## Element 4. Products

Most people can begin to visualize a potato chip factory or a car manufacturing plant by starting with the end product. Visualizing a finance and accounting factory can also begin by viewing its output—reports, for example—as end products. We'll also think about the "by-products" of knowledge work operations, just as manufacturers do for conventional production operations. Many of these knowledge work by-products can be reduced and eliminated. Think of the inbound customer queries that are the costly, unintended, and avoidable by-products of confusing instructions.

———

Initially many people struggle to see how these four essential elements could possibly apply to knowledge, or office, work. But in fact, these elements are already in place. Knowledge work is already arranged in informal "factories." And most of these existing factories even informally use industrialization principles, such as division of labor and standardization. But these elements of industrialization, and the historically profound innovations they enable, are underused and underformalized. That's because they are overlooked or misperceived. To see them, we have to start in the brain, not in the organization.

## How the Brain Ignores These Elements: Three Perceptual Errors

In manufacturing, these four elements of industrial work are obvious. For the most part, they're tangible. People won't bother to debate their existence. When it comes to tangible assets, the overconfidence bias and the physical world are in sync and difficult to misinterpret.

But it's a different story in knowledge work. Here, the four elements are not obvious. They're largely *in*tangible.

Overconfidence doesn't handle intangibility very well. And we've seen that it doesn't mind being at odds with facts or the physical world. Consequently, these valuable industrialization elements are easily overlooked. This *oversight is the first of three perceptual errors* that hide the knowledge work industrialization opportunity. The initial oversight implicitly and gently nudges the door closed on the opportunity. Try to reopen this door the wrong way and the overconfidence bias notices instantly. The next thing you know, people are passionately asserting, "No, I would've noticed that." And as soon as these words have laid down the challenge, the perceptual door has been explicitly shut. It's almost impossible to reopen without heated debate that ends with embarrassment. Someone will have to back down (learn how to preempt this in Chapter 12, "Managing Industrialization").

Keep pushing this subject with knowledge workers. Provide ironclad evidence, and many will double down on the initial denial. The industrialization opportunity—a historic innovation opportunity—remains overlooked and underused. But now it's trapped in an endless loop of perceptual errors that are reinforced by overconfidence, inaccurate assumptions, and self-defeating circular logic. Think of a Möbius strip (see Figure 5-2).

**FIGURE 5-2**  Industrialization opportunities for knowledge work remain trapped in an endless loop of perceptual errors—just like the loops of a Möbius strip.

## *The Path of Least Embarrassment*

One perceptual error identified, two more to go. Like missing the gorilla on the basketball court, acknowledging obvious oversight errors is embarrassing. It offends our overconfidence bias like a slap in the face that leads to a duel. It upends our conventional, technology-based view of business improvement value. The path of least resistance, and least embarrassment, is to **deny** the feasibility of the industrialization opportunity, irrespective of the work elements. "So what? Maybe these 'elements' exist, but they don't apply. Our work is unique." Deny quickly and move on. Don't even consider analysis or a feasibility pilot test. This *denial is the second error*. It reinforces the first error: oversight. It locks the door on the vast, potential productivity gains from knowledge work industrialization. It ensures that these remain overlooked and underused. This paves the way for the *third error: rationalization of the status quo*.

Paradoxically, businesspeople consider the current lack of knowledge work industrialization as proof that it can't be profitably industrialized in the first place. "Why isn't anyone else in our industry doing it? There's your evidence. I told you it's not feasible—and I'm right!" Nobody wants to be wrong, no matter how much it might cost the business.

To help you remember, here's a quick recap of the three errors:

1. Oversight
2. Denial
3. Rationalization of the status quo

## The Better-Mousetrap Dogma

Overconfidence is a doddering old granddad. It doesn't notice (yet another oversight) that digital upstarts are *already industrializing knowledge work:* robots write news articles, algorithms replenish retail inventories, and artificial intelligence apps estimate your auto damage for insurers. Nonetheless, businesspeople love these market-based rationalizations of the status quo, even if they're founded on oversights. One major reason is that, throughout their careers, they are taught that markets are ruthlessly efficient. Businesspeople believe that markets deliver an unerring, unquestioned message regarding innovation: if you build a better mousetrap, the world will beat a path to your door.

Knowledge workers are convinced that the market will search out and recognize valuable innovations. And if it hasn't, the reasoning goes, then the innovation must not be valuable. Therefore, since the world has not beaten a path to the door of knowledge work industrialization for over a century, then this innovation must not be a better mousetrap.

Sure, this logic is circular. It encourages inaction. It's self-defeating and self-serving, but our biased brains leap to embrace it. Overconfidence loves the shortcut it enables: *do nothing.* Most people find it impossible to consider exceptions to the better-mousetrap logic. But of course, the world is *full* of exceptions. Technology historian David E. Nye points out some real whoppers:

> History is replete with examples of innovations that were over-
> looked or underutilized. The Chinese invented gunpowder but
> used it only for fireworks. The Aztecs invented the wheel but used
> it only on children's toys. The ancient Greeks invented a small
> steam engine but thought it a mere curiosity. The Romans invented
> poured concrete, but the process was forgotten and was rein-
> vented centuries later. . . . Innovation on a particular device may
> cease for decades or even centuries before someone reconceptual-
> izes its design or its use.[1]

Chapter 3 mentioned Hero of Alexandria and his steam engine. You can see what it looks like in Figure 5-3.

And Chapter 3 also described one of the newer, more enduring uses for the wheel, namely, the rolling suitcase.

Compared with the examples above, knowledge work industrialization is a fairly obscure innovation. And it's intangible, so it's not hard to see how it could easily be overlooked and underused. Consequently, if you are charged with persuading others to consider relaxing their better-mousetrap dogma, you might want to bring along Professor Nye's list of overlooked innovations—particularly the steam engine. It failed the better-mousetrap test of feasibility for 2,000 years and remained stuck in the "boring" long tail of history before it was rediscovered and launched the world's greatest gain in productivity. After all, if the market can overlook the steam engine, it suddenly seems quite possible, even probable, that it would overlook the idea of knowledge work industrialization.

directional nozzle

steam exhaust
causes sphere
to spin

pivot

steam rises
through tubes

water vaporized
in heated kettle

**FIGURE 5-3**   Hero of Alexandria's steam engine—just one of many overlooked innovations of history. If the market can overlook this invaluable improvement, it can certainly overlook knowledge work industrialization.

Image source: Encyclopaedia Britannica/Illustration Source, reproduced by permission.

## Better-Mousetrap Business Contradictions

Of course, most will not consider that overlooked, ancient Greek steam engine plans are very comparable to, or relevant for, today's businesses. No problem. There are plenty of overlooked "better mousetraps" within today's businesses that provide stunning, inexplicable contradictions. Here are a few of these real-world, painful paradoxes.

- **A memory technology leader can't remember.** One of the world's leading digital-storage-technology producers has a costly memory problem. Although the company delivers world-class, global-scale memory systems for Fortune 200 customers, it loses valuable warranty-service-contract revenue because it fails to keep rigorous records for its installed base of customer equipment. That's not so unusual.

- **An "errors and omissions" leader suffers from . . . errors and omissions.** A global insurer dominates a professional-services market segment with its "errors and omissions" policies that protect architects, software developers, and attorneys from the liabilities of high-risk errors. Paradoxically, the insurer's own error rate for newly issued policies is almost three times the industry average.

- **A leader in global news reporting can't cover its own stories.** An international news-reporting organization represents the "gold standard" by which all journalism is measured for accuracy and timeliness. Unfortunately, the firm's internal management reporting group cannot deliver the same white-glove level of service. Executives struggle with a proliferation of late, inaccurate reports with confusing titles and illegible formats. Many executives can't even determine how many employees work in the organizations they manage.

## Starting Within

Expect to encounter overconfidence obstacles at every successive level of detail. The steam engine oversight might cause everyone to pause at a summary, conceptual level. And the business contradictions might provide examples that seem closer to home. However, the three perceptual errors of Möbius strip logic will simply relocate to the next level of detail. And the rationalizations of the overconfidence bias may take on a different tone:

- "It's too complex to document."
- "We need more information to act."
- "There isn't enough similarity to standardize."
- "That's a short-term gain; we need to think long term."
- "We have to do it this way because that's what customers want."
- "We've already tried that—and it didn't work."
- "IT is automating the business processes; let's wait until the IT folks finish."

- "That's operational; we need strategic improvement."
- "It's a great idea, but now is not the right time."

Ask yourself, "When is the *wrong* time for a great idea?" Never, of course. But these statements often pass unchallenged when respected coworkers espouse them. And the frequency with which these are used can make them part of the culture, causing knowledge workers to nod acceptance of these non sequiturs that reinforce the status quo.

## Countering the Anecdote Avalanche: The Five Whys

As the investigation of knowledge work operations begins, the four elements of industrialization do not calmly present themselves in the neat, tidy, and clearly divided list that we derived from our virtual plant tour. When interviews with knowledge workers begin, expect to be overwhelmed with an avalanche of anecdotes packed with arcane operational detail.

In the real world, these rush at the interviewer, all at once, in a chaotically messy swarm that seems hopelessly overwhelming—like insects protecting a nest.

But—and here's the important part—*this chaotic swarm is highly manageable*. It's not as chaotic as it appears. These efforts can be nimbly managed by focusing on a few critical details of operations—the Five Whys. This simple technique (from manufacturing) is outlined in the story below.

Let's imagine that Bob from the insurance company in Chapter 1 decides to interview some of his knowledge workers. Of course, he'd have to wear a disguise to get honest replies. If he begins in the contact center, he might be presented with the most dramatic anecdotes available—perhaps about customers who have been reduced to tears. Bob might ask the customer service rep precisely when it happened, only to hear: "I can't be sure. It wasn't my customer." This might make Bob wonder if he's encountering the business equivalent of an urban myth.

No matter. Bob can press on and begin to counter the avalanche. He can ask the Five Whys, just like they do in conventional factories. To knowledge workers, this term will sound mysterious. In reality, it resembles the conversational technique of a three-year-old who relentlessly asks "Why?" to every answer provided. Yes, it's as simple as that—and astonishingly effective. Of course, Bob's technique will be a bit subtler than the three-year-old's. And Bob should carefully select his target. Perhaps he should choose an operational "by-product," such as an inbound customer query or complaint. These usually provide excellent illustrations of avoidable, virtuous waste:

**Bob:** "Why (#1) was this customer calling?"

**Rep:** "I'm not sure, but I presume that their policy was canceled."

**Bob:** "Why (#2) are policies typically canceled?"

**Rep:** "They don't pay on time."

**Bob:** "Why (#3) not? Do we know?"

**Rep:** "It varies, but a lot of them are confused by the invoice."

**Bob:** "Why (#4)? What's confusing?"

**Rep:** "Lots of customers I talk to don't recognize our company name on the envelope. They toss it."

**Bob:** "Why (#5) haven't we fixed that if we know about it?"

After the interview, Bob does a bit more investigation. His global company owns multiple smaller insurance companies that operate—and sell—under various individual brand names. Policyholders easily recognize their individual company brand names, but the global parent company's name means nothing to them. Someone in corporate operations, however, decided to save money and standardize. With the best of intentions, the parent company purchased one envelope with the parent's global brand name on the outside as the sender. It's used to centrally mail out *all* the invoices for the individually branded companies. Their brand name appears only on the invoice inside. Understandably, when this envelope arrives with its unfamiliar, parent company's brand logo, many policyholders fail to even recognize it. They toss it out—with their invoice inside—thinking that it's a junk mail campaign. After all, they already have insurance; they don't need any more. The cycle continues and the invoice goes unpaid until the policy is canceled.

Passionately presented anecdotes can initially seem like horror stories—overwhelming. But ask the Five Whys. These often reveal that non-technology root causes (like the printing on an envelope) are to blame for the problem.

The Five Whys can be especially effective for anecdotes that purport to describe deficient IT systems. Often, the technology is adequate, but the data quality is the problem. Typically, data quality is poorly monitored. Take a sample. Don't be surprised if you find that the data are junk. Some of the information may date back decades. It's never been cleaned and standardized over the course of several system upgrades and conversions. It's no surprise then that a "data warehouse" often resembles a landfill.

The consequences are costly. Research indicates that data quality issues reduce labor productivity by up to 20 percent—and prevent 40 percent of all business initiatives from achieving the targeted benefits.[2] One survey of global financial-services firms confirms the lack of attention to data quality: 55 percent of the respondents maintain no defined data quality strategy.[3] They manage data quality on a one-off, ad hoc basis and delegate responsibility for it, in a decentralized manner, to various operating organizations.

## Touring the Anthill of Knowledge Work Operations

In knowledge work, waste is not obvious, *even to the workers remediating it*. Their error correction activity involves the same keystrokes, mouse clicks and screen views as value-added activity. The only difference is perception. As a result, the very definition of "wasted effort" can be highly subjective. It can vary from worker to worker. Everyone is highly autonomous. Sometimes people work together cooperatively on a task. Other times they work alone and are self-directed. Division of labor is present in knowledge work. It's just practiced too informally to be fully productive.

People are busy. They seem to know what they're doing, even though there are no instructions or blueprints. Many of their tasks are similar, even identical; you might call the tasks broadly "standardized." However, the standards are so vague, under-documented, and loosely measured that any benefits are negligible.

Still, everything appears to be under control. And in its own inefficient way, it is. Operations are very loosely "industrialized." But the industrialization in an office tower is about as formal as that found in a flint-tool production site from 30,000 years ago. *From a distance,* knowledge work operations present an impressive, even overwhelming, spectacle. *Without looking closer,* it seems impossible that 30 to 40 percent of all these workers' activities are actually avoidable, albeit well-intentioned, wasted effort.

It's not like a factory. It's more like an anthill.

Ants evolved to dominate the insect world about 50 million years ago.[4] No competitors have displaced them since. Their success is often attributed to their mastery of division of labor—industrialization. Ants also maintain well-defined organizational layers and groups. They work together cooperatively to accomplish such tasks as swarming intruders, hunting prey, and farming fungus. They also work individually. They manage to communicate across colonies that can include a million members. They build structures up to 25 feet tall, without instructions or blueprints. *From a distance,* their achievements present an overwhelming spectacle to behold. And they are, as you can see in Figure 5-4. Everything looks under control, and it is.

However, if you look closer at the ants, you get a different impression. Maybe you've owned an ant farm or watched a nature film shot with a camera inside an anthill. Underground, everything looks pretty chaotic (see Figure 5-5). The tunnels are inefficiently designed. They are full of trash. Many are dead ends, yet ant after ant proceeds down these, only to turn back around. The ants are kept busy with rework. They spend an inordinate amount of their time stuck in traffic jams, crawling around obstructions, or just backtracking because of poorly marked dead ends. They move a leaf fragment, seem to mysteriously change their mind, then move it back again. To the lay observer, this looks like well-intentioned, but wasteful, effort, or virtuous waste, just like the efforts of knowledge workers.

**FIGURE 5-4**   From a distance, an anthill appears to be a marvel of organizational capabilities, attributed to ants' division of labor—industrialization.

Image source: Shutterstock.

**FIGURE 5-5**   A look underneath the surface of an anthill reveals a labyrinth of inefficient tunnels: dead ends, trash, traffic jams. Ant colonies—just like knowledge work operations—are rife with avoidable work.

Image source: Eric Feferberg/AFP/Getty Images.

Now imagine that you're assigned to interview the ants as part of an operational improvement effort. Your goal is to get their input on the feasibility of further standardizing their operations. How would you imagine that conversation might sound?

**Ant:** "Why do we need to improve operations? We've dominated the market for 50 million years."

**You:** "There is much more value that could be delivered to shareholders: You're in first place but performing significantly below potential. In a mere 5 million to 10 million years, some genetically modified start-up species could steal your whole market share. You wouldn't just be out of business, you'd be extinct. Like T. Rex. Or Kodak."

**Ant:** "Well, the first problem is our information biotechnology. It's impossible to communicate easily with other divisions of the colony. Last time I counted, we were using more than 15 different pheromone biotechnologies. And this colony is still way understaffed. We're down to less than a million ants."

**You:** "We could make some really simple, nontechnology improvements. We could standardize and document your "tribal knowledge" into operating instructions. The variance in leaf fragment processing is over 7x for identical tasks. We could map your fragmented process flows and lean these out. And have you seen all the time wasted on tunnel travel? We could easily build the tunnels on a grid, just like Manhattan's street system."

**Ant:** "You obviously don't understand the operation. No two leaf fragments are identical. Each has to be handled, trimmed, and transported differently. Are you claiming that an oak leaf is processed the same way as a magnolia leaf? You're joking, right? And the tunnels—they're designed and built by the users. After all, they're the experts. They know best how to do their own work, including tunneling. They're our sandhogs. Are you implying that they can't even recognize the obvious? The shortest distance between point A and point B? That would insult them."

How can you respond? The ants hold the high ground of familiarity with the detail. Unfortunately, it's subjective. It's locked away in their heads because almost nothing in this knowledge work anthill is documented or widely visible. It's hard to make commonsense, inarguable comparisons.

The ants—and your knowledge workers—are certainly employing *some* of the principles of Adam Smith (remember: standardization, specialization, and division of labor). They're doing pretty well. But today's knowledge work organizations have yet to attain the level of industrialization first achieved by Ford back in 1914—that is, mass production. Instead, they're doing something different, which resembles the *predecessors* of Ford and his peers. It's called the American System of Manufacturing; you can read about it in the sidebar.

## The American System of Manufacturing

This is the name given to the principles governing industrial factories in the late nineteenth century. At the time, it delivered breakthrough gains, and it was the envy of Europe—thus the name. Today, it appears quaint.

In the late 1880s, many manufacturers lacked the technology to reliably produce interchangeable parts. Instead, their parts were merely "compatible." They were cast in the same molds and formed with the same equipment. However, metallurgical science, measurement systems, and mechanical engineering had not sufficiently advanced to enable "once-and-done" mass production of durable, close-tolerance components. Consequently, most of the critical parts of a sewing machine, bicycle, or pistol produced under the American System required hand fitting by skilled craftsmen.

Manual production labor had been reduced, but not eliminated. The remaining semiskilled tasks typically involved reaming holes, fil-

(continued on next page)

ing edges, and polishing surfaces. Individual parts of a single product were often marked with a common number to keep them together. And factories sent their hand files to the machine shop for resharpening—by the train-car load.

Now that you understand the American System, you can, unfortunately, see that it's alive and well in today's knowledge work organizations. The difference is that all of today's hand fitting and polishing is digital. There are no telltale train-car loads of dull files.

## A Two-Pronged Approach

The best way to succeed at achieving your knowledge work industrialization effort is to think of it as a simultaneous, two-pronged approach: one perceptual, the other practical. You must constantly overcome, or at least circumvent, a never-ending stream of potent perceptual roadblocks. At the same time, you must devise practical operational changes that more rigorously adapt the principles of industrialization to existing knowledge work. Of course, these are intertwined. The success of one directly influences the outcome of the other.

Begin by developing two lists. The first is perceptual: biases, contradictions, faulty logic, and false trade-offs. The material included earlier in this chapter is a start. However, the most effective examples are compiled from direct experience in the business. Begin observing. Ask the Five Whys. Soon you'll notice these quirks of human perception everywhere, not just in your business. Overconfidence renders everyone "above average." Difficult questions are swapped for easy ones. Invisible gorillas are everywhere. These are the "doors of perception" that hide knowledge work's timeless industrialization opportunity.

Back in the real world, it's time for the second list: the practical list. Begin by compiling and monitoring a small number of critical, highly focused operational facts—typically the uncomfortable ones that nobody likes to gather in knowledge work: productivity, quality, and variance. The challenge here will be to avoid the temptation, and the advice of the organization, to develop an excessively broad data set that attempts to "boil the ocean."

Start with a general inventory of knowledge work operational data. What do executives currently use to discuss and manage operations performance? Here are some other places you can look, and categories you can use, to help populate your list:

- **Cost.** Look for unit costs, such as transactions or cost per customer. Don't be surprised, however, if you find that most costs are managed as budget line items.
- **Service.** Search out measures, such as cycle times for service delivery, customer onboarding, or first-contact resolution of problems. Again, don't be surprised if all you can find are vaguely worded and highly positive customer satisfaction survey results.
- **Productivity and quality.** Outside of contact centers and other organizations with obviously similar work activities, there are typically few metrics to be found in knowledge work in these categories. You're looking for things like daily error rates, reason lists for customer inquiries, or units per hour.
- **Instructions and guides.** Are there practical "cheat sheets" close at hand? Sticky notes? Summary, easy-to-follow guides, scripts, or shortcuts? Instead, you may find lengthy, web-based tools that are user-unfriendly. These instructions may even require their own instructions!
- **Prior initiatives.** These may include business process maps, surveys, and one-time analytical efforts.
- **RPA analysis.** Typically, robotic process automation (RPA) efforts provide insights on work activities along with volumes and frequency.

Having this inventory provides an insightful landscape of the management information currently in use. It helps manage the avalanche of anecdotes. You will be able to cut through the detail and focus your questions for the Five Whys and the most valuable missing metrics to get started.

## Industrialization: The Perception Paradox

Now we're ready to start our industrialization effort. When it seems overwhelming, remember that it's all perceptual. And it's easy. Maybe it's too easy. That might contribute to the perception paradox. When innovators first began to industrialize conventional manufacturing, their technical reach exceeded their grasp: they imagined interchangeable parts, but the enabling technologies wouldn't become available for nearly a century. In knowledge work industrialization, the situation is reversed: The technical grasp already far exceeds our reach. Producing interchangeable parts for knowledge work, such as data elements, has been within our technological capabilities for generations. All we have to do is adopt conventional manufacturing's discipline—and alter our perception.

Begin to gather the information available for two of the four elements that you'll need for Phase I of your knowledge work factory construction. The first is organization charts; you'll need these for determining nameplate capacity. Gather all the existing org charts you can find. Expect a jigsaw puzzle operation, so find a conference room with a large table. The following chapter provides guidance.

The second element you'll need is work products. Building an inventory of these can be a tall order. That's covered in Chapter 7.

## CHAPTER 5: **TAKEAWAYS**

1. Four essential elements of industrial work provide the building blocks for the foundation of the knowledge work factory:
   - Capacity
   - Processes
   - Work activities
   - Products

2. All four elements are currently in place within knowledge work operations and, at large scale, viewed from a distance, represent "a spectacle to behold." But close scrutiny reveals vast inefficiencies and improvement opportunities. Analogies include:
   - The American System of Manufacturing, late nineteenth century
   - The anthill analogy

3. Three interconnected perceptual errors related to the overconfidence bias obscure visibility of the four elements and the knowledge work industrialization opportunity:
   - Oversight
   - Denial
   - Rationalization

4. The widely held belief that the competitive marketplace unfailingly adopts valuable innovations ("better-mousetrap dogma") does not reconcile with overlooked innovations throughout history:
   - Gunpowder
   - The wheel
   - Poured concrete
   - The steam engine

CHAPTER 6

# WHAT'S THE CAPACITY OF YOUR KNOWLEDGE WORK FACTORY?

Now that you've seen the essential parallels between industrial work and knowledge work, we're going to set about industrializing your knowledge work organization. We're going to begin this journey by talking about organization charts. Sounds boring? Nope—that could be your overconfidence bias kicking in again. You'll be surprised how these seemingly mundane documents came into existence, how they evolved, when they peaked, and why. You may be thinking, "If they peaked, how did people track organizations once they declined?" If that is what you are wondering, then you've already developed the healthy skepticism needed to industrialize knowledge work.

## Nobody Knows Anything—but Why Not?

William Goldman, the renowned screenwriter of *Butch Cassidy and the Sundance Kid*, *All the President's Men*, and *The Princess Bride* (to name a few), once said about the movie industry: "Nobody knows anything. Not one person in the entire motion picture field knows for a certainty what's going to work. Every time out it's a guess and, if you're lucky, an educated one."[1]

As we've seen, this observation could just as easily apply to the overall management of knowledge work operations throughout business. It's that apparently organized-from-a-distance/haphazard-up-close dichotomy we've explored in our anthill analogy in the last chapter. Was Goldman referring to knowledge work, too? *Nobody knows anything.*

But Goldman's scathing assessment of Hollywood *shouldn't* apply to knowledge work operations. Remember the four elements of the knowledge work factory? Here's a quick recap of these "industrialization" elements:

1. Capacity
2. Processes
3. Work activities
4. Products

In our journey together, we're going to develop each one of these elements. But look at that list. Which one of the four should be the *easiest* one to tackle? Which one should be the lowest-hanging fruit, the best documented, and the no-brainer place to begin?

The first one, of course: organizational capacity. What could be simpler? The number of employees, as well as their physical and organizational location, should be an easily found, inarguably well-charted certainty—a baseline. After all, organization charts for business have been around for nearly two centuries; they were originally developed to help manage railroads back in Victorian times.

## Full Steam . . . *Backward*

What if you could take a railroad superintendent from, say, the 1850s and transport him (it probably wouldn't have been a "her" back then) to the present? What would he expect to see? Given the bold march of progress, he'd surely expect that the organization charts of the future—that is, today—would have evolved dramatically. They would blow away anything he'd seen before. They'd be standardized. Automated. Stored in a digital repository. And they'd have an intuitive graphical user interface, or GUI, much like Google Maps, to help you navigate through the enterprise. You could easily drill down from the macro to the micro, with appropriately descriptive details served up nicely at every level. This would allow everyone in the business, from the boardroom to the front lines, to quickly understand each organization's purpose, activities, size, and location.

This electronic organization chart would serve as a hierarchical directory—a taxonomy—of management responsibilities and even operating performance. By tapping selected icons on a screen, managers could compare similar operating performance metrics across the business, just as railroads internally benchmarked their cost per mile in the mid-1800s. Our time traveler would be awed by the technology, but even more impressed by the operational efficiencies it made possible. He'd be convinced that today's managers are armed with org charts that allow them to easily and intuitively access the subtle, fact-based details they need to drive productivity and business effectiveness.

Of course, that never happened.

Alas. Let's see what our Victorian visitor would *really* recognize:

He'd be stunned, all right. But not by the progress. To the contrary. He'd be stunned by the lack thereof. Sure, quill pens have been replaced by spreadsheets, yet errors now lurk in cell formulas, not ledger pads. And while today's knowledge work executives routinely claim that "our people are our greatest assets," they do a better job managing the inventories of their *office supplies* than managing their organization capacity. Despite today's technology, such basic knowledge work activities as recording and reconciliation remain virtually unchanged from those in the counting house of a Dickens novel. Today's organization charts are, well, a train wreck. Why? "Nobody knows anything."

## The Jigsaw Puzzle

Here's a story that illustrates the point. Remember Nick Clearsight, the private equity activist investor from Chapter 4? Well, the newest target in his improvement crosshairs was the U.S. commercial lending operations of a well-known global bank. Nick sent his improvement team to investigate. Here's what happened:

"Organization charts? I haven't seen any lately, but I'm sure we have these somewhere around here. Let me get back to you." The senior vice president of human resources (SVP of HR) was responding to a fairly typical request from Nick's team. Sadly, his reply was as typical as the request. *And the request really wasn't complicated.* The improvement team was merely trying to determine the size of this bank's U.S. commercial operations. How many total employees were there, sorted by organizational group and geographic location? This shouldn't be hard to answer.

Wrong. It was very difficult. The team interviewed not only the SVP of HR, but also the president of the Americas division, the CFO, and the COO. "Nobody knows anything," thought the leader of the improvement team, and then he instructed his people to consult *external*, rather than *internal*, sources of information.

That's correct. It was faster—not to mention more accurate—to get the information the team members sought from places like Wikipedia, financial statements, trade publications, and regulatory filings. Using those sources, they tallied the total number of employees in the commercial banking division and came up with between 4,500 and 5,800. By visiting external recruiting websites, they were able to estimate salary costs. In just one day, they were able to get a decent summary of the organization.

Fast-forward a week. That's when the improvement team finally received the bank's "org charts." The client rep seemed surprised as he handed off his trove to the improvement team: "I never thought we'd be able to pull these together. I've been working with HR, finance, and IT. We had to dig back into the *archives* for some of these."

What, then, did he deliver to Nick's team? More than 300 pages of diagrams, sourced from three separate, often-overlapping files, all served up in multiple formats: Excel, PowerPoint, Word, PDF—even some JPEGs. As the members of Nick's team glanced over them, they saw the "usual suspects" of challenges confronting them:

- **Narrow views.** Each page included few employees, typically from 3 to 20.
- **Duplication.** Some managers and workers randomly appeared on multiple charts.

- **Structural inconsistencies.** These were rife:
  - Titles and hierarchies featured a dearth of descriptions, compounded by confusing categories: "Managers," "Directors," and "VPs."
  - Management spans of control varied widely: the number of direct reports ranged from 0 to 15.
  - Management layers—the levels of reporting (top to bottom)—varied from 3 to 9.
  - The structure was inconsistent. Similar groups appeared in both centralized and decentralized forms.
- **Unclear labeling.** Organizations had cryptic, conflicting names; acronyms went undefined.
- **Missing demographics.** Half the pages had no location information.
- **No description.** What does each group do? Who are its customers? Who knows?

The team thanked the client rep and immediately requisitioned the largest conference room available. There, the members of the team printed out hard copies of the "organization chart" files and went to work. Using scissors, tape, and colored highlighters, they began to assemble this jigsaw puzzle into a new, consolidated diagram—an effort that took them three solid days. But the jigsaw puzzle let them visualize the organization. With their experience, they were able to start to fill in the missing pieces.

Afterward, over the course of the following week, they reviewed their preliminary chart with managers across the organization. The goal was to validate the diagram. Here are some of the responses they noted when they presented the new org chart to bank employees:

- "No, I don't know what that organization does."
- "I don't recognize that acronym. I have no idea who they are."
- "Actually, I think this organization reports to me. Let me check and get back to you."

- "We have a matrix organization. I report to two bosses—no, three."
- "I only report to one executive. I'm not in the matrix."
- "I manage between 300 and 400 people in my group. I can get back to you with an exact figure."

## Why Labor-Cost Data Go Missing, or Technology to the Rescue . . . Not!

Next, the improvement team spoke with both the central IT department and the HR technical team that maintained the organization's "human capital management" software. It was a widely used, industry-standard application. Just about everyone was broadly familiar with its features and functions, which included an automated organization chart feature— exactly the kind of functionality our Victorian trainman would have drooled over.

But this bank, like virtually all other companies these days, never bothered to use it. The software also included an optional finance-and-accounting module. This would allow the organization charts to display the employee headcounts *and* summary labor-cost data for each group, location, and management level.

Simply using these *existing* features would deliver a major step in the direction of the Google Maps–style user interface we described above. But few CFOs today coordinate their technology selection with the chief HR officer. Why bother? Their bosses—the CEOs—see little need to strongly encourage (read: "mandate") valuable coordination of technology platforms between these two organizations. How could that possibly help the business and improve earnings? And so what if the IT group was well aware of these unexploited features? How did that differ from any other technology deployed across the enterprise? The IT group perceived its mission as fulfilling management requests. If the management people didn't ask for it, then they must not want it. The IT group didn't need yet another spending request smack-down. It didn't want to once again be portrayed as bleeding-edge, impractical futurists.

And besides, in practice, who ever used the term "human capital management"? Or referred to employees as "assets"? Sure, that *sounds* great: everyone is always quick to say that "our people are our greatest assets." But do the hard work of cleaning up the jigsaw puzzle of the company's organization charts? Here's what you'll hear:

- "Why?"
- "Sounds like a waste of time."
- "That's not my job."

Automate these organization charts with the industry-standard technology that the company already owns and operates? Connect to the relevant labor costs that already reside in the compatible general ledger technology? Again, here are the answers that Nick's team received:

- "Of course, it's possible, even easy. But that's a C-suite decision, way above my pay grade."
- "I'm sure that if they saw it as valuable, they'd have done it already."
- "Everybody else in our industry does it our way, so it can't be too bad. In fact, it must be OK."

(*Alert:* Better-mousetrap dogma at work!)

So this is why organizational capacity goes uncharted and labor-cost data go missing. This is how the office equipment inventory winds up more clearly categorized and more rigorously tracked than knowledge workers—who also happen to be the most valuable, costly, and underproductive assets in the business. But it did not begin this way. Paradoxically, it began as a productivity breakthrough.

## The Man with the One-Track Mind

The earliest surviving railroad organization chart is vastly superior to today's charts. It was developed in 1855 for the New York & Erie Railroad by Daniel C. McCallum (see Figure 6-1).

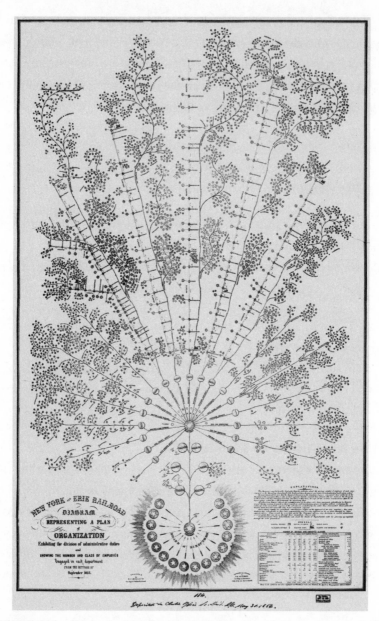

**FIGURE 6-1**   The earliest modern organization chart for business, created in 1855 by Daniel McCallum for the New York & Erie Railroad.

Image source: Wikimedia Commons, public domain.

Most people who see this document today will think it quaint. After all, the senior execs are in the "wrong" place: they're at the bottom. And the chart looks like an antique rendering of an ivy plant or a tree. Plus consider the context: "Railroads? That's ancient history; it can't be applicable to my business today." That's yet another overconfident oversight. And by the way, the tree shape was intentional. It represented *the flow of data for management operating reporting* (more about that below).

As a senior executive, McCallum was a knowledge worker. His organization chart perfectly reflects the definition of knowledge worker activity, i.e., the use of creative thinking to solve a nonroutine problem. His nonroutine problem: the railroad had grown too large to continue effectively managing by rules of thumb and tribal knowledge. Recall the ancient Babylonian merchants from Chapter 2? Their inventories grew too large to manage by memory alone. That nonroutine problem spawned the creative thinking that delivered standardized record-keeping (accounting) and specialized workers (accountants). Same organic genesis.

Hmmm . . . Today's nonroutine problem facing knowledge workers? Their work has grown too large to manage by memory alone? Nope. *Perceiving* this fact is today's problem. There's plenty of existing technology and nontechnology improvements available to solve the management problem. Using the yardstick of self-aware perception, Babylonian and Victorian management make today's digital age management look like hunter-gatherer laggards.

Pardon the digression—but this huge oversight warrants the attention. Back to our story.

McCallum created his chart to help him standardize and specialize three fundamental knowledge work management capabilities—for railroads:

1. **Visualization.** Create an unmistakably clear portrait of the business that integrates its inventory of human assets, its geographic footprint, and related infrastructure: stations, sheds, and switches.

II. **Definition.** Identify the typical management roles, titles, and related scope of responsibilities (organizational and geographic, centralized and decentralized) across the enterprise. Quantify the inventory of the "human assets."

III. **Operation.** Describe the flow of data required from local (detail) to enterprise (summary).

We'll dive into these categories in a little more detail momentarily. But for now, it's important to recognize that it takes little effort to see that these fundamental knowledge work management capabilities for railroads apply to any business. And although he didn't use the term, McCallum created a "knowledge work factory" for the Victorian era. Using simple, nontechnology methods, his quaint-looking org chart standardized many of the perceptions and activities of the railroad's managers (knowledge workers). It described the first of the four industrialization elements (capacity) so thoroughly that it enabled integration of the other three: processes, work activities, and products. Yes, that's right, products! Think of cost per mile. Although a railroad is a service business, McCallum (and others to this day) think and manage in terms of virtual products, such as "cost per freight ton-mile" or "cost per passenger-mile." Why can't today's managers similarly adapt product-based thinking to manage their knowledge work? Of course they can, once their perceptual capabilities catch up with those of the ancient Babylonians. We'll explore knowledge work "products" in the next chapter.

Today, McCallum's elegantly simple innovation—the enhanced organization chart—remains overlooked, lost to business history. However, the term "train wreck" lives on throughout business as a metaphor for catastrophic error. And it's often an apt description of the disastrously costly errors that pervade knowledge work. The difference is that many of today's knowledge work train wrecks occur digitally and discreetly. Sure, the high-profile disasters are impossible to overlook: product-launch misfires, endorsement debacles, and marketing-campaign snafus. But the smaller, activity-level errors—the long tail of invoice problems, correction, duplicative effort—occur with such frequent regularity that most people simply write these errors off as the unavoidable costs of "business as usual." But the costs are neither small nor unavoidable. Cumulatively, they're a silent, slow-motion train wreck (see Figure 6-2) that continually erodes earnings.

**FIGURE 6-2** The cumulative costs of the small, activity-level errors constitute a slow-motion train wreck that erodes earnings.

Reproduced with permission from the Wisconsin Historical Society, image number WHi-78385.

## A Prescient, Purposeful Tool

Referring to McCallum's poster merely as an organization chart verges on insult. It is, in fact, a multifunction tool that more closely resembles the graphical user interface (GUI) on a modern computer than a simple chart of job positions and reporting relationships. Of course, it serves that latter purpose, acting as an inventory of the railroad's human resources. But McCallum also intended it to function as the schematic design, or directory, of management operating reports for the railroad's managers and board of directors.[2] As we develop our knowledge work factory, we will need organization charts that more closely resemble this railroad management artifact than the complex matrices invented by mid-twentieth-century management gurus.

Let's drill deeper into how McCallum's 1855 chart helps standardize and specialize the three fundamental knowledge work management capabilities we mentioned above.

## I. Visualization

The chart is a spatial data-visualization tool, the Google Maps of its time. Look up any modern list of design objectives for a successful data-visualization tool, or GUI. This 1855 chart checks all the boxes. It neatly packs large amounts of data into small spaces. The labeling is crystal clear. There are no arcane terms or acronyms known only to insiders. Anyone can understand it. The data on resources, both employees and equipment, are arranged intuitively. At each rail station, the job positions and employee quantities are listed.

The chart also works on multiple levels, i.e., summary and detailed. For example, it can be viewed at a distance. Standing several feet away, one can easily comprehend the scope of the network: the number of trunk lines, the geographic regions, and the supervisors' responsibilities. But the chart also allows the viewer to zoom in on individual details for each station. Icons indicate where telegraph offices and dining facilities are available. All you have to do is move closer to the chart. It's the Victorian equivalent of scrolling on the wheel of your mouse to enlarge the view of a Google map.

McCallum's single sheet thus effectively depicts all major aspects of what was then one of the longest railroad networks in the world. It provides a visual footprint of the physical business. In its miniature form, this single document serves as a "floor plan" for McCallum's knowledge work factory. Once all the managers share a common definition of operations, it can be further detailed with illustrated boundaries of their coordinated responsibilities. (Contrast that to the modern-day bank's jigsaw puzzle charts discussed above, in which the managers don't even know what other organizations do.)

McCallum could also use this visualization tool to help his board of directors understand the business. He could supplement it with quantified facts about products, processes, and work activities—the other elements of industrialization—to demonstrate his understanding of where profits were made and lost: which lines were profitable, which cargoes, which assets, which customers. Our bank managers? Good luck.

## II. Definition

McCallum's chart describes and quantifies the organization's inventory of "human capital," as well as summarizing people's roles, skills, and responsibilities. In other words, it fulfills standard organization chart requirements. It solves, or preempts, the jigsaw puzzle questions that impeded Nick's improvement team, and the organization at large, in the global bank example described above. First, it depicts the overall structure of the organization. It provides an inventory of employees arranged along a number of dimensions: management level, geographic location, organization, etc. Next, it defines who's in charge of each organization and how these executives report up through the management structure (vertical descriptions). Finally, it describes "who does what" (horizontal descriptions).

## III. Operation

The chart provides a framework, a schematic design, for operational reporting. Caitlin Rosenthal, assistant professor of history at UC Berkeley, described how McCallum used his organization chart to manage the operational reporting that informed everyone from the boardroom to the rail yards:

Even as McCallum decentralized decision making along the railroad, he also insisted that targeted metrics had to be reported back to its board of directors. That data flowed down from the branches of the tree to its roots, where McCallum and the board could use the information for oversight and long-term decision making.

McCallum therefore designed a system of hourly, daily, and monthly reports that enabled him to calculate practical metrics, such as cost per ton-mile and average load per car. By comparing the profitability and efficiency of different routes, the board could identify opportunities for improvement.[3]

## Capacity (Management) Is King

As the railroad network grew, it became increasingly difficult to centrally and profitably manage capacity utilization of the railroad's costly, highly leveraged infrastructure. Efficiently managing this *tangible* capital depended on efficiently managing the *intangible* human capital (just like those Babylonian merchants). Centralized scheduling snafus produced costly delays, inefficient routes, unprofitable pricing, and increased risk of train wrecks. Thus, McCallum's diagram was designed to redistribute management decision making from centralized control to regional coordination.

Notably—and germane to this chapter—McCallum's diagram could be used to calculate *capacity*. It summarizes the inventory of the intangible "human capital" assets of the railroad. It clearly describes the jobs, management spans, levels, and locations of all of the railroad's 4,715 employees. These data can be used to calculate the net capacity of the organization, the "available hours." For a railroad, just like a factory, most of these available hours would be assigned to operate equipment and facilities. The scope of the infrastructure would determine the minimum number of employees and the distribution of required skills. This chart makes those capacity quantities and relationships obvious. But for whom?

It was for the workers in the railroad's knowledge work factory. They produced the most valuable products in the business: the operating schedules and profitability reports that helped keep the trains safe and fully loaded and the fares profitably priced . . . i.e., the "scheduling factory." (This is where we would find Raylene, from our Chapter 1 tire factory story, had she worked for the New York & Erie Railroad back in 1855.) Capacity data constitute the primary feedstock for any scheduling factory.

McCallum's scheduling factory might have resembled Raylene's in terms of size—less than a dozen individuals. Compared with organizations today, the railroad was an operation with a very lean overhead. Only 5 percent (247) of total employees (4,715) could be categorized as selling, general, and administrative (SG&A) expense. These are the railroad's "knowledge workers." Their available work hours represent the capacity of the railroad's knowledge work factory. This is where the scheduling "subfactory" for the railroad would reside. After deducting the agents and clerks (180), who were service workers, about 67 "true" knowledge workers, based on our contemporary definition, would remain. This is roughly 1.5 percent of the total employee headcount—a lean management benchmark for today's executives!

It's easy to see why our time-traveling railroad superintendent, accustomed to McCallum's simple, effective graphical tool, would, at a minimum, expect the same functionality to reside in today's digital work environment. And after seeing today's legions of knowledge workers, he might easily wonder how the business community could lose sight of this valuable innovation. (*Answer:* The same way that civilizations have routinely overlooked other valuable breakthrough innovations: gunpowder, concrete, the wheel, and the steam engine. See "The Better-Mousetrap Dogma" in Chapter 5.)

## The Knowledge Worker "Exemption"

Despite these types of stubborn facts, knowledge workers have, over the years, felt a certain sense of entitlement when it comes to the type of organizational innovations espoused by people like McCallum. They seem to be willfully detached from operational facts—in denial. Why is this?

Management writer Peter Drucker, whom we first mentioned back in Chapter 1, had a hand in this. For knowledge work, he conflated "innovation" and "productivity," proclaiming (without data) that:

1. "Continuing innovation has to be part of the work, the task and the responsibility of knowledge workers," and (more ominously)
2. "Knowledge workers have to manage themselves."[4] Too much emphasis on starchy items like org charts, it's been argued, stifles the freewheeling culture that's required for innovation.

But that's a specious argument. It implies a false trade-off: organized *or* innovative.

Why make that assumption? You shouldn't. And why further assume that the Silicon Valley, garage-based start-up is the innovation model for large, multinational corporations? Don't do it.

In fact, a seven-year study, undertaken during the 1980s, demonstrated the false trade-off inherent in the "organized versus innovative" assumption. It showed that the largest, most innovative, and most valuable companies at that time (with names like Intel, National Semiconductor, Texas Instruments, HP, and Motorola) routinely maintained some of business's most detailed, rigorous org charts, replete with well-maintained horizontal and vertical descriptions and up-to-the-minute accuracy.[5]

# Five Lessons from a Century of Organizational Sidetracks

So we've seen that McCallum "innovated" his elegantly simple, multidimensional organization chart in response to the (knowledge work) management problems confronting the largest railroad of its day. It worked. Without technology.

Over the intervening century, U.S. knowledge work jobs grew nine times faster than all others to dominate the economy.[6] McCallum's org chart visualization approach is more relevant and valuable today than ever. Yet it remains systematically overlooked and undervalued. This is true despite a century of failed alternatives. These efforts can be grouped into five major categories. And although none have worked well or become widely adopted, each offers valuable insights. These insights highlight fundamental fixes that you can implement quickly—and see the results of, beginning in just 30 days.

Let's get started. A century of lessons. Followed by 30 days of fixes and results.

## 1. Paradox: Knowledge Work Rises, Org Charts Rejected (1900–1920)

By 1910, organization charts had been formalized. They no longer resembled trees. However, their use was still not widespread. Writing in 1914, Willard Brinton, a mechanical engineer with a passion for data visualization, complained that organization charts weren't used widely enough.[7] Industrial engineers at the time tried to promote the widespread use of organization charts, but it didn't matter. Management then, as now, failed to understand how organization charts could be used to standardize knowledge work management, or the value this delivered.

But then, in early 1914, mass production became a global obsession, particularly after Henry Ford doubled his company's minimum daily wage to $5. He was using standardization as a disruptive force, overturning conventional thinking to deliver unprecedented, breakthrough gains during a decade of industrial productivity stagnation. His new assembly-line plant was achieving annual productivity gains of 22 percent while the U.S. economy slumped along at 1.5 percent each year.[8] This productivity growth soon spread to other tangible-asset-based businesses, but not to office, or knowledge work, organizations. The numbers of knowledge workers grew relentlessly, seemingly with little regard to organization charts and the capacity management they enable.

Perhaps management perceived that the rising tide of industrial productivity would also lift the boat of knowledge workers. Regardless, knowledge workers somehow obtained a free pass to sit out the continuing productivity boom of the Industrial Revolution during the early twentieth century—despite numerous attempts to bring them aboard the productivity train.

**Lesson No. 1:** Knowledge workers and their managers routinely, overconfidently overlook the simplest, most valuable innovations like organization charts.

## 2. Technology Vendors Institutionalize Inefficiency (1920s–1940s): Scientific Office Management

The Ford factory's success soon launched a movement to directly adapt the industrialization methods from the factory to the office. One of the leading proponents of this "scientific office management" effort was C. C. Parsons. The critical role that organization charts played in the industrialization of office work was obvious to him when, in 1917, he wrote:

> Indeed, every factory in existence has of necessity felt the influence . . . of improved shop management, efficient operation, and increased output at reduced costs. Keenness in competition has necessitated the adoption generally of improved machinery, scientifically installed . . . shop management has reached a high state of development.
>
> A like scientific adoption of efficiency methods in offices has not as yet become the universal practice. We are just at the beginning of the productive efforts in the campaign to revolutionize the work of the office . . . with the same high grade machinery that is provided in the factory.[9]
>
> . . . The *plan of every organization ought to be shown by a chart* in order that each component may know just what his position is in relation to all the others.[10] (Emphasis added.)

Since the proportion of knowledge workers in businesses was growing rapidly, this advice was more important than ever in 1917. On McCallum's org chart for the railroad, knowledge workers represented a mere 5 percent of the total 4,715 employees. Over the next half century, their share of the organization grew significantly. In a textbook published by Parsons in 1917, he included a full copy of the enterprisewide organization chart for the National Cash Register Company, now NCR Corporation. Of the total 4,618 employees at the time, 23 percent were knowledge workers. Today, even in manufacturing companies, knowledge workers often constitute a majority of total employees. Recall that in the tire company that Toby and Nick discussed in Chapter 4, knowledge workers represented 60 percent of the total.

Over the course of the period from 1917 to 1940, those involved in the "scientific office management" movement tried, but failed, to instill factory discipline in office, or knowledge, work. Their efforts coincided with an explosion of growth in new technology for office workers: filing systems, tabulating machines, and the predecessors of computers—punch card systems. Despite well-documented, successful efforts, management and knowledge workers easily avoided adopting these proposed improvements—better mousetraps.

Instead, the new office-technology vendors adopted a reassuring sales pitch that will sound familiar today: "No need to redesign office operations or organizations. Install our technology and let it do the 'management engineering,'" as office work transformation was termed at the time. The new technology had everything transformational already "built in." Simply purchase, install, and sit back. Then watch the organizational streamlining begin and the improvement benefits add up.

Modern business historian Thomas David Haigh insightfully summarizes the all-too-familiar results: "In fact, even the largest and most clerically intensive firms, such as insurance companies, seldom applied systematic management techniques to office work. The purchase of office machinery was, in reality, more often a symbolically effective alternative to managerial rationalization than its companion."[11]

A century ago, large-scale office technology deployment was one of the most acceptable and effective ways to avoid adopting the (nontechnology) principles of knowledge work industrialization: standardization, specialization, and division of labor. It still is.

**Lesson No. 2:** New technology vendors have always exploited the overconfidence bias that pervades management's perception of knowledge work operations. Today, vendors continue to promote a "false dawn" of convenience: Let the technology do the automation for you—like an organizational Roomba. Sit back and watch it streamline your organization and operations.

> The more things change, the more they stay the same.
> —Jean-Baptiste Alphonse Karr, Les Guêpes, January 1849

---

## 3. Measuring Points and Happiness, Not Productivity (1940s–1960s): The Hay System

The next wave of rekindled interest in organization design and charts began after the scientific office management movement had fizzled. In 1943, Edward N. Hay began a management consulting company (Hay Group) with the goal of standardizing criteria for job descriptions, performance evaluation, and compensation. It became known informally as the "Hay System." Early versions of the system allocated points for grading management capabilities and job requirements and also recommended compensation levels based on organizational characteristics, including size. Once compensation became involved, many executives, particularly at large organizations, quickly developed a keen interest in organization charts.

But Hay Group soon morphed into a broad-based "people development" advisory firm. Perhaps the disruption of the 1960s and 1970s caused by financial engineering and the start of the private equity movement diverted management's attention. Executives soon faced other, more rapid ways to turbocharge their compensation rather than accumulating points like trading stamps.

In 2015, Hay Group was acquired by international recruiting firm Korn Ferry. Today, the website confidently proclaims that "People want more than money . . ." Plug in the search term "productivity" on this site and get directed to a 4,000-word article entitled "Happy People Spark Serious Productivity." It claims that happy employees are 30 percent more productive. Perhaps this is true, but there is no mention of standardization and specialization, so these benefits are still available—on top of the purported 30 percent "happiness gain."

Standardization and specialization deliver plenty of upside beyond the happiness gain. By way of comparison, Ford's industrialized plants were *30 times* more productive than its most efficient competitor's plants, which used conventional artisanal methods of fabrication.

Consequently, the smart money should be backing executives who are "happy" to use McCallum's organization chart–driven approach to standardize and specialize knowledge work management.

**Lesson No. 3:** Motivation alone won't increase organizational productivity in knowledge work. Capacity and operations standardization must be directly designed and actively managed.

## 4. Organization Chart Psychology—Unproductive (1960s–1990): Organizational Theory

The next wave might be described as the "golden age of organizational theory," and it spanned roughly 30 years from 1960 through the late 1980s. Also termed "organizational studies," it is "the examination of how individuals construct organizational structure, processes, and practices and how these, in turn, shape social relations and create institutions that ultimately influence people."[12] Not surprisingly, this thinking gave rise to a constant flow of new theories that were almost impossible to support with facts. This caused one prominent scholar at the time, Dwight Waldo, to comment cynically, "The modern period in organization theory is characterized by vogues, heterogeneity, claims, and counter-claims."[13]

However, at least one prominent organizational theorist, psychologist Chris Argyris of Harvard, identified the contradictory, counterproductive knowledge work operations resulting from perceptual bias.

> Managements, at all levels, in many organizations, create, by their own choice, a world that is contrary to what they say they prefer, and contrary to the managerial stewardship they espouse. It is as if they are compulsively tied to a set of processes that prevent them from changing what they believe they should change. If this is true, then management could be in a very fundamental sense not in control.[14]

Today we have the benefit of a large body of research work, some of it Nobel Prize–winning, that conclusively explains many of the cognitive disconnects and perceptual biases that Argyris describes. Despite this rigorous new science of behavioral economics, managers who want to capitalize on the opportunity must overcome the compulsive ties to the processes that are "contrary to the managerial stewardship they espouse" and that "prevent them from changing what they believe they should change."

In short, achieving this objective is fiendishly difficult because of instinctive perceptual bias and circular, self-perpetuating logic. It's like a virus.

**Lesson No. 4:** Psychologically based organization design does not provide the solution. Management processes can often be irrational, producing unintended, contradictory outcomes. But let's not write off psychology. It can help unwind the numerous biases that drive irrationality in business.

## 5. Brutally Productive: Zero-Based Budgeting (Reborn in the Early 2000s)

The latest rage in private equity investing involves zero-based budgeting (ZBB). Former U.S. president Jimmy Carter adopted the approach when he served as governor of Georgia in the 1970s. ZBB is a method of budgeting in which all expenses must be justified for each new period. This method starts from a "zero base," and every function within an organization is analyzed for its needs and costs.

Organization charts are essential for ZBB. In what can be a brutal process for newcomers, each group must provide reviewers (often hostile acquirers) with the following types of information:

- What its organization does—activities, processes, products, i.e., industrialization elements
- How these elements contribute to the goals of the business

Reviewers then decide what to include in the budget as essential. Everything is reviewed to determine alternatives that may be more effective.

Remember the Five Whys analysis that Bob used in Chapter 5 to drill into the root causes of inbound customer queries in the insurance call center? Just apply the same simple, relentless questioning for each organizational group in the enterprise. Then repeat this agonizing process year after year and see how many employees can take it. How long will they remain?

**Lesson No. 5:** Knowledge work organizations require "nudging" to adopt even the simplest, most valuable improvements (see Lesson 1, above). But why not design it (i.e., the nudging and the improvement adoption) as a natural, routine aspect of knowledge work management? Why not institutionalize the improvements into the operating processes and the organization charts, just like manufacturers do? Once and done. Capture the benefits of the experience curve and avoid the redundant, inefficient brutality of annual ZBB.

## Fundamental Fixes—Implement Now!

Despite nearly a century of management trends involving organization design, and the charts that are supposed to document it, today "nobody knows anything." Interview any knowledge work organization and you will encounter the same paucity of description and data that initially impeded McCallum in the mid-1800s. Sure, that's a problem. But it's also one the simplest, fastest ways to improve knowledge work operations.

And it's an ideal first step to begin the journey of building your knowledge work factory. Remember in Chapter 5 how the detail will come rushing at you, from individuals in the organization, as this task begins? Simply ask them for the organization chart for their area. Then get to work with them on the following list of "hands-on" near-term improvements.

I.  **Visualization.** Create an unmistakably clear, consistent, easily comprehensible representation of the business. It should be designed to be understood by internal employees, external shareholders, and even the general public. Like McCallum's chart, it should be predominantly qualitative. It should tell its story visually, requiring minimal text and numbers to communicate its message to users.

   a.  Put the jigsaw puzzle together. Start at the top. Include the entire organization on a single, manageably sized poster.

   b.  Keep it simple. Use simple labels and as few as possible. Eliminate acronyms. Even the world's largest organization should be limited to a handful of summary pages—five or six at most.

   c.  Tell a consistent, visual story. For example, ensure that the chart aligns with the segments and cost centers reported in the financial statements: no "secret decoder rings" should be required.

   d.  Layer the detail. The chart should work at a summary level—at a glance. It should also include additional layers of detail, allowing the user to zoom in.

   e.  Get creative. McCallum used simple graphics and artwork to tell the story of his company's geographic footprint. These helped depict the directional flow of equipment and management reporting information. You can be just as creative, without the "vines" and "leaves." Use symbols and icons.

The better the job done by the organization chart on visualization, the easier the tasks for definition and operation.

II. **Definition.** Quantify the inventory of human capital assets, or employees: quantity, skills, and location. Specify the typical management roles, titles, and related scope of responsibilities across the enterprise (e.g., by organization and geography; centralized and decentralized).

  a. Include up-to-date headcounts.

  b. Quantify the characteristics of the organization structure:

  - Management levels (from the top of the organization to the front lines)

  - Spans of control (average number of direct reports per manager)

  c. Add links to summary-level compensation (don't worry; it's already posted on the web).

III. **Operation.**

  a. Create (or at least begin) an inventory of existing performance reports by organizational area:

  - Operations level

  - Job-position level

  b. Develop summary descriptions: responsibilities, decision rights, performance targets.

## Benefits Begin in 30 Days

So what kind of benefits could you expect to begin seeing within 30 days?

1. Reduction of redundant, conflicting operating reports
2. Standardization of management spans and layers
3. Establishment of consistent (if temporary) performance metrics for:

  - Operations

  - Job positions (employees)

4. Creation (or at least the foundation) of a more consistent inventory of performance metrics

5. Consistent documentation of summary descriptions: responsibilities, decision rights, performance targets

Now that you've got a handle on the capacity of your knowledge work organization, it's time to gain a better understanding of the "products" it creates every day. Are they hidden? Some more than others. Get the details—and a story that I think will hit close to home—in Chapter 7.

---

## CHAPTER 6: **TAKEAWAYS**

1. The first organization chart, developed for a railroad in 1855, far surpasses most modern charts and even functions as an early knowledge work factory by:
   - Visualizing the entire business (largest in the United States at the time)
   - Defining management roles, decisions, and asset responsibilities
   - Quantifying organizational capacity clearly and unmistakably
   - Defining data flows for performance reporting and "product" definition
2. More than a century of subsequent organization chart innovation attempts have failed to meet or exceed the functionality of this original chart. These efforts offer lessons that point out costly flaws in organization design to be avoided.
3. Improvements in today's typical organization charts provide two near-term advantages for knowledge work improvement:
   - Deliver the first of four essential elements needed for "industrialization"—capacity.
   - Produce meaningful operational improvement benefits that begin within 30 days.

---

CHAPTER 7

# RECOGNIZING THE "HIDDEN PRODUCTS" YOUR KNOWLEDGE WORKFORCE BUILDS

Factories crank out tangible things to sell. Your knowledge workers, by contrast, provide a *service*, right?

If only it were that simple. This chapter explores the "hidden products" that your knowledge workforce builds every day, what they're worth, and who's in charge of it all. The answers might surprise you.

## The Library of Babel

Although he died in 1986, the Argentinian writer Jorge Luis Borges wrote surrealist stories that still resonate in today's tech culture. One is a particular favorite among today's digital rock stars. "The Library of Babel," published back in 1941, describes a universe of books that contain every possible permutation of the characters of the alphabet. Though the vast majority of the books contain gibberish, the knowledge that *every possible permutation* exists in the library also holds out a tantalizingly promising possibility: somewhere in the stacks, there must be a book that contains a perfect index of the library's contents—its inventory. This directory would be like a Rosetta Stone that could decode all the other books and the logic of the shelving system. In Borges's story, the librarians search the shelves in suicidal despair, seeking in vain for this holy grail of books—this Rosetta Stone.

Sound farfetched? Of course. But it's easy to see how this story stimulates the creative juices of modern digital adventurers, eager to discover the next Rosetta Stone algorithm that can unlock vast swaths of the untamed internet, today's metaphor for the Library of Babel. Most will not succeed. Yet digital gamblers embrace these lottery-style odds and the prospect of a winner-take-all payoff. That's one big-picture, romantic view of Borges's story.

But for savvy business executives, there's another, less romantic and more costly view. For them, the Library of Babel analogy represents a poorly organized, mob-managed, internal data warehouse of the "products" of knowledge work. It exists in multiple locations throughout every business. Frustrated librarians, in the form of data wranglers, search the digital shelves in despair. (Just think of Alex, the data dude, from this book's Introduction.) But there's a straightforward solution for executives. They don't have to find a directory. They can simply mandate one to guide their operation through this profit-robbing gibberish.

## Call in the BOM Squad

If you're seeking to industrialize your knowledge work operations, you needn't look far. The Rosetta Stone that can organize these Babelian libraries is nothing more than what manufacturers call a "bill of materials," or BOM. This is the document that defines how a product is made. It's a hierarchical list of the quantities of raw materials, components, and subassemblies needed to manufacture an end product.

Creating and managing hierarchical BOMs for the products of a knowledge work factory is relatively simple: the inventories are mostly digital. The overwhelming challenge is, as always, perceptual. Workers and executives will overconfidently maintain that the output of knowledge work cannot be viewed as "products," standardized with BOMs, and centrally managed as they are in a factory. And yet these very activities are performed in their organizations, on an ad hoc basis, right before their eyes. The anthill of knowledge work operations generates an anthill of digital data inventory. And like the Library of Babel, at a first distant glance, it presents an overwhelming spectacle to behold. The stacks are massive. Every book is in place. Only when someone is assigned to use these tomes, like Alex, the data dude, does the suicidal despair of Borges's librarians become clear.

Each of these wasteful libraries is created with the most virtuous intentions. Don't believe me? Consider the following anonymized, composite stories.

## *The Other West Wing*

Julie is an accountant who was just appointed controller at one of the nation's largest hospital networks. The secret to her success? Relentlessly detailed work, combined with uncanny responsiveness to senior management—she was proudly "proactive." Sounds like a perfect personality type to manage effectively, right? Not always. You might call this tale "The Accounting Library of Babel."

When this story starts, Julie had been at her current hospital for about eight years, since shortly after the completion of its new west wing. Back then, she was a senior accounting manager . . .

And here's where this story *really* begins. Put your Borges-lens glasses on and see how virtuous waste hides in plain sight.

### The Innocuous Request

Shortly after the west wing opened, the hospital director casually asked Julie and her team to compile a breakdown of the past year's maintenance costs for the new wing. It was a one-off request and not terribly difficult: Julie's team completed the report in just four days. The director was satisfied. He thanked Julie and moved on.

But Julie perceived a twofold opportunity. (1) She could be ready whenever another similar maintenance report was requested, and (2) she could advance her career by having that information at her fingertips, with prescient speed and precision.

The solution was simple: She'd keep the maintenance costs for the west wing in a separate cost category. She'd expand the detail. Then, when that next request appeared, she'd have that report done in *minutes*!

Now, one might wonder: Did she ever ask that director why the original report was requested—or if there might be more like it forthcoming? Of course not. Why would Julie second-guess senior management? It wasn't her place to probe. She preferred to "read" the situation; after all, that's what had always worked for her.

### Bert to the Rescue

"Just relax, Jules. I'll handle this," said Bert, as he waved her out of his office.

Bert was a seasoned CPA. He'd been an accountant at this very hospital for 31 years now; he remembered when the hospital broke ground for the *east* wing.

No one knew the chart of accounts like Bert did. He knew every line item. Most were identified primarily by numbers, or prefix codes, followed by brief text labels. Bert was the master of prefix codes. You tell him what cost you wanted, and Bert could rattle off the six- to eight-digit code of every single line item you needed for your report. It was a point of pride, and he could do it all *in his head.*

So, Bert reasoned, Julie's request to carve out the west wing maintenance costs was simply an expansion of his existing system—a mere matter of adding more suffixes. Easy. He scrolled through all the accounts on his screen and cherry-picked the ones he'd need to fulfill Julie's request. Here was the first one, an existing hospital maintenance account:

- 0005-22—Painting—Walls

Using his usual approach, Bert "expanded" the account by adding a new *sub*account (23), with its logically suffixed name (West):

- 0005-23—Painting—West

Simple! Bert saw no need to write down any kind of "key," no BOM, no directory. The system seemed so clear and obvious. He was confident that costs couldn't possibly get misposted to the wrong line-item account.

Besides, he personally reviewed the day-to-day journal entries of the junior staff; he'd be able to catch what few errors might arise.

Bert plowed ahead, creating an entirely new cost center to aggregate and subtotal the 100 line items he'd just identified for Julie's new "West Wing Maintenance Report," should it ever get requested again. He labeled the new cost center, logically enough, "West." He'd remember what it meant.

## The Under-the-Radar Product Factory

Let's step back. Across the enterprise, there are nearly 2,000 employees in the finance department. That includes literally hundreds of strong-willed, independent managers like Julie. And every day they create more one-off products like Julie's "West Wing Maintenance Report," with no BOMs.

Why? They trust their perception of the needs of management, the business, and their own organization. And they trust their judgment because they're at the front lines—closest to their operations and the needs of their business customers. So in their view, they're *doing something that needs to be done*. They view their efforts as *virtuous*.

Julie and her peers would never consider themselves "product developers." The thought, and the title, simply would not cross their minds. And since they don't regard themselves as *developers* of products, they would never consider themselves *managers* of the products they've developed. To the contrary, Julie and her colleagues see themselves as passionate advocates of white-glove, concierge service for the business. Thus, no amount of detail is too much. No response time is too fast. Julie didn't become controller by delivering mediocre service.

Now, peering through your Borges-lens glasses, look at all the finance people supporting all the Julies. For every manager like her, there are *lots* of Berts, proudly delivering the new products (reports, cost centers) for the Julies. They don't "waste their time" on things like documentation. They see no need for BOMs. That would (they'd reason) just add more bureaucracy and more effort. It would only slow everything down. People like Julie and Bert anticipate needs and get things done.

They also, intuitively and overconfidently, follow their own misperception of the principle of least effort (Chapter 4) and don't squander time on directories. In their thinking, the Berts of every organization are always available to explain. They can keep track of everything—or at least everything that they work on.

With the best of intentions, everyone was focused on improving his or her own area. But collectively and inadvertently, the finance department was building its own Library of Babel. The "shelves" of the general ledger were always expanding, groaning under the weight of a seemingly infinite number of one-off permutations of accounting line items—38,000 and counting!

From a distance, everything appears orderly and under control. It's a spectacle to behold. But wandering deep within the stacks are data dudes like Alex. They're like archaeologists, excavating artifacts, piecing together shards of data created by hundreds of people like Bert.

We'll return to Julie and Bert in a minute. But let's first take a closer look at BOMs and their importance to your knowledge work organization.

## A BOM by Any Other Name . . .

A bill of materials, or BOM, has six major uses. It:

1. Defines the product
2. Provides manufacturing (or production) instructions
3. Controls changes and variations
4. Schedules production activities
5. Facilitates order entry
6. Helps establish costs and pricing

The earliest recorded BOM dates to an advertisement in 1744.[1] It shows a Franklin stove, then the latest, most efficient heating device on the market. The components and their quantities were listed, along with the sequenced instructions for customer assembly. Just like that, it fulfilled at least the first two of the six major uses of BOMs.

Unlike managers of knowledge work, manufacturers embraced these valuable uses of BOMs. Over time, they developed bills of materials into components of larger production control systems. Advancements were made over the decades between the emergence of mass production (1913) and the widespread arrival of business computer systems (1960s).

And as the functionality and scope expanded, the name began to change. During the 1970s and 1980s, the process of creating BOMs became known as materials requirement planning (MRP), and it was handled by IT systems. With the arrival of high-performance, decentralized computers, the scope of these systems grew to include other functional areas of the enterprise, most notably finance and human resources (HR). By the late 1980s, the name of the system changed to enterprise resource planning (ERP), to accommodate the expanded capabilities.

Today, most finance and HR departments have failed to integrate their data or operating processes with these time-proven, manufacturing-oriented technologies. They continue to operate just like Julie and Bert. With their narrowly focused good intentions, they continually expand the Accounting Library of Babel.

## "We're Performing a *Service,* Not Making *Products*"

Knowledge workers don't naturally include "producing products" when they think of their daily routines. This is reinforced by the false trade-off that constrains conventional thinking: operations can either deliver products (which are tangible) *or* perform services (which are intangible).

On the surface, this makes sense. A "product" is typically defined as "an article or substance that is manufactured or refined for sale." *For sale.* Those are the two words that send knowledge workers' thinking down a limited path. That's because most of what knowledge workers create, especially in the finance department, is never sold. So they're certainly *making* things, but they don't perceive these as *work products*. When you phrase it that way, the *products* become much clearer. Still, most knowledge workers are convinced that all they do is provide *intangible services* (never mind those stacks of reports) and consultative expertise for their customers, either internal or external. They're professionals, vested with more autonomy and discretion than production workers.

If you really press them ("What products are you producing?"), knowledge workers tend to identify the obvious, final, macro-level outputs of their operations. These are often the most tangible. For example, accountants in the finance department may point to external, published reports: financial statements and tax returns. Insurers, like Bob in Chapter 1, will identify new policies as their group's products. Raylene, at the tire factory, might name "schedules" (but more likely "tires") as her group's product. Tom, at the global media giant, would name completed, paid advertisements.

All of these answers are correct. And they could be used to broadly manage operations. But most knowledge work organizations never bother to keep product inventories, costs, and BOMs. That's like an auto manufacturer identifying its product as "completed cars." Sure, that's correct, but it's much too general. How much can "completed cars" help you if you're working in the tail-light subassembly plant? Without standards and BOMs to direct your work, you'll improvise. It's the same lack of information that drives Julie and Bert to furiously improvise products for their customers—and informally store the BOMs in their memories.

As we'll see in the next chapter, knowledge work managers like Julie could keep an inventory of reports and the standard data elements to constrain them. They could calculate the average times and costs to produce them. They could measure the reports' effectiveness. But first, they must reject the false trade-off of "products *or* services." And that could undermine their professional self-perception.

## A Hundred Years of Pushback

For a century, these professionals have recoiled at the notion that their organizations operate as knowledge work "factories" that deliver "products." Many resent the suggestion that they can improve by adopting conventional, factory-floor industrialization methods:

- "That's just more work!"
- "Who needs all that formality? I can remember this myself."
- "Where would we post it?"
- "Who would read it?"
- "It's faster for me to just tell someone; it's fastest of all if I simply do it myself."
- "Besides, our customers—the business executives we serve—*want* personalized service and explanations."

It's simply inconceivable to these knowledge workers that the ERP system that is used to manage the plant floor could just as easily help manage the general ledger, the financial close, and the production of management operating reports.

After working, and thinking, this way for generations, they're not open to perceiving *products*. Why not?

- There are no "bills of materials," or parts lists, that describe the subcomponents of products and how these fit together.
- There are certainly no "shelves" for storing inventories of raw materials for supplying production operations.
- There are no formal staging areas for incomplete work in process.

Knowledge workers will tell you, quite simply, that these product and inventory analogies are irrelevant.

But they won't stop there. They'll try to convey the unfathomable complexity of their operation: thousands of accounting line items, hundreds of business-line customers (i.e., their personal Library of Babel). That's because it always seems impossible to visualize and comprehend the full scope of intangible knowledge work activities. Julie and Bert have their hands full keeping details of their small corner of the finance department in their heads. Visualizing and comprehending the full scope of their division certainly seems impossible. And extending this effort to encompass the operations of the enterprisewide finance department? That seems imponderable.

Of course, none of this is true. False complexity is just an overconfident misperception, as always. The brain takes one of its usual shortcuts and declares, "Impossible!"

But wrapping your mind around the accounting line items of the entire enterprise is no more difficult than visualizing and comprehending the typical corner grocery store.

## Cleanup on Aisle Five

Imagine you're at the grocery store. And by "grocery store," I mean your average-sized neighborhood supermarket. This store stocks about 50,000 items.

Fifty thousand. Sounds like a lot, right? Yet the shoppers who visit the store are hardly overwhelmed. They comfortably navigate the aisles, guided by the dozen or so overhead signs and the intuitive arrangement of products.

Meanwhile, the employees and vendors restock the shelves nightly. Over the course of a year, the entire inventory of products will be replaced (sold) an average of 19 times. Merchandising managers monitor every square inch of shelf and floor space. They aggressively attempt to increase this inventory turnover. If products linger too long in the store, these are promptly replaced, and shelves are reconfigured. Logical, right?

Now, imagine the finance department as a grocery store. The "shelves" are the individual accounting line items that constitute the general ledger. Imagine the numbers recorded in the cells of these line items as the products stocking the shelves of our "general-ledger grocery store." But unlike a retail grocer, nobody in the finance department is managing the shelves of the general ledger. Finance employees like Bert can individually decide to create and name 100 new accounts (digital shelves) to track west wing maintenance costs.

There are no controls. Bert's counterparts in other divisions are similarly creating series after series of one-off line items, or shelves. They each know where they stashed their data and how they labeled them. But it's not useful for others. Imagine shopping for what you're looking for in *that* kind of market.

Ideally, the general ledger should be standardized and intuitively arranged like the floor plan of a grocery store. Bert and his counterparts in other divisions would "shop the aisles," quickly and intuitively, just like they would at a grocery store. There they would spend as little time as necessary to find the standard accounting line-item data they need to perform their primary job: conducting analysis for their internal business-line "customers." Instead of creating personalized line items and squirreling them away where no one can find them, Bert should spend his time with the various hospital departments, fine-tuning their revenue forecasts and monitoring their progress against those plans.

But no. Bert is designing digital shelving: accounting line items. To these, he's adding his own cryptic, quirky labeling scheme with no instructions, no "directory." And he's also spending large amounts of his time reworking the defective components and products that arrive in his department "not in good order." These are the mangled, unreconciled journal entries that will delay the financial close. They are booking errors caused by other cryptic, quirky general-ledger line items, similarly created by other "Berts" and likewise lacking instructions or directories.

Why doesn't the CFO maintain a couple of "merchandising managers" to keep the accounting general-ledger "store" in order? Because there's typically never been an inventory of general-ledger items. No one thinks of these as frequently used "components" that are assembled into more complex "products" (e.g., reports) that are used and reused across the business.

Now, let's suppose that the CFO of the hospital network hired the grocery store's employees to perform a quick inventory of the company's general-ledger store. Here's what they'd find:

- Roughly 45,000 (mostly empty) shelves, or line items.
- 50 line items (shelves) that contain 60 percent of all expense data.
- 500 line items that contain 83 percent of all expense data.
- 44,500 line items that contain just 17 percent of the remaining expense data.
- No central directory for this general-ledger data store.
- Aisle signs that consist primarily of numbers; recall Bert's codes, such as "0005-22—Painting—Walls."

Imagine that you walked into this store. The items that you use the most would all fit on the endcaps of the aisles. These are the 500 line items that contain 83 percent of all expense data.

But that's not where they are. They're scattered throughout the vast, nearly *vacant* shelves. Nobody in the finance department even knows how many shelves exist! There are no merchandise managers to analyze the products and ensure that the shelf stocks are balanced and replenished with useful, standardized products. And every day, workers keep *adding new shelves and aisles* with only a couple of items on them. Like Julie's maintenance report, nobody knows if these products will ever be requested again. And if they are, the hope is that the employee who stocked the shelf is still working for the company and can remember the location of the report.

The resemblance to Borges's imagined Library of Babel is as uncanny as it is unintended.

## Serious as a Heart Attack

Meanwhile, back at the hospital, Walter, the head of the cardiology department, was on hold, waiting to speak to Julie. He needed an update to the standard analysis of the shortfall from the quarterly revenue plan. And he needed it now: the CFO's office was breathing down his neck.

The entire hospital network, as it turned out, was coming up short on the corporate-mandated quarterly revenue plan (as always). And so the CFO's office was grilling each of the hospitals' department heads to understand how they intended to "close the gap." Walter felt the pressure acutely: cardiology provided his hospital's largest revenue stream. This is why he (like all the other department heads) was grilling his accounting team for analytical forecasting support to explain and close (partially) the revenue gap.

Frustrated, Walter gave up and decided to try again later.

### Back on Planet Bert . . .

Bert usually handled this revenue-reconciliation task for cardiology. He had a handy crib sheet of effective tricks to reduce the shortfall.

Still, Bert couldn't get to Walter's request today. Instead, he turned to the huge stack of journal entries—basic debits and credits—he needed to correct. Of course, Bert was massively overqualified for this task. But nobody else had that Bert-like intimacy with the individual line items to make the required fixes in just one or two days.

The erroneous journal entries piled up continually. That's because there weren't any useful instructions or documentation—no BOM—explaining how to enter them in the first place. There was an online guide, but it was much too general—not to mention long out of date. Thus, the various department staffers each made their own best guesses on how to code the different revenues and costs. It was a valiant effort, but it still resulted in an error rate of 35 percent.

Most of these could be corrected by Julie's lower-level team members. A few, however, required Bert; he knew these stubborn errors best. Otherwise, the staffers would be forced to call around and investigate every single entry. Even then, there was no assurance they'd get the corrections right and properly reconcile the accounts. And if the accounts didn't get reconciled quickly, then several critical trial balance reports would get delayed. That, in turn, could jeopardize the timely completion of the monthly close. That wasn't the type of attention that Julie wanted from the CFO's office.

## The Lesser of Two Evils

Julie was trapped between opposing forces from corporate: close the books accurately *and* explain why revenue had fallen short of plan this quarter.

She looked up to see Bert standing in her doorway. "Want me to switch gears to cardiology?" he asked.

Julie shook her head. "Stay on the rework. We can't miss that deadline for the close." Like everyone else in her position at the company, Julie prioritized the financial close, with its regulatory implications, ahead of management's "need to know" about the revenue shortfall.

Back in his office, Bert sat at his computer, relaxed. He knew this fire drill well. It was the same thing, over and over, as long as he could recall, despite decades of technology upgrades.

Although he had to admit, things seemed to be getting worse lately. The revenue variances were getting bigger. The financial close was getting tougher to complete. The board of directors was getting more frustrated and impatient every year. Bert wondered if the C-suite team might be seeing some turnover. No matter. That's never changed the work in the past.

## Bert's Test Drive

As he pored through the journal entries for corrections, Bert noticed that a lot of them had to do with maintenance. This was an opportunity to "test-drive" his new cost center for west wing maintenance. Of course, this detour would take the rest of the afternoon, and it wouldn't help with the revenue variance, but Bert believed this was a good investment of his time. It would let him see how his new design worked in practice. After all, Bert thought—just like Julie—you never knew when the hospital director might want to review the west wing maintenance costs. They'd be ready!

# The Shared Services Initiative: The Perils of Unrecognized Products

The Shared Services Initiative (SSI) was one of the enterprise's most important improvement efforts. The CFO and the senior managers in finance jointly decided to centralize as many of their organization's similar work activities as possible. They wanted "division of labor," although the term never crossed their minds. The goal was to become more efficient by "colocating" similar job positions. These SSI workers would become more efficient by concentrating on a narrow range of similar, or "standard," work activities gathered from across the enterprise to enable high volumes and frequent repetition. Again, nobody thought in these terms, but the SSI project was counting on exploiting the benefits of standardization and specialization.

Although the SSI team members didn't recognize it, the SSI project directly sought productivity gains via the three pillars of manufacturing industrialization: standardization, specialization, and division of labor. But they didn't think of their operations as a "factory" filled with knowledge workers. And they didn't perceive that their workers delivered "products." They simply assumed that any centralization must be good centralization. After all, they'd already seen their competitors adopt the same strategy. Therefore, they concluded that centralization must be a better mousetrap. So they began to improvise their way into an unrecognized industrialization effort.

And that was the problem. Nobody involved with the SSI project was quite sure how to proceed or how everything was going to work. Nothing about existing operations was well documented. The SSI project work plan was one page long and short on details.

If the organization were a factory, the team members would know how it was going to work. It wouldn't be mysterious. They would simply transfer the products to another location to be manufactured. They would compile the bills of materials, the production specifications, and the labor standards and determine the new manufacturing capacity required. That would let them establish the specs for designing the new location, such as infrastructure needs, workforce size, and skills. And they could also quantify the existing capacity that would be freed up by the transfer, ensuring that the effort achieved the planned savings.

Consider the two ways they could've proceeded:

- **Option A.** Product-based planning
- **Option B.** Org chart–based planning

## *Option A: Product-Based Planning*

The members of the SSI team could adopt a product-based approach if they embraced the notion that their organization operated like a (disorganized) factory. They could begin by identifying the unrecognized "products" produced by their employees. How? By taking inventory. Then they could work backward from these to create BOMs. And from the BOMs, they could generate realistic, quantified schedules of work activities, labor requirements, and physical infrastructure needs. But it never occurred to the members of the SSI team to think of their knowledge work organizations as similar to factories. So, naturally, they did not consider Option A. (Spoiler: They did not want to consider Option B either, but we will return to that topic later.) Here's how they improvised their improvement efforts.

### The SSI Team's Improvised Planning

Eager to show progress, they began the SSI project by first acquiring physical infrastructure. They selected a site in the Midwest, leased an enormous, low-rise, campus-style office building, and began to notify current finance employees that they would soon be expected to relocate there. Next, the SSI project leader sent an e-mail to all finance department employees to better understand the work activities to be centralized. This was an electronic survey form, requesting that they list their daily work activities and estimate the time, in minutes or hours, that they spent on each. The survey listed about a dozen activities as examples, followed by blank lines with a note to add any other activities, with descriptive detail.

As he was correcting the journal entries—and trying to carve out time to visit with Walter to discuss the cardiology revenue forecast—Bert received his copy of the SSI survey in his inbox. "Wow," he thought as saw all the blank lines, "these folks must want a lot of detail. Fortunately, I have it!"

Each day for the next two weeks, Bert diligently added to the SSI activity list, generating almost three pages of single-spaced detail, just like his west wing maintenance project for Julie. Meanwhile, hundreds of Bert's colleagues were completing their surveys with similar zeal and detail. And after spending hours describing the uniqueness of their work, they would be loath to devalue their efforts by consolidating and standardizing it. Later, this would prove to be a major roadblock when the SSI team attempted to "lift and shift" activities to the central shared services center. The team had never considered that every action it took, even a survey design, could generate unintended, and often counterproductive, consequences.

### Meanwhile, Back at SSI Headquarters . . .

Not surprisingly, the survey results overwhelmed the SSI project team. They had expected perhaps a hundred activities. Thousands arrived. The original plan was to have an analyst compile the activities into a central spreadsheet. But the list of activities soon hit 10,000—and the analyst had only entered about half of the returned surveys.

The SSI team quickly abandoned its compilation effort. As a sanity check, one of the SSI team members casually decided to total the self-reported times of the 10,000 activities that made it into the spreadsheet. The sum exceeded the total existing organizational capacity of the entire finance department. On average, each participating finance employee perceived and reported that he or she performed the work of four. In other words, the respondents reported that, based on their activity lists, they were each effectively working *32 hours a day!*

This isn't surprising. Recall from Chapter 3 that 93 percent of U.S. automobile drivers rank their abilities as above average. Overconfident, subjective perception is always at work—even with accountants. Unfortunately, the SSI team based its improvement effort on a foundation of *self-reported data.*

The SSI team's survey was intended to create an inventory of the (obviously) "standard" activities that could be relocated and consolidated within a single site. But it's dangerous to rely on perception and assume the obvious. Consequently, the survey was generating the unintended consequence of "complexifying" the work, instead of simplifying it—just like Bert's uncontrolled ledger line items for the west wing. The Accounting Library of Babel was always stealthily expanding. Now it was annexing the SSI team's improvement effort.

### Option B: Org Chart–Based Planning

It didn't have to be this way. Even if the SSI team members didn't want to perceive their organization as a knowledge work factory, and even if they didn't want to think in terms of "work products," they could still fall back on organization charts. They could have taken a lesson from Daniel C. McCallum's 1850s organization chart for the New York & Erie Railroad, as we've discussed in Chapter 6. If they had clear, up-to-date organization charts, they could have easily sent Bert a summary of his group's capacity. Even without defining any products, the SSI team could have asked Bert to allocate his group's time across a simple checklist of activities. Sure, it would have depended on self-reported information, but the tendencies of Bert's overconfident perceptual bias would have been limited by one inarguable fact: the organization's capacity.

## The Costly "By-Products" of Improvised Improvement

The story of the SSI project and its survey results highlights only one of several widespread problems with knowledge workers' self-directed, improvisational improvements—when "products" go unrecognized and BOMs are not defined. The result is the dictionary definition of a "by-product": a secondary and sometimes unexpected or unintended result.

In the SSI example, the most problematic by-product was the overwhelming volume of poorly structured, counterproductive data—the "data lake"—that the well-intentioned survey unintentionally produced: subjectively developed, inconsistently defined, unbounded in scope, and mathematically incorrect—by 400 percent.

Similar problems plague knowledge work operations initiatives everywhere. They arise from the improvised improvements common to knowledge work: the unconscious, undisciplined application of the elements of industrialization.

The costly by-products of industrialization creep in stealthily and are easily overlooked. They're the antithesis of the three pillars of industrialization, i.e., standardization, specialization, and division of labor. Specifically, they result from the *accidental* division of labor, *casual* standardization, and *subjectively defined* specialization. Examples of common by-products include:

- **Product proliferation.** Without a product orientation, employees naturally focus on work activities, a more daunting conceptual and managerial challenge (as we will see in Chapter 10). The result is that knowledge work products grow in both number and complexity without BOMs or centralized directories. Managing work productivity becomes fiendishly difficult without product-based unit measurement. And as the SSI team discovered, casual standardization efforts can have the unintended consequence of increasing operational complexity and uniqueness.

- **Process mutation.** Some activities get transferred to the new location. Others get left behind. This creates a new "mutant" business process that straddles both locations. Often, the resulting process includes even *more* activities than the original. Executives will often remark, "We centralized (or, we outsourced), but the work didn't seem to go away." Now you know why.

- **Fragmented accountability.** After the redesign, many of the job responsibilities are neither centralized nor decentralized. An undocumented version of "job sharing" is thus unintentionally implemented. And the job positions, activities, and responsibilities are typically inconsistent from location to location, or even among different employees at the same location. Managers, coworkers, and customers struggle to understand who is accountable for what. And when they inquire, they hear, "It depends."

- **Stranded expertise.** Bert's know-how, along with the BOMs in his head, would be lost if he refused to relocate and instead opted for early retirement. The cardiology department would lose his insights for targeting the factors that increase revenue and meet the CFO's goals. Nobody would be able to decipher the thousands of general-ledger items he'd left behind—and everyone would be terrified to delete them.

- **Overwork: working below one's pay grade.** "It's faster for me to just do it than to try to explain it to you." This common excuse, in the absence of a documented bill of materials, underscores the cost—and risk—of keeping this information in one person's memory. Expertise is diverted from high-value tasks, like reconciling Walter's cardiology department revenue plan. Instead, it's squandered on analyst-level activity, like correcting the journal entry errors to complete the financial close on time.

## Taking Inventory of the Overlooked Products Your Knowledge Workers Create Every Day

So now you know your knowledge workers are spending their days creating products—even if they generally don't think of them as such. How, then, can you take inventory? Where should you look for descriptions of knowledge work "products" and their quantities? Here are some obvious hiding-in-plain-sight places to consider:

## External Sources

Typically, external sources lack essential detail; however, these do have a couple of advantages. First, they are generally inarguable. The Berts of the world will find it difficult (but certainly not impossible) to quibble with these sources. Second, external, public sources enable competitive benchmark comparisons at a summary level.

1. **Financial statements and quarterly reports.** Depending on the industry, these may provide quantities of widely recognized knowledge work "products." It's a long shot, but examples might include totals of accounts, customers, transactions, production statistics, and more.
2. **Regulatory reports.** Many highly regulated industries—such as utilities, insurance, and healthcare—are required to file details of their operations. Often these exist at the state level. It might require some digging, but it can be well worth the effort.
3. **Industry associations.** Members sometimes participate in "industry roundtable" surveys and studies.
4. **Information services providers.** These will usually involve a purchase. The costs, quality, and relevance will vary widely. Consider products such as:
   - Equities analyses
   - Marketing surveys
   - Benchmarking surveys
5. **Satellite services.** Yes, you read right: outer space. For example, hedge fund traders subscribe to service providers that use satellite-generated photos to count cars in retailers' parking lots, track shipments from mines, monitor oil inventories, and more. These types of outside-in analytical services are just the tip of the iceberg for the future.

## Internal Sources

These knowledge work assets are worthy of extensive investments to upgrade, standardize, maintain, and widely circulate inside the business. Of course, they are hiding in plain sight and are rarely in good order:

1. **Organization charts.** These charts should form the baseline for all knowledge work analysis and improvement but rarely do. The SSI team could have saved itself lots of heartache and delay by starting with clear, updated org charts, instead of an activity survey.

2. **Revenue forecasts.** Why didn't the SSI team begin with these internal forecasts? Instead of sending around a loosely defined activity survey, the team could have rounded up the revenue plans. The team members could have met with Bert and Walter to review the cardiology department's revenue plan. There, they would have discovered detailed descriptions and quantities of products: surgeries, tests, post-op case support, and more.

3. **Marketing and sales departments.** Sure, the marching orders for overall revenue growth and margin targets typically come from the highest levels of corporate. However, down at the day-to-day levels of business operations, these dollars have to be converted into nuts-and-bolts budgeting items. Bert has to help Walter translate— i.e., reverse-engineer—these new revenue dollars into additional new surgeries for the cardiology department. And then the sales team has to recruit health plans to send the patients to Walter's locations. Here you can often find excellent examples of widely recognized, quantified products that correlate with revenue and costs. That's why Walter was anxiously looking for Bert. He wanted help to explain and close his revenue reporting shortfall in the cardiology department.

4. **Operating statistics (source data).** Many of the existing operations-related technologies in knowledge work organizations capture statistics on volumes and frequencies of "machine tasks." Look for transaction volumes, cycle times, user log-in information in IT sys-

tems for call processing, order management, and customer relationship management. *Warning:* Extensive data wrangling may be required.

## Inspirational Example: A Case Study in Simplification and Standardization

Around 1910, a young, inexperienced executive named Lynn Webster Ellis was thrust into managing the marketing and advertising operations of a global enterprise, recently formed through several mergers. In his book *Data on Advertising Department Records*, written in 1917, he described a company in chaos, desperate for advertising to support the aggressive growth needed to fund the cost of the acquisitions.[2] His book reads like a modern story, and the operational challenges that Ellis faced are pervasive today, a century later, in marketing operations. (See Figure 7-1 for an example of leading-edge office technology circa 1920.)

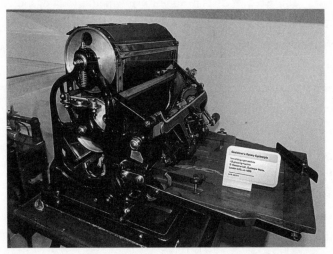

**FIGURE 7-1**   Here's an example of leading-edge knowledge work technology circa 1920—the cyclostyle, an early copier machine. Technology vendors, then as now, claim that their products will "standardize" operations. But standardization doesn't happen by accident—or by buying the latest technology.

Image source: Reproduced without alteration from the original photograph on Wikimedia Commons by Dr. Bernd Gross, CC-BY-SA 4.0 License.

Like the SSI team, Ellis had no improvement experience, so he improvised. Unlike the SSI team, however, Ellis began with a keen awareness that he had inherited a chaotic mess. And he also knew that chaos begat more chaos. He did not fool himself into believing that the existing advertising staff—or anyone else, for that matter—held the answers for improvement. Like the SSI team, Ellis began with a survey. But that's where the similarities end.

The Ellis survey began at the top of the organization with summary-level, inarguable data. Later, he would use these summary insights to selectively drill down and invest scarce, valuable time on the critical details that determined productivity. He began by taking an inventory of the "products" produced by his new organization. He used internal sources: the files from the previous year. He consulted his internal customers, the regional managers, to understand their pending sales goals; think of Walter, Bert, and the cardiology department. Although Ellis didn't use the term, his "products" consisted of display ads in print media, catalogs, direct-mail campaigns, trade press articles, speaking presentations, and more.

By quickly establishing the overall demand parameters for his department's products, Ellis made his task manageable. He avoided the Library of Babel syndrome. During the next year, he and his team calmly and methodically identified the root causes of the types of costly by-products that the SSI team encountered. Of course, they did this through improvisation, and they never used any of the terminology used in this chapter. Figure 7-2 provides just one example.

Ellis and his team rapidly identified the false complexity that drove costly internal product proliferation. For example, they no longer allowed their internal customers to specify the minute details of ads. Instead, these customers could broadly identify the colors, shapes, and sizes of ads. Then the employees in Ellis's organization fit these specs into their newly standardized templates for ads. This allowed the advertising department to narrow their inventories to the point where external vendors and printers could take over most of the inventory duties. Large retailers now use this technique for inventories and call it "collaborative planning, forecasting,

## A Knowledge-Work Standardization Tool circa 1917

### ORDER FOR ADVERTISING LITERATURE AND NOVELTIES

Subject ————————————————————————————————

Job number ——————————— Date of order ——————————— Date expected ———————————

Form number of advertisement ——————— Last job number ——————————— Quantity ordered ———————————

Number of pages ——————————— Size (approximate) ——————————— inches high x ——————————— inches wide

Postage ——————— cents; estimated cost, each ——————————— cents; total $ ———————————

Stock: Cover ——————————————————————————————— Ink ———————————————

Inside ——————————————————————————————— Ink ———————————————

Requested by ——————————————————— Authorized by ———————————————

For the benefit of ————————————————————————————————

——————————————————————————— Department Division —— Branch —— Line —— Dealers

Circulation:  Sale —— Exhibitions —— By mail from the branches or the home office —— By the salesmen and dealers

Envelope stuffers —— Catalog insert

Immediate distribution: Dealers ——————————————— Branches ———————————————

Reserve stock ————————————————————————————————

Remarks on circulation ————————————————————————————————

Copy to be furnished by ——————————————— Date ———————————————

Remarks on copy ————————————————————————————————

**FIGURE 7-2** This is a reproduction of one of L. W. Ellis's knowledge work standardization tools: a standard order form for advertisements. Forms like this gave Ellis control over his organization's work products, and the forms also limited variation—in other words, he standardized operations with a nontechnology approach.

Reproduced from L. W. Ellis, *Data on Advertising Department Records*, (New York: A. W. Shaw Company, 1917), 7.

and replenishment," or CPFR. Unfortunately, most marketing departments today have yet to adopt the standardized, template-based approach that Ellis pioneered. After a century, and despite the advent of sophisticated technology, they continue to suffer the costly effects of product proliferation.

Considering the productivity gains he achieved, it's a sad commentary on the culture of business during his time (and ours) that people in Ellis's organization complained about time spent standardizing and documenting. "It's just a bunch of useless red tape," they would complain. But Ellis had a ready retort: "There is no detail of operation too small for your earnest attention—once. But after . . . you are criminally negligent if you don't write it down where it can't get away."[3]

His coworkers should have thanked him. In just a year, he'd expanded the group's productivity fourfold—while reducing its budget by 20 percent.

## Let's Build!

You're in great shape at this point. You've got more than enough useful information to start building your own knowledge work factory. And we'll begin this in Chapter 8.

---

## CHAPTER 7: **TAKEAWAYS**

1. Although knowledge workers deliver numerous "work products," they prefer to perceive that they deliver "services," shunning simple, proven, product-based management methods used by manufacturers.

2. Decentralized, informal knowledge work management methods create staggering levels of costly, ever-increasing—and avoidable—operational complexity:
   - Work product proliferation
   - Business process mutation
   - Fragmented accountability
   - Stranded expertise
   - Overwork: "working below one's pay grade"

3. The avoidable "false complexity" of knowledge work impedes the success of industrialization efforts (e.g., shared service centers, outsourcing, centralization) that depend on standardization, specialization, and division of labor.

4. Knowledge work organizations can adopt bills of materials to gain product-based management capabilities that avoid the "false complexity" eroding effectiveness:
   - Formal product definitions and inventories
   - Instructions for production
   - Capacity estimates for planning
   - Data for costs and productivity

# CHAPTER 8

# BUILDING YOUR OWN KNOWLEDGE WORK FACTORY

We've been building toward this point in the book for a long time. Now we're going to put these insights to work, so you can build your own knowledge work factory. You'll see what's simple, and what isn't. You'll witness a frontline struggle between the forces of industrialization and advocates of the status quo. You'll get winning ideas from a thought leader who "lost" a battle with Henry Ford. And you'll be treated to a brilliant cameo performance from one of our heroes from earlier in the book.

Curiosity piqued? Let's get started.

## Building the Factory: Overwhelmingly Simple

It's amazing how much a little knowledge can change your worldview. Not long ago—as in, back in Chapter 5—the prospect of transforming a knowledge work organization into a knowledge work *factory* seemed daunting. Remember the offices full of workers and the sheer number of tasks being performed?

But now everything is flipped on its head. Suddenly, the prospect of building a knowledge work factory seems too easy. Calculate employee productivity? Merely divide organizational capacity by work-product volumes? Is that all there is? *Long division?!*

This can't be right. It's too simple. "Simple," however, doesn't mean "easy," as Chapter 12 will show. Overconfidence bias is whispering warnings in your ear: "Don't kid yourself. It has to be more complicated. Surely, this must require a team of data scientists, reams of algorithms, and monumental computing power . . . lots of new technology. After all, if there were a simple, better mousetrap, someone—*everyone*—would be using it already." Ask those around you, and as always, they will overconfidently reinforce these fears.

Stop. Right there. *Ignore them.* They haven't read the first seven chapters in this book. This isn't a time to stress. It's a time to recap everything you've accomplished thus far:

- You documented and quantified organizational capacity. Remember the insights from railroad man McCallum and his org charts in Chapter 6?
- You identified and took an "inventory" of the knowledge work products that these organizations generate. Remember the BOMs, or bills of materials, from Chapter 7?
- You've focused on operational data that, in many cases, are overlooked. Remember the 50 line items (out of 45,000) that contained 60 percent of all expense data from our "general-ledger grocery store"?
- All along the way, you rejected demands from employees and management to delay, to study further, to engage in false precision, and to fall prey to the siren song of analysis paralysis.

As you arm yourself with this knowledge, and generate unconventional, challenging new insights, you'll also notice an interesting change. Suddenly, everyone seems a bit less confident in their conventional perception. Who knows what surprises your data might hold?

Let's find out!

## Secrets of the Deep

To crank up your knowledge work factory, simply divide the work products into the organizational capacity. It's really that simple. Start at the top of the organization: the summary level. This might be an entire business, a business line, or a functional department like finance or a contact center.

Some of these data probably already exist. And here are the kinds of reactions you'll hear:

- "But we already do that!"
- "We're close to the industry averages!"
- "There's not much variance."
- "There's no reason to drill down; everything is the same."

These are typical misperceptions. Ignore them. Keep drilling.

At the summary level, business-to-business performance variance may well appear minimal. That's because all of the wide—read: "valuable"—variance at the *lower* organizational levels is obscured and unexplored.

Keep diving. You want to go down, down, *down*—all the way down to *individual-employee data:* numbers of products produced, transactions completed, or calls processed. This is the analytical "ocean floor," where the unexpected, valuable variance lives (see Figure 8-1). Think of the bizarre creatures that live near the bottom of the ocean—with lights on their heads. That's what you're seeking. At these depths, the variance starts to get crazy, defying everyone's overconfident expectations. It's not unusual to find a variance of 2x to 7x for the simplest, identical work activities. That's where the wild things are: the strange, valuable "long tails" of wide variance.

## Crossing the Great Divide

Remember Bob, our VP of operations for a top-10 U.S. property and casualty (P&C) insurer from Chapter 1? When we last left him, he was charged with boosting his organization's productivity by at least 15 percent. This was a daunting challenge, considering that the CEO wanted to grow the business, but not its headcount.

And so Bob was diligently working his way through his various operations teams in search of productivity. He wanted his managers to agree that they could process more work and agree to a quantified target. He had interviewed the executives in several of his operating groups: new policy applications, underwriting, processing, issuance, and policyholder services.

**FIGURE 8-1**   To find the organization's true levels of performance variance, go all the way down to *individual-employee data*, i.e., the "ocean floor" of operations. That's where the valuable "long tails" of wide variance hide.

Image sources: Shutterstock and Helmut Corneli/Getty Images.

Bob wasn't having as much luck as he had expected. The execs would agree to 5 percent, or maybe 7 percent if Bob was lucky. And what were Bob's managers using as the basis of their arguments? *Summary-level data and averages.* That's right: financial, ledger-line info with hundreds of rows of distracting detail—exactly the kind of reports that accountants like Julie and Bert (Chapter 7) take pride in creating. Sure, it *looks* impressive. But it's *summary.* It's *surface.* It doesn't take the requisite "voyage to the bottom of the sea" to reveal the staggering individual-employee performance variances that hide massive opportunity gains in productivity and effectiveness. And insights for innovation also lurk there.

Having interviewed his other managers, Bob now turned to his manager of claims, his largest organization. This is the story of their conversation.

Meet Laura. She'd managed the company's P&C claims organization for 12 years. Laura sat across from Bob at the company cafeteria, patiently explaining her conventional perception of reality in claims processing: "Bob, I know that we're under pressure. From corporate management, the board, activist investors . . . I get it. The company needs to increase productivity. But you need to understand that the claims processing organization is unique, especially compared with your other organizations. To compound the situation, we're severely shorthanded. I've got scads of unfilled positions. So if you're looking to increase productivity, I suggest that you let me increase headcount. I urgently need more claims processors. More processors, more productivity."

"Actually," Bob replied, "I was planning on asking you to *reduce* staff."

Laura blinked.

"No terminations," Bob assured her, "but an 'effective' reduction. I need a 20 percent capacity increase to handle the new business growth expected for next year. (Bob purposefully inflated the required capacity gain, certain that Laura would try to negotiate down.) Since corporate wants the added capacity without added staff, it's effectively a 'reduction' for your team—higher productivity from your existing claims processors."

Laura paused. "Pardon my candor, Bob, but that strategy is a nonstarter. It would be *catastrophic*. I don't think you're seeing the unintended consequences."

Bob: "Which are?"

Laura continued, "If I push my claims processors to meet productivity goals, our claims losses will go through the roof."

Bob: "Why would losses necessarily rise?"

"It's simple," Laura replied. "If our claims processors even *suspect* that we're measuring them for processing speed, they'll simply overpay each claim to make sure they meet their productivity quota. Effectiveness, or caution, goes out the window. Claims loss levels will skyrocket. Can you imagine the negative earnings impact of a 10 percent rise in claims losses paid, or overpaid? That would've been a *third* of the auto division's earnings last year."

Bob frowned appreciatively. "Wow. You always surprise me, Laura. I'm impressed."

Laura smiled. "Thank you, Bob."

"Because," Bob continued, matter-of-factly, "after speaking with every other manager in my shop, I've learned that none of them maintains any meaningful productivity data—especially effectiveness stats like claims overpayment. Not only are you tracking the productivity of the claims processors, but you're obviously *linking it* to claims loss levels—that's an effectiveness metric. Very cool."

Laura waffled, "Wait a second. I never said—"

Bob continued, "A 10 percent rise in loss payments? Wow. I need to share your reports with the other managers. That's exactly the kind of detailed performance management capability we need to implement across this organization."

"Well . . . ," Laura began, "I'm not actually *tracking* anything. I'm just telling you what everyone who works in claims already knows—common, industrywide knowledge."

Bob raised his brows. "Really?"

"Yes, unfortunately," Laura replied. "Look, Bob, I've spent 20 years of my career in claims processing. Everyone agrees on this one. You can't get *both* high productivity *and* low loss severity. It's a trade-off. So we have to choose."

Bob held his tongue. Laura was his most progressive manager—or so he had thought. Now she was adamant that it was "impossible" to have both quantity *and* quality—discouraging. Finally, he asked, "Are you familiar with the corporate internal improvement team?"

"Of course."

"Well," Bob replied, "the team is getting some assistance from an external resource. Kind of like a consultant. He's directing the team's efforts, and the team members would like to have access to whatever data you have."

Laura nodded again. "No problem. I'll be sure to mention it at our weekly leadership meeting tomorrow. I can also send out a memo to the entire claims organization."

"Thanks, Laura," said Bob. "That will be a big help. I think you'll like this guy. I imagine he'll bring an unconventional perspective to the review of claims processing."

"Okay . . . ," said Laura, cautiously. "What's his name?"

"Nick Clearsight."

(Hold on. I need to take you, the reader, aside here. As I'd mentioned back in Chapter 1, Bob is a composite character, based on real people. And so is Laura. But do you remember when things got extra sticky for our real-life composite characters at the tire factory in Chapter 4? That was when I created our fictional *knowledge work factory* superhero, Nick Clearsight. As you can see by now, Bob and Laura can use a facilitator—an "insight coach." So it's only appropriate that we bring in Nick to speed things along.)

## Where the Long Tail Hides

After lunch, Bob thought about Laura's auto claims group. He knew that it performed at roughly industry-average levels, maybe even a bit higher. Everyone in the company, and on Wall Street, tracked these summary averages. Laura's team processed an industry-average number of claims per employee—average productivity. And the team paid an industry-average amount to settle each claim—average effectiveness.

These industry averages were compiled from numerous sources: industry group surveys, research firms, and regulatory filings. And all these summary-level comparisons, or benchmarks, tended to cluster closely around the mean. In other words, *no single company was consistently far ahead, or far behind, its competitors.* Typically, companies fell within just a few percentage points of each other—the difference was often less than a point.

Sure, there was the occasional exception when a price war erupted, new products were mispriced, or catastrophic damages exceeded the ranges that underwriters predicted. And in-depth, apples-to-apples comparisons were difficult because each company maintained a different product mix. But overall, the appearance was one of a tight-running pack.

This is a fertile breeding ground for the overconfidence bias. People in the industry—people like Laura—will seize on this tight clustering as further proof (confirmation bias) of the prevailing conventional wisdom: there is no high-performing outlier. In other words, there's no one else to look to—no industry leader—for additional best practices when it comes to optimizing claims processing. It's a performance innovation stalemate. "We can't see competitors using a better mousetrap," all the Lauras of the world will tell you. "Therefore, it must not exist. We'll wait for new, innovative technology."

If it's persistently believed that everyone's performing at about the same level—that there's market equilibrium—it's even easier for managers like Laura to conclude that there are no great insights to be gleaned from digging deeper into the detail of their own operations. If it was pointed out that claims processing was a knowledge work factory, they could confidently agree. And furthermore, they could point out that *their* factory was obviously optimized based on this market equilibrium—just like all the other claims factories. If and when a better mousetrap came along for claims processing (more productive, effective, and innovative), everyone would learn about it and adopt it. In the meantime, everyone must already be using the best mousetraps available.

## Shallow Water, Shallow Insights

The overconfidence bias of Laura—and of everyone like her in the industry—will adamantly maintain that all the opportunities for productivity improvement have been fished out. And that's an interesting word choice, because it overlooks the long tails that are hiding deep down on the "ocean floor," as we described it earlier, within *every claims processing organization*, or every knowledge work organization. The fact that you don't see outliers on the surface is no guarantee that the depths aren't teeming with them. And in fact, they are.

Remember the fat-tail perceptual bias from Chapter 3? It's the belief that only a few, valuable "big rocks" provide breakthrough improvement opportunities. The invention of the steam engine is an example. Overconfidence says that the *little* rocks in the long tail don't matter very much. They were the "boring history," back in Chapter 3, that preceded the big-rock application of steam power. Overconfidence says, "Don't sweat the small stuff. Instead, find the big-rock breakthroughs. That's where the money is."

As a result, businesspeople overlook three types of opportunities hiding among the long tail's small rocks. *The first is consistency.* Sure, the inconsistent performance—the variance—takes an obvious toll on productivity, frequently squandering more than 20 percent of organizational capacity. However, this inconsistency also erodes service quality (think of risk and compliance errors) and degrades the customer experience.

*The second opportunity is effectiveness.* The benefits of even the smallest improvements in effectiveness can frequently far exceed those of all productivity gains. Think of increasing the conversion rate for the prospects pursued by a sales team, or, as we'll soon see, reducing the overpayments for property damage insurance claims. Increased effectiveness is the ultimate goal of knowledge workers' efforts, yet it is rarely measured, particularly at the individual-employee level.

*The third "small-rock" opportunity that's overlooked is innovation.* The long tail of small rocks is, historically, today's favorite hiding place for tomorrow's big-rock opportunities. Recall that the steam engine was conceived in ancient Greece, hundreds of years before it was "invented" in England. In other words, the design for this better mousetrap languished, overlooked, in the long tail of "boring history"—concealed in the small rocks—for 1,600 years before it was reinvented. Every business has numerous unexploited, small-scale "steam engine" innovations lurking in their long tails. For example, Laura's group could coordinate claims-loss data with Bob's other organizations, such as sales and underwriting, in real time, to fine-tune policy pricing and loss risk assessment. This innovation is simple, mundane, highly valuable, and truly un-sexy. That's one reason why it's overlooked. As we saw in the Introduction to this book, marketing execs and CEOs prefer to pursue sexy new mobile apps. Why not pursue both? (Hint: another false trade-off—operational vs. strategic.)

Unfortunately, most businesspeople don't ever see the facts about small-rock opportunities. And even if they did, they wouldn't let these facts get in the way of their misperceptions. They'd rather spend almost all of their time looking for the big rocks, the fat tail of improvement: breakthrough inventions delivering game-changing opportunities. When they glance at the industry averages for claims processing, they notice that these are tightly clustered with low variance. Almost instantly, they overconfidently conclude, "Everyone is about the same. There's nothing here to learn. It's not worth investigating. Don't waste your time digging deeper."

*Ignore this directive!* Instead, recognize it as a "tell," the evidence of a possible oversight. Do the exact opposite: Dive! Dive! Dive!

Crank up your new knowledge work factory. Divide the work-product quantities into the organizational capacity at the individual-employee level. *Voilà!* Long tails emerge. A variance of 2x to 7x—maybe more. They're hiding down at the individual performance level. That's where you find those valuable, overlooked small rocks of opportunity. Down here, it's a diamond field of valuable opportunities. Just pick them up. It's deceptively simple.

## The Return of Nick Clearsight

So whatever happened after Laura's lively exchange with Bob? Let's find out.

Laura agreed—albeit with trepidation—to meet this Nick Clearsight at the company's espresso bar off the main lobby. Via e-mail (their only contact to date), he had promised to review some of his findings with her. "Not to worry," he had written. "It's all good news."

Being told *not* to worry, of course, made Laura worry. For two weeks now, she and her team had continually transmitted reams of operating data to Nick and the corporate improvement team. Nick asked very few questions of her people and even fewer of her. She knew that Nick had even less experience with claims processing than Bob. How could this "mystery man" possibly prove useful? He hadn't spent decades in the claims trenches, like Laura.

Now he sat across from her and smiled. "Laura, the members of your team have been fantastic. Wonderfully responsive. They actually have pretty good data. Better than most."

Laura perked up. "Better than most claims processing organizations?"

Nick shrugged. "I wouldn't have a clue. I seriously doubt it, though. What I was referring to was the overall *comprehensibility* of your data, irrespective of the industry. *That's* what was better than most. Nearly 40 percent of them were understandable and usable as is. That's almost double the norm."

Laura stiffened. Was that a compliment? Did he just say that 60 percent of her data were useless? Could that be true? "So," she replied, "did you find *anything* you think is useful?"

"Oh yes," Nick offered. "The performance data for individual employees were invaluable—a real gold mine. This information is readily available in your system—what I call 'source data'— but I couldn't find any internal operations reports that use it. Does your organization produce any? Do you track performance of individual claims processors?"

Laura fell silent. "Of course not," thought Nick. He'd seen it so many times before: Without *individual* performance measures, the employees were effectively "self-managed." They operate with their own instructions. Management has not set estimated times, or quantified targets for productivity or effectiveness. In other words, the *management* of work was not separated from the *performance* of work. Laura's claims processors, Nick knew, managed their own individual workdays, tasks, and goals.

Her organization wasn't operating like a claims processing factory. It was more like a Victorian workroom, full of salaried claims processing "artisans." They performed the work as they've been taught *and as they saw fit*. It resembled work in Charles Dickens's time, except with one big difference: In Victorian workrooms, there were few salaries. Workers were paid only for the items they produced—the piecework model drove productivity.

"Actually," Laura said, "the overall performance averages are pretty constant for our organization. We closely track overall averages of claims processed, based on total headcount. We also watch average losses paid per claim. This is reported weekly, sometimes even daily, on an organization-wide basis." She sat back, satisfied. "So, we have overall averages. There's no need to look at individual-employee performance. It's costly."

"Costly?" Nick replied. "It was just a couple of mouse clicks for our team—"

"Oh, heavens no," interrupted Laura. "I'm not talking about the cost of preparing reports. Those are negligible, I agree. I'm not even talking about the labor costs of the claims processors. These are important, but I mean really, how much can individual productivity performance vary? Maybe 5, 10, even 15 percent per employee—at the most? It's not even worth tracking, in the big scheme of things. No, Nick, I am talking about the unintended costs of measuring individual-employee productivity. Are you familiar with the term claims loss 'severity'?"

Nick nodded. "'Severity.' Yes, it's the amount paid to settle a policy-holder's claim. But how does this link to the cost of reporting?"

"It's simple," Laura explained. She was in her comfort zone now. "If we start reporting individual performance and setting quantified daily quo-tas, claims loss severity will rise. The processors will speed through their work. Quality will suffer. They'll take shortcuts, like overpaying the claims simply to get them off their desk to make their productivity goals, their daily quotas."

Nick interjected. "I understand completely. However, there's a problem with that conventional wisdom."

"What's that?"

"The data contradict it—your data."

Laura paused as Nick clarified. "Let's start with productivity. The highest producers in your organization process far more claims than those in the bottom quartile—roughly two-and-a-half times as many." Nick slid a chart to Laura. This long-tail chart of individual-employee performance told the story. (See Figure 8-2.)

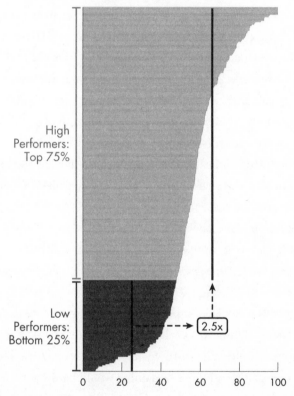

**Claims Processed per Employee***
(Identical Work Activities)

**FIGURE 8-2**  The individual-employee data were inarguable: the high performers (top 75 percent) in Laura's organization processed 2.5 times as many claims as the low performers (bottom 25 percent).

*These employees are known in the industry as "claims adjusters," and they process insurance claims from policyholders.

(In a word, *whoa!* We need to step outside Nick and Laura's conversation here, just to underscore the magnitude of what Nick just revealed. Based on conventional management expectations, that is one exceedingly large variance for claims processing efficiency: 250 percent! It's *15-50 times higher* than Laura's overconfident misperception. Remember, she was expecting 5 to 15 percent, tops. And you'll recall that at the [dangerously misleading] *summary* level, Laura's teams all fell within just a few percentage points of one another. This was also consistent with the industry average variance range [about 1 to 2 percentage points]. But down at the murky ocean floor, within each claims team, individual-employee productivity variance per claim processed is running up to 100 times greater than the summary-level, industry-average variance. As Nick will tell you, this is hardly unusual for knowledge work. *Spoiler alert:* Reducing this variance translates into meaningful labor efficiency improvement for Laura: effectively a 25 percent capacity gain that can be used for the planned growth. More valuably, increased productivity also improves employee effectiveness. In this case, it actually *reduces* overpayments of claims losses, as we'll see next.)

Laura squinted skeptically. "My top three quartiles are processing two-and-a-half times as many claims as my bottom quartile? That doesn't feel right. I'll need to check the numbers."

"Of course," nodded Nick. "No problem. But I'm curious. When you say it doesn't 'feel right,' what are you comparing it with?"

Laura was vague: "It doesn't feel right, based on my experience—my expectations."

"Well, this is a valuable improvement opportunity. The capacity gain alone is certainly significant," replied Nick. "Do you realize that the workload of the entire bottom quartile of your processors could be absorbed by the remaining staff? And those remaining would hardly even notice it. It would amount to adding just one more claim per day for each of them—they currently each process over 60 claims daily."

"That's 25 percent. That *would* be a big capacity gain," Laura admitted. "But I think we would've noticed a gaping hole like that if it really existed. And even if we didn't notice it, which is doubtful, then I'm positive that *someone* in our company or the industry would've noticed this by now. Why isn't one of our competitors operating at that level? Tell you what. I'll withhold judgment until I check your numbers."

Nick smiled. "Understood. Anyway, this capacity gain is peanuts compared with the reduction in loss payments."

"I don't think so," snapped Laura. "Like I said, the processors will simply pay the claims to clear their desks. They'll overpay to make their numbers."

"Again," replied Nick, "your data show just the opposite."

Laura was silent with disbelief.

"It's true," said Nick. "Claims losses will actually plummet if you can bring those low performers up to par. Today, they overpay each claim by an average of 50 percent, compared with the other 75 percent of high-productivity processors. Laura, you're getting the worst of both worlds with the low producers. First, their low productivity squanders 25 percent of capacity—through low efficiency. Second, their low quality gives you higher losses in the form of overpaid claims—low effectiveness." He slid another printout across the table. "Here's the chart." (See Figure 8-3.)

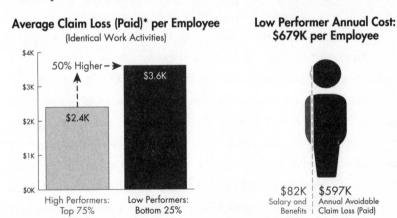

**FIGURE 8-3** The chart that Laura saw looked a lot like this. Her low performers pay out 50 percent more per claim, and overall, each of these low performers costs the company nearly $700,000 annually.

*Average claim loss (known in the industry as "severity") is the average amount paid per insurance claim.

Laura looked at the chart and felt queasy. "We can't show this to the team. Or anyone, for that matter," she said quickly. "This is unfair to the low performers. We don't need to shame them."

Nick: "I'd say it's unfair to their coworkers—the high performers. And actually, these low performers are shaming you, Bob, and the whole company. Not to mention the shareholders."

Laura: "Maybe they can improve. We've got to give them a chance, Nick. Especially if we need capacity to grow next year."

"Sure," replied Nick. "But to do this, you'll need to start reporting individual-employee performance. You don't have to post their names. Just bar charts: quartiles. People will know where they fall—which quartile."

"That'll be a big culture shock," said Laura.

Nick waved away her fears. "Not really. The managers on the floor estimate that at least a third of these low-performing claims processors have already received written warnings about their work habits. I don't think any of the processors will be surprised; everyone on the floor knows who is performing and who's not. Besides, you're concerned about the wrong population of workers: the low performers."

"We have to be fair and even-handed," Laura responded.

Nick pressed on. "Your thinking may be well intentioned, but there's more downside risk for the business with your high performers. You should be concerned about being fair to *them*. It's unfair to allow the low performers to work as they please with no documentation and no penalties. This makes it more likely that the high performers will leave and the low performers will hang around. The current approach incentivizes the low performers and their supervisors to erode the company's earnings. The claims overpayments by low performers currently squander about 20 percent of the auto division's earnings. This is not a trivial matter. These losses are measured in the hundreds of millions."

Laura was nervous. "I presume that Bob also has all this info on claims processing operations?"

Nick nodded. "We're going through his entire organization with the corporate internal improvement team, doing the same simple analysis, and we'll reconvene in about a week."

"All we're doing," he added, "is dividing work-product volumes into organizational capacity. It's the same as what you're doing at the summary, organizational level. The only difference is that we drill down as far as possible, down to individual employees. That's where we always find the big, unexpected variances. And that's the big value opportunity."

Think about that. The only difference between what Nick's team was doing and what Laura had been doing was drilling down deep, down to the "ocean floor." The result? Hundreds of millions in overlooked value.

Laura wondered aloud, "Are you finding the same thing everywhere?"

Nick nodded. "Same as always, for knowledge work. All businesses, all industries. Never changes."

"And bear in mind," Nick added, "that none of these findings include operational improvements to the high performers, you know, the top 75 percent. We'll come back later and work on improving the business processes at a more granular, activity level of detail. I know there's probably another 20 to 30 percent in gains that could be achieved in that way alone. That's also the best time to identify automation opportunities—like robotics."

## The 100-Year-Old Secret in a Productivity Death Match

In 1914, two titans of productivity improvement, Frederick Winslow Taylor and Henry Ford, each put their methodologies to the test in the emerging automobile industry. Only one survived. But you can benefit from both sides of this epic battle. Specifically, you can begin your industrialization journey by adopting some of the strategies of the "loser," i.e., Taylor. Doing so will rapidly deliver breakthrough improvement benefits and establish your first-stage "knowledge work factory." Afterward, you can take your "factory" to the next level by implementing an activity-based productivity improvement approach (Chapter 11). That's exactly how Ford did it. This is the 100-year-old secret. And the tale of two real-life automakers is the best way to understand it.

The early 1900s had many similarities with today. At the time of the Taylor-Ford showdown, new breakthrough technologies were flooding the U.S. economy: radio broadcasting, neon lighting, air conditioning, powered flight, and Brillo Pads, to name a few. Factories adopted electrified production methods. However, despite these advances, U.S. annual productivity growth in durable goods, electrical machinery, and textiles was low, hovering around 1 percent. Between 1900 and 1919, some industries—such as chemicals, furniture, and primary metals—actually became *less* productive. Even with the unprecedented influx of new technology, overall growth of the U.S. economy during this period limped along at 1.5 percent annually—an early twentieth-century productivity paradox.[1] It resembles the 1.6 percent productivity growth rate—the modern productivity paradox—that has haunted the digital economy from 1970 to 2014.[2]

Taylor, famous for his 1911 treatise, *The Principles of Scientific Management,* was retained by the Packard Motor Company to implement his productivity improvement methods in the company's plant. In retrospect, you may wonder why Packard would bother with anything other than an assembly-line strategy. After all, Ford's management team had already implemented its well-publicized moving assembly line in 1913 and doubled production over its industry-leading 1912 levels. Couldn't everyone see the obvious? The better mousetrap?

As always, it was far from obvious at the time. In fact, it was downright radical. Resistance came from all sides, including from Ford's own shareholders, plant workers, and managers. And why shouldn't it? After all, even without the assembly line, the Ford management team had used conventional methods to *double* its production in the year ending in 1912.[3] These methods generally resembled the best-practice techniques championed by Taylor. The "conventional" Ford plant had been the subject of glowing articles in trade publications. This "best-practice" plant was the envy of the industry. Why fix a production model that wasn't broken? No competitors had better mousetraps. To conventional auto manufacturers of the day, it was far from clear—even doubtful—that the assembly line would ultimately prove to be the *only* competitively viable, large-scale production strategy.

But by year-end 1914, the numbers spoke for themselves. The contest was decided, and Ford would dominate the market for the next decade. Using Taylor's methods, Packard produced almost 3,000 autos at an annual rate of roughly two-thirds of a car per employee. During the same period, Ford's plant produced an average of *20* cars per employee for a total of over 250,000 autos. Comparing individual worker output, Ford's methods were 30 times more productive than Taylor's.[4]

Ford's productivity growth also trounced that of the U.S. economy. In the 10-year period ending in 1919, as annual U.S. productivity growth chugged along at 1.5 percent, Ford's productivity grew 15 times faster, at 22 percent each year. Ford managed to escape the productivity paradox of the time.[5] And its factory methods were poised to boost the productivity of the entire U.S. economy over the next two decades as others adopted mass production.

## Breaking Up Is Hard to Do: Separating the Management of Work from the Performance of Work

"What are you talking about? Of *course*, we separate the management of work from the performance of work. We always have. That's nothing new."

Don't be surprised if you hear these replies repeatedly as you crank up your first knowledge work factory. Expect people to hold this perception. And they're directionally correct. This separation has always existed. Taylor became famous by writing about its critical role in productivity. Ford became an industrial icon by acting on and then advancing the concept. And if asked, Laura, in claims processing, would confidently assert that her organization separates the management of work from the performance of work. Everyone is correct. But as always, the devil is in the details. And so is the value; see the sidebar.

## Division of Labor: Three Levels

Industrialization methods can be segmented into three categories, based on successively detailed, increasingly rigorous, and increasingly productive levels of labor specialization.

### *Organizational Level (Laura)*

Most knowledge work organizations, like Laura's claims processing group, use an informal, almost accidental segmentation approach. Labor is defined, measured, and managed at the organizational level. Typically, organizational definitions are highly informal and inconsistent (Chapter 6), making comparisons difficult. This is the least rigorous specialization method. Workers are almost entirely self-directed. They often decide how—and how much—work will be performed.

### *Job-Position Level (Taylor)*

Here, job positions are studied, often with cameras and stopwatches, to identify best practices, or "the one best way" to perform the work. Standards are documented, quantified, and implemented across

*(continued on next page)*

the relevant job positions. However, since standards originate with the most productive workers, this approach implicitly assumes that workers develop, maintain, and ultimately "own" their skills. Management's job is to standardize and transfer the best skills.

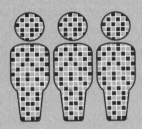

## Work-Activity Level (Ford)

Activities are studied and questioned: Why are these grouped in a way that requires worker skill, or extensive learning? Why are some of these activities performed? Why can't the root causes of many activities be eliminated? Why can't the remaining activities be streamlined? Redistributed? Among unskilled workers? Machines? Why not redesign the *product* to help reduce and streamline activities? Why can't machines be specialized to perform certain activities? (If these questions sound familiar, it's because they're basically the Five Whys for work activities.)

From a practical standpoint, it's best to avoid these unresolvable, philosophical discussions. As you initially launch your knowledge work factory, simply drill down into the detail. Find the best-performing workers. Document their best practices. Write these down and convert them to rules. (This is the "Taylor side" of the productivity equation.) Finally, transfer these rules to everyone else—especially the low performers. Measure everyone's performance constantly. Reduce the variance.

Both the Taylor and the Ford management teams employed these methods prior to their 1914 auto-assembly death match. And both received acclaim; the trade press featured the Ford Piquette Avenue plant as a best-practice factory, prior to the arrival of the assembly line.

But it's hard to learn much that's helpful for your modern-day knowledge work factory from 1914 magazine puff pieces. And Ford neither recorded nor generalized his thoughts for a wider audience. Taylor did. Sure, he lost the productivity contest to Ford (but who didn't?). And yes, modern-day manufacturers will chuckle at Taylor's quaint, outmoded language describing the principles from his 1911 treatise. However, if you're looking to build your knowledge work factory from scratch, Taylor's writings are directly relevant. He published detailed records of his work and his productivity thinking. He illustrated his points with real-life stories of basic, manual work tasks, such as moving iron ingots, shoveling, or laying bricks (borrowed from our old friends Frank and Lillian Gilbreth). And Taylor laid out straightforward, generalized instructions like the ones below:

> The managers assume, for instance, the burden of gathering together all of *the traditional knowledge* which in the past has been *possessed by the workmen*, and then of classifying, tabulating, and *reducing this knowledge to rules*, laws, and formulae which are immensely helpful to the workmen in doing their daily work.[6] (Punctuation and emphasis added.)

Notice that Taylor regards "traditional knowledge" as the source of value for productivity improvement. In other words, *he never questions the inherent skills of the workers.* Challenging this notion relentlessly was Ford's recipe for success. And the following chapters (9 through 11) will show how you can do it in knowledge work. But as you launch your first knowledge work factory, you may want to learn to walk confidently before you attempt to run. If so, follow the development principles outlined above by Taylor. Note his focus on transferring possession of know-how (traditional knowledge that comprises intangible assets, i.e., competencies) *from* the workers *to* the company and its management. He wants to boil it down to "rules, laws, and formulae." He wants it documented. These are best practices by another name. This transfer is a critical point for industrialization success. And it's always a point of contention between workers and management. We'll outline simple but counterintuitive management techniques to preemptively avoid this roadblock in Chapter 12.

## What You Have in Common with Henry Ford (*Hint:* A Lot More Than You Think!)

Think that you don't have anything in common with Ford's century-old industrialization team? Think again. The members of the Ford team faced an uncannily similar technology and economic environment to yours as they developed their breakthrough "industrialization" techniques. Consider what they faced:

- **Productivity paradox.** New technologies failed to increase business productivity.
- **Perceptual bias.** Craftworkers were the specialized knowledge workers of their day. Even the experts, like Taylor, did not perceive that division of labor could be *further* applied to achieve a productivity breakthrough.
- **Glaring oversights.** The enabling technologies and methods were everywhere. Many were "overlooked" and unconsidered. Examples include:
  - **Conveyors.** Breweries, foundries, and grain mills had used these for over a century. The Ford plant included a foundry with a conveyor prior to the implementation of the assembly line. And since the Civil War era, meat-packing operations had used overhead trolleys to bring the work to stationary, low-skilled workers. No need for conventional butchers.
  - **Interchangeable parts.** Metallurgy and machine-tool accuracy had advanced by the 1880s to make this feasible for a wide range of products: sewing machines, guns, and bicycles.

— **Mass production techniques.** The British navy used continuous-flow mass production techniques to bake biscuits for seamen for generations before the assembly line; decades prior to the auto-assembly line, Heinz and Borden similarly mass-produced their canned consumer goods.

These examples demonstrate that the concept of continuous-flow mass production—including bringing the work to the workers—was hardly a new idea. The breakthrough was the radical idea of applying these same nontechnology principles of industrialization—standardization, specialization, and division of labor—to the highly skilled, sophisticated activities of auto manufacturing. The breakthrough was *perceptual . . .* as always.

Feel the momentum building? All of the *perceptual* hurdles you've cleared are now paying off with relatively straightforward executional guidelines rooted in historical precedent.

Together, we've blazed the path to your own knowledge work assembly line. The next chapters will help you optimize it.

## CHAPTER 8: **TAKEAWAYS**

1. Create a basic knowledge work factory by simply dividing work products into the relevant organizational capacity—but dive down to individual-employee productivity levels, similar to a conventional factory.

2. When individual knowledge worker performance is measured and analyzed, several unexpected and unconventional insights typically emerge:

   • Wider variance—Compared with summary-level performance figures, i.e., organization-wide, individual performance varies significantly for identical work. Top-quartile workers' performance can often average 2x to 7x that of bottom-quartile workers.

- Lower efficiency—This wide variance often consumes 15 to 25 percent of organizational capacity, delivering an unexpectedly costly operational efficiency penalty.
- Surprising effectiveness—High productivity in knowledge work operations often delivers higher effectiveness, as well as higher efficiency. Conventional perception often frames these objectives as mutually exclusive, i.e., a false trade-off.

3. The best way to close the individual variance gap is to begin by adopting Frederick Taylor's methods for recording and transferring best practices from high performers to low performers. But don't stop there—see #4, below, for the next step.

4. Achieving "better-than-best-practice" performance requires adopting Ford's methods of work-activity-level improvement: redesign, elimination, standardization, and automation (addressed in more detail in subsequent chapters).

# PART III

# THE TURBOCHARGE

# CHAPTER 9

# OPTIMIZING YOUR KNOWLEDGE WORK ASSEMBLY LINES

At this point you've managed to build a basic knowledge work factory. That's a profound achievement. It provides critically important key performance indicators (KPIs) that quantitatively measure the productivity of organizations and even individual employees. That capability alone is light-years ahead of virtually all other knowledge work organizations, and most importantly, your competitors. Astonishingly, it's even ahead of many conventional manufacturers: nearly 10 percent of *all* U.S. manufacturers maintain *no* key performance indicators.[1]

This is a good time to recap progress. First, we calculated the total "nameplate" organizational capacity of the knowledge work factory. We documented this with simple, easy-to-understand organization charts in Chapter 6. This provided an unmistakable visualization of the operations capacity of each organizational group. Next, we "took inventory" to identify the quantities of work products produced by each of these organizational groups in Chapter 7. Finally, in Chapter 8, we divided each organization's capacity by the quantities of these completed knowledge work products to calculate average productivity. We extended capacity/output quantity measures "all the way down" to monitor the daily productivity of individual employees. Now, we can improve performance by pinpointing and actively managing underperforming organizations and individuals.

But we've only solved half of the productivity paradox—the *easy* half. Specifically, the capability to improve the *low* performers. But overall competitive capability ultimately depends on the *high* performers. We still need a plan to improve *their* productivity and effectiveness. We need to achieve better-than-best-practice performance.

## Curator Versus Innovator

Remember the Taylor-versus-Ford showdown? And remember how we were going to start with Taylor and then advance to Ford? Well, we've reached that point in our journey. The Taylor-style knowledge work factory turns out to be a mixed blessing. On the one hand, it's valuable because it delivers productivity gains immediately, without new technology. It lets you manage knowledge work with numbers. On the other hand, it simply can't deliver the winner-take-all breakthroughs in productivity, effectiveness, and automation that Ford's 1914 Model T factory realized—or that Amazon now seems close to achieving. That's because Taylor-style factories both rely on and are constrained by the "best-practice" improvements of existing high performers. They're captives of the "current state"—the status quo.

Under Taylor's methodology, management's job is to act as a curator, rather than an innovator, of best practices. Think of these best practices as existing "bundles" of work activities that have been invented or devised by the top-performing workers. Following the Taylor method, managers remain at an arm's-length distance from the workers. From there, the managers observe, measure, identify, and document "the one best way" to perform each of these practices. Then they use these to develop guidelines, or "templates," to standardize the practices of all, especially those of the low performers. In this way, the high performers, with management's active intervention and oversight, pull up the low performers.

So far, so good. But where do we go next? How can we challenge the status quo of "the one best way"? Who says it's best? Best compared with what? Can it be better? In other words, where do we find superior practices to develop templates for improving the *high* performers? Is it even possible to make such templates in a methodical manner? Can we systematically and incrementally improve the high performers? Or are we doomed to wait for a lightning strike of innovation? A "big-rock" breakthrough? These are the right questions, but they are seldom asked—especially by the industry incumbents. Answering these questions is challenging. And so most knowledge work improvement efforts fizzle out when they hit this perceptual brick wall.

We've now reached the point where we began this book: the productivity paradox. But instead of talking about it, we're encountering it—head-on. It appears that the improvement path has vaporized, leaving a void. Our brains struggle. Instinctive perceptual biases rush in to rationalize and compensate.

*But what if the void itself is a misperception?* What if it turns out to be just like the cognitive biases and optical illusions that tricked our brains back in Chapter 4? What if we could improve our perception and push through these cognitive barriers?

We can. And this chapter will show how to do it.

First, let's ponder the valuable possibilities of simple improvements that *may be* hidden in this void, obscured by perceptual oversights—improvements that might even be achievable with templates, in a methodical, predictable manner. We'll move quickly, before perceptual biases drag these possibilities out of sight.

Consider these five productivity paradox improvement possibilities—"The Five Maybes":

1. Maybe we don't need a breakthrough innovation—i.e., a "big rock"—in order to improve.
2. Maybe we don't need any new technology in order to improve and to automate more.
3. Maybe we can use timeless improvement methods, like industrialization.
4. Maybe the improvements are extraordinarily valuable.
5. Maybe only a widespread *perception* problem makes these improvements nonobvious.

"Impossible!" is how most people automatically react. "I would have noticed these improvements if they were that valuable. And if I didn't, someone in our company, or one of our competitors would have noticed." (Read: "Let's do nothing.")

How many of our familiar perceptual biases appear in the statement above? The overconfidence bias, the principle of least effort, the fat-tail bias, and the better-mousetrap dogma have all conspired to convince people that they've reached a void. So they make a U-turn on this vital leg of their improvement journey.

This is how the productivity paradox manifests itself in the mundane details of day-to-day improvement thinking. Recall how the fat-tail bias (Chapter 3) obscures perception of improvement opportunities? CEOs and senior executives are routinely disappointed by the lack of improvement and digital automation opportunities they find in their own operations. But they don't search in the long tail. And roughly 90 percent of CEOs and senior execs don't even bother to contact their own CIOs for IT-related business innovation. Instead, the majority turn to industry publications and newsletters in search of more interesting external examples, aka better mousetraps. The second most popular source is their "personal network."[2] Is that the golf course?

## Outachieving the Overachievers

How do we get past these misperceptions? Where do we go next?

We need a map.

Actually, we need a "how to" template. We need guidance from high performers who have successfully improved. After all, they've shattered the barriers of a best-practices factory to discover better-than-best practices. They were willing and capable of unbundling, "blowing up," and reconfiguring their existing best practices, even if they had invented them. They quickly discarded the latest technology and equipment if they found better methods.

But these individuals and their methods are hard to find. As noted earlier, entrepreneurs seldom have time to keep diaries. Chapter 5 pointed out the overlooked long tails of serendipitous, undocumented, trial-and-error efforts that precede a recognized breakthrough like the steam engine, the Microsoft operating system, or the Ford Model T assembly plant. If we're lucky, a few details might show up as footnotes in the memoirs of the marketplace victors, years after the fact.

And that is precisely where we will find our templates (and inspiration) for developing better-than-best-practice improvements. The managers and supervisors of the early Ford plants who pioneered the Model T moving assembly line achieved celebrity status, just like today's tech stars. Scholars, journalists, and Ford preservationists interviewed many of them. Others wrote memoirs detailing their trial-and-error efforts to create Ford's first mass production assembly line. From these records, we can piece together our template.

This chapter will shuttle back and forth between the present and the past. Examples from the Ford workers of 100 years ago will demonstrate how to recognize, define, and integrate business processes. Then, after we identify the principles they used to systematically develop better-than-best practices and improve processes "on the fly"—all while their business was in overdrive and striving to meet hyper-aggressive growth targets— we'll return to the present to see how these can work today.

For some context, Chapter 10 will explain how to extract the detailed work activities from the business process maps and analyze them separately. Identifying a manageable set of "universal" work activities will make the task of industrialization easier. Finally, Chapter 11 will put it all together and explore the benefits of a Ford-style, fully industrialized knowledge work factory.

## Meanwhile, Back at the *Daily Planet* . . .

Remember Tom from Chapter 1? He worked for the global media company and was trying to unsnarl his organization's perception of its customers' priorities. He's going to be the "voice of the present" for our time-traveling journey in this chapter.

Tom had just received a presentation document from his internal improvement team describing their progress to "improve the customer experience." That's a polite way of putting it. More to the point, the team members handed him a massive spending request. They wanted Tom's approval to make an immense technology investment that would, in their words, "automate all the business processes that influence the customer experience."

The size of the proposed expenditure was breathtaking, even for a global business of this size. Everything imaginable was baked into it, which included bids from the most prominent technology providers and systems integrators in the marketplace. It was all to be cloud-based and available for any mobile device imaginable, worldwide. The list of proposed applications was huge. Some were upgrades; others were new:

- Customer relationship management (CRM)
- Promotion planning
- Promotion optimization
- Marketing campaign operations management
- Digital asset management
- A plethora of social media technologies
- A 3D visualization tool—replete with artificial intelligence capable of delivering machine learning to model pricing, margins, and profitability
- An automated revenue attribution tool

Tom winced as he read the last item on the high-priced wish list: a revenue attribution tool. For Tom, this epitomized the entire proposal: inwardly focused technology overkill. "Given recent, lackluster revenue trends," he thought acidly, "isn't it a bit premature to need high-powered technology to finely parse and attribute revenue?"

But these were just Tom's concerns about the initiative's *pricing.* Even more unsettling was the time frame. It stretched for *years.* Tom had heard from Larry, the IT team leader, that the number of business processes to be automated topped 2,000. The more Tom learned about the effort, the more questions arose in his mind. Why would it take so long? Why had it taken a year just to complete the proposal? For that matter, why was everything in the proposal wholly dependent upon new technology? Wasn't there something that could be done right now with what's on hand? And how could there possibly be 2,000 business processes?

Tom decided to get some answers.

## Do the Gemba Walk

Tom was an ardent practitioner of "management by walking around," also known as MBWA (yes, that's a real term and a real acronym). He'd adopted this approach on his own, during his early career in aerospace engineering. He'd found that his job as an assistant designer was easier—not to mention more rewarding—if he had firsthand knowledge of the plant operations. When he first came across "MBWA" in a manual, he couldn't help but laugh. It seemed like a joke. Nothing that simple and obvious could be a management discipline.

But later, while attending lean improvement training at his manufacturing campus, Tom learned that Japanese manufacturers had their own term for these: Gemba walks. Taiichi Ohno, one of the two Toyota executives who established the fundamental principles of lean manufacturing, is credited as a developer of Gemba walks.[3] The objective of these walks is to get firsthand observation of workflows, value streams, work areas, and employee activities.

The reasoning is simple and sound: Without this basic knowledge, executives must rely exclusively on reviewing results and doing "reverse engineering" to draw conclusions. Or even less reliably, they must depend on the opinions and observations of others (think of Laura, the claims executive from Chapter 8). Of course, managers will always need to analyze data and listen to others, but by *walking around* they'll have firsthand observations to provide context for their perceptions.

The aircraft plant where Tom used to work was pretty straightforward: you could recognize, say, a jet engine being attached to a wing. So Tom knew that Gemba walks would be more challenging as he walked the "factory floor" of sales and operations within this massive media conglomerate. But he intended to give it a try. He wanted to get a sense of real-life operations before he reviewed the 2,000 business processes that Larry's IT team had "uncovered."

We'll get back to Larry in a minute. But first, as mentioned, we're going to shuttle back in time to the days of Henry Ford.

## Cast Iron Charlie

It was April 1908, and engineer Charlie Sorensen had just been ordered by Henry Ford to team up with plant superintendent Ed Martin and "go out and run the plant, and don't worry about titles."[4]

Sorensen was a movie star–handsome, notoriously stubborn Dane whose family had immigrated to upstate New York in 1885 when he was 4. At age 19, Sorensen began his 40-year industrial career in a Detroit foundry. In 1905, he landed a job as a pattern maker in the foundry operations at Ford Motor Company. Henry Ford nicknamed Sorensen "Cast Iron Charlie" due to his affinity for low-cost, cast-metal production methods. Sorensen had an uncanny ability to translate Ford's ideas into three-dimensional models—a particularly valuable data-visualization skill, given that Ford couldn't read blueprints. The two men formed a close relationship that lasted over 30 years.

When Sorensen received his title-free promotion to "run the plant," the company had just announced the new Model T. Orders began to flood in, but the car wasn't yet in production. Ford's plant on Piquette Avenue, considered the most advanced in the world, still had its hands full producing the Model N, a good seller for the company. Somehow, Sorensen and Martin had to figure out how to massively increase production, all within the crowded Piquette Avenue plant. (Later, they'd have to scale it up and improve it in Ford's new Highland Park factory.)

On a typical day, Sorensen arrived early at the Piquette plant and went straight to the shipping department to review the quantities of cars produced and shipped. This quickly highlighted for him which areas of the plant were experiencing problems. The review also determined the route of his daily walk through the plant—his Gemba walk.

Of course, Sorensen didn't call it that (it would be another 70 years before the term was formalized), any more than he referred to his process as "MBWA." Yet over time, as he walked through the plant each day, he noticed glaring, fundamental inefficiencies in the assembly operations— hiding in plain sight. How could these possibly go overlooked?

For example, the cars were assembled on the third floor—the very top floor of the building. As Sorensen noticed, this required the company to spend an exorbitant amount on labor, just to wrangle all the parts onto an elevator to haul them upstairs.

After the parts arrived on the third floor, workers had to constantly shuffle them around to make room for assembly. In Sorensen's words, "the job of putting the car together was a simpler one than handling the materials that had to be brought to it."[5]

Sorensen then had an insight—something that no one, not even the top performers, had considered. *Why not assemble the cars on the ground floor?* Even better, *why not feed the parts downward, from the top floors, via roller conveyors?* The current situation, Sorensen noted wryly, essentially resulted from "the unthinking rejection of the aid of the long-accepted principle of gravitation."[6]

## Question Everything

How could anyone overlook something as basic as *gravity?* It's actually very easy to do, especially if your definition of "auto assembly" is too narrow. And at the time, it was. "Auto assembly," prior to Sorensen's insight, was defined simply as "the final fitting together of parts."

People who relied upon Taylor-style factory-improvement methods would likely end up focusing on the "one best way" to accomplish *only those assembly tasks.* Never look up—or down. Thus, without questioning this conventional definition, they would focus on optimizing *a minority of the total labor involved,* that is, just a few "vertebrae" of the long tail. And if they looked around at their competitors, their confirmation bias would be reinforced. They were all "trying to build cars on the third floor." No breakthroughs to be found, right? If no one else was using a better mouse-trap, it certainly didn't exist. That's how it appeared . . . to everyone except Cast Iron Charlie.

Based on his direct observations during his daily walks around the plant, Sorensen developed a broader definition of the assembly process— and factory operations—than almost everyone else in the company, or even the industry. Importantly, his definition of the assembly "business process" included *everyone in the plant.* Therefore, this—naturally— included the work activities spent on wrangling the parts up the elevator and around the third floor. Sorensen looked at everything. He considered every single person on the factory's organization chart. He then perceived their work activities as these extended throughout the plant's various, often-overlooked, processes . . . such as costly parts-wrangling.

Sorensen thereby revolutionized everything by moving assembly downstairs.

Or not.

As much as he wanted the plant to work *with,* and *not against,* gravity, he was faced with a pressing reality: There was simply no time to recon-figure the plant before the new Model T would begin production. He was forced to compromise—and improvise. If his workers would be stuck humping parts up the elevator, then Sorensen resolved that they'd at least do it as methodically and efficiently as possible.

To free up space on the third floor (and throughout the storerooms), Sorensen and others at the plant implemented "just-in-time" inventory planning. The phrase had yet to be coined, but Sorensen and his team employed the technique nonetheless. Although they purchased materi-als in bulk, they had their suppliers hold on to their inventory and only deliver it to the plant in small batches, and only when it was needed.

Sorensen and his team also implemented "velocity-based inventory planning," another term not yet developed. They did this by bringing the bulky, slow-moving inventory items—such as chassis, engines, and axles—to the third floor for storage. Meanwhile, smaller, easy-to-handle, higher-quantity, faster-moving items—such as fasteners, trim, and accessories—were sorted, prepacked, and stored in a different building. These were brought up to the third-floor assembly room at more frequently scheduled intervals to coordinate with final assembly.

Soon, they began to stage and sequence materials directly adjacent to where they would be needed by the mechanics during assembly operations. Sorensen noted—and this is huge—that they were essentially *moving a stockroom to the car as it remained in a fixed position*. That's the big leap. From there, it was a relatively straightforward mental step to the next iteration: This "business process" would be much easier if it were simply reversed. They should move the car to, or through, the stockroom as it was being assembled.

## The 1908 Beta Test

Sorensen and his colleagues kept pushing the envelope on this bring-the-car-to-the-parts concept; after all, experimenting with work design was fun for these young engineers. After several weekends of secret test runs, Sorensen and three helpers decided they were ready. One Sunday morning in late July 1908, they hitched a tow rope to an auto chassis and manually demonstrated one of the most valuable business processes in history—the moving assembly line—to Henry Ford and two senior executives of the company. As Sorensen recalled decades later, the tow-rope demo was hardly a slam-dunk. In fact, the benefits were not readily perceived:

> The only ones in Ford Motor Company who looked at this crude assembly line idea were Mr. Ford, C.H. Wills (chief designer and metallurgist), and Ed Martin (plant production manager). Mr. Ford, though skeptical, nevertheless encouraged the experiment. Martin and Wills doubted that an automobile could be built properly on the move. Wills was particularly hostile. "That way of building cars," he said, "would ruin the company."[7]

Ford Motor Company ended 1908 with total production and sales of 6,398 autos.[8] It took the company *five more years of tinkering* with process improvements, technologies, and product design (not to mention an entirely new factory at Highland Park) before it was able to realize the moving assembly line that the men had demonstrated that Sunday morning.

So what happened between 1908 and 1913? You don't hear much about these supposed "dark ages" at Ford—but you should. They're important. Because even *without* the moving assembly line, Ford—with the help of Sorensen and his team—blew the doors off the competition. *Even then*, they were held up as best-practice exemplars, as noted in a magazine article entitled "Building an Automobile Every 40 Seconds."[9] That's right: one every 40 seconds, *without* the moving assembly line.

After the moving assembly line was implemented, production surged yet again—on the order of about two to three cars every minute. Production for 1913 reached 189,088 cars—more than twice the number featured in the article.[10] By continually pursuing better-than-best practices, the Ford team kept beating its own numbers. By year-end 1916, production had tripled, reaching 585,388 cars.[11] In fact, in an overcrowded marketplace, Ford produced more than five times as many autos as its nearest competitor.[12]

### Production Figures for 1915

| | |
|---|---|
| Ford | 501,492 |
| Willys-Overland | 91,904 |
| Dodge | 45,000 |
| Maxwell | 44,000 |
| Buick | 43,946 |
| Studebaker | 41,243 |
| Cadillac | 20,404 |
| Saxon | 19,000 |

---

### Business Process Principles: A "Better-Than-Best" Template

Business processes must encompass every worker in the factory.

Every work product (Chapter 7) is delivered by processes.

Processes divide every worker's time into sequential work activities.

Total process work activities = total organizational capacity (Chapter 6).

Every work activity is evaluated for standardization, specialization, and division of labor (people and machines).

---

there excess wrangling of parts (data elements)?

re there opportunities to free up space? What would these "prefab ventory packs" look like?

ave you optimally sequenced assembly?

ave you cut out back-and-forth wasted effort?

see how the answers could affect businesses today, let's rejoin Tom, global media giant, back in the twenty-first century.

## ngling "Escalations" Up the Elevator

routinely received a running list of customer complaints. Some were r; others were severe. The severe types were deemed "escalations" ypically required some sort of intervention—and a concession by ledia company. These were often do-overs of ads, known as "make- s" in the media business, run to satisfy disgruntled customers whose ad been run or billed incorrectly.

Seems like a good first step for a Gemba walk," thought Tom, and he to the customer-billing department to learn more.

Sorensen was quick to disavow sole ownershi
idea. Later in his memoir, he sums up its evolution.

> Henry Ford had no ideas on mass production. H
> a lot of autos. He was determined, but like every
> time, he didn't know how. In later years he was
> originator of the mass production idea. Far from
> into it, like the rest of us. The essential tools and
> line with its many integrated feeders resulted from
> which was continually experimenting and improv
> production.[13]

Sorensen's memoirs provide a number of lesson
stunning is one covered in Chapter 6: When it c
*nobody knows anything.* Not even Henry Ford. We c
ception. Sorensen and his team confronted the same
void that we've now reached with our Taylor-style k
tory. Yet they figured out a way to get breakthroug
ment from the industry's highest performers—to dev
practices. They did it by stubbornly improving the w
loosely defined factory business processes—and igno

We can do the same in our knowledge work fact
inarguable success and the details in the various mem
olate a simple template of business process principles t
tion and improvement for *our* knowledge work indu
The first principle is the most significant: *processes mu
worker.* The remaining principles depend on this basic i

Think about your knowledge work factory from a S
of view. Ask yourself:

- Is assembly on the third floor instead of the first?
- Is the work floor crowded?

While there, chatting with the workers (to learn about how bills were generated, how they were delivered, and how issues got resolved), Tom was stunned to discover a pocket-sized, printed instruction manual that the department had created for new employees. The thing was a gem. It had clear, easy-to-follow steps for all the basic billing activities. The steps were even illustrated, with clear diagrams of what to do and when. This little instruction manual effectively provided end-to-end business process maps of sequential work activities for the customer-billing department.

Tom was equally stunned to learn that this trove of information had never been used by either the sales or IT department, even though it had been shared with both of them. The members of the sales team considered the work "below their pay grade." And the IT team members believed they'd get better information, not by reading the clearly laid-out steps, but by studying the computer screens and keystrokes of the billing department staffers.

"So *that's* where the 2,000 'business processes' are coming from," thought Tom. "They are transactions, clusters of keystrokes. You don't have to be clairvoyant to see where this will lead: a big, shiny, expensive box that automates the existing—that is, the incomplete, often wrong—tasks. No end-to-end process breakthroughs coming anytime soon from *that* fragmented approach."

Later, Tom spent a half hour in the office of one of the billing staffers, who had offered to show him typical examples of overdue customer bills on the escalation list. Most of these weren't complicated; many customers weren't paying because the amount being billed in the first place was incorrect. Here are the typical problems that the staffer explained to Tom:

- "This was billed wrong. The customer's ad ran in the wrong media channel."
- "This ad went out to the wrong demographic areas."
- "The ad had incorrect pricing. It didn't include the promotional discount that the sales rep had promised the customer."

- "This one had incorrect customer data. We billed the wrong subsidiary; they're not authorized to pay for ads. Turns out that the wrong subsidiary was entered into the system as 'the client' in the master file—so this error keeps repeating."

*There's a pattern here,* Tom realized. All the errors were simple. All were easily avoidable, "upstream," at the source. And rather than ask for permanent fixes, the customers were taking advantage of these errors. It was easy for them to exploit the company's mindless billing practices and thus delay paying their bills. Tom had to sigh. He honestly couldn't blame them.

And while some of the bills had aged 90 to 120 days, the sales reps wouldn't pick up the phone to resolve them. Not their job. Below their pay grade.

Meanwhile, back in the early 1900s . . .

## Avery's Taxonomy

A couple of years after his 1908 assembly-line demonstration, Cast Iron Charlie was hard at work in Ford's new Highland Park plant. Here, he was assisted by Charles Avery, a former schoolteacher with a college education—a rare and valuable asset at the time. The two of them were rapidly implementing assembly lines for all the subcomponents that they could. However, these processes were neither connected nor balanced—"integrated" was the term they used. Parts surpluses, or shortages, could occur at various points within the plant without much warning, undermining their goal of continuous-flow production.

In a career move that would have far-reaching implications, Avery had decided to quit his job in education (he had actually been a teacher of Ford's son, Edsel) and learn factory work instead. Seeing the opportunity, Sorensen put Avery through an eight-month, hands-on, shop-floor training regimen, where the former teacher proved to be a quick-learning student.

Next, Avery moved to the office where he worked directly for Sorensen. He was assigned the design responsibility for connecting and balancing all of the subassembly operations. Using the firsthand knowledge he'd gained on the shop floor, Avery aimed to sketch out an enormous, single, interconnected workflow for the plant—to integrate all of the end-to-end operating processes.

This workflow, as it turned out, was a masterpiece. It effectively represented a classification system, or "taxonomy," for everything in the plant. Remember Daniel McCallum's 1855 railroad organization chart from Chapter 6? It was the same simple style of genius.

Avery's taxonomy stitched together every existing assembly line in a prioritized hierarchy. Every business process was designed to connect and feed the final assembly of the car. Avery worked out the time sequences to balance the flow of products across the network and ensure that all the right parts arrived in the right places at the right time. The taxonomy was essential for achieving the continuous-flow production dream foreshadowed by Sorensen's 1908 tow-rope demonstration. Within a few months, Ford productivity soared to historic levels, transforming the world of manufacturing productivity.

Thirty years later, in his memoir, Cast Iron Charlie was brutally honest in his assessment of the breakthrough: "We weren't as smart as we have been credited with being. All we were trying to do was develop the Ford car. The achievement came first. Then came logical expression of its principles and philosophy."[14]

## Back to the Future: Tom Visits IT

Over the course of several weeks of Gemba walks, Tom had put himself through his own Avery-like shop-floor training program: he'd learned the ropes of advertising operations, sales, and customer service at this global media giant. Now he was back at the IT department, scrolling through that daunting list of more than 2,000 business processes on Larry's large-screen computer monitor.

He and Larry were maybe one-tenth of the way through the list when Tom asked Larry to stop scrolling. He was starting to wrap his head around this problem.

"Let me ask you something," Tom began. "Does your schedule define a 'currency conversion' as a 'business process'?"

Larry nodded.

Tom: "And how many currencies do we support, across our geography and customer base?"

"I don't remember exactly," said Larry. "But it's over 40. Maybe 50 total."

"So then, currency conversion," said Tom, "accounts for about 50 of the total 2,000 business processes in your list."

"No," countered Larry. "That's only half of it. Literally. You've got to realize that there's both an *inbound* and an *outbound* conversion process for every single currency."

Tom: "So, we can say, about a hundred."

Larry nodded.

And so Tom pressed on. "So let's call it a hundred currency conversions. That's about 5 percent of the total 2,000—"

Larry: "No."

Tom blinked. "'No' again?"

Larry shook his head. "'No' on the '2,000.' It's up to about 2,500 as of this morning. We just keep uncovering more and more processes. Every single day."

Tom scratched his head. "But I think we've only got about 3,000 employees, total, in all of sales and ad operations. It's hard to imagine that we've got almost as many processes as we have people."

Larry shrugged. "I wouldn't know. I have no idea how many employees are in the area. We focused solely on analyzing the activities they performed on their workstations—with an eye toward reducing and automating these activities."

Tom steered the conversation toward another issue he had observed firsthand: "What about the customer-billing process? Are you automating that?"

Larry shook his head. "No. That's a stand-alone system. It's relatively new and up to date. We implemented that one about four years ago."

Tom posed what he thought was the obvious question: "Then why do we have so many customer-billing errors?"

Larry gave him what he knew to be the obvious answer: "Most of them are *user* errors. When we implemented the new system, we tried to get the salespeople to help us take advantage of all its features—it's pretty sophisticated. We wanted to autogenerate the customer bills. It's totally feasible."

Tom: "So what went wrong?"

Larry tossed up his hands, resigned. "The salespeople," he explained, "were always too busy to help us configure these features. They'd tell us, 'We're supposed to make sales, not design technology!'"

Tom: "And . . .?"

Larry: "And so they told us to make the new system just like the *old* system—the one they were all familiar with. So that's what we did. We had to get the system up and go live—deadlines rule."

## Cast Iron Tom

"How," wondered Tom, as he returned to his office, "did this project ever get so complicated?" It was supposed to *simplify* business processes, and yet left unchecked, he knew this would all crash and burn.

Absentmindedly, he looked up the definition of "business process" in Wikipedia; perhaps that would clarify things for him. Here's what he found:

> Business process . . . a collection of related, structured activities or tasks that in a specific sequence produces a service or product (serves a particular business goal) for a particular customer or customers.[1][2][3] A business process may often be visualized (modeled) as a flowchart of a sequence of activities with interleaving decision points or as a process matrix of a sequence of activities with relevance rules based on data in the process.[2][3][4][5] 15

Tom blinked. "'Interleaving decision points'? 'A process matrix of a sequence'?" It was mind-numbing.

But then Tom had an "aha moment." He'd discovered a major contributing factor to this confusion: too many words. He stopped reading at 150 words—why should it take that many to define a business process? And within those 150 words he noticed an onslaught of redundancies, circular references, and seven—*seven*—footnotes. All these competing sources claiming authorship.

Out of curiosity, Tom next looked up the definition of "manufacturing process." Here's what he saw:

> *Manufacturing process* . . . the steps through which raw materials are transformed into a final product. The manufacturing process begins with the product design, and materials specification from which the product is made.[16]

It was like a breath of fresh air. The first sentence (12 words) defines the process; the second tells you how to reverse-engineer its design from the product's bill of materials (BOM). Total word count: about 30.

Tom thought back to his early days at the aerospace manufacturing plant. Everything there was infinitely more complex; yet it was more effortlessly managed than his current organization. Everyone and everything in the plant was part of a process.

Then Tom turned his thoughts to Larry and the IT team. They were all furiously automating thousands of tiny transactions—work activities—and calling them "business processes." They never looked any further than the borders of everyone's computer monitors. It was no wonder that, despite massive investment, almost nothing ever seemed to get truly automated. Their fragmented automation approach would never deliver meaningful business benefits.

Tom resolved to fix this problem.

## *Building from a Bigger Perspective*

Tom used his direct observations from his Gemba walks to form a broader definition of "business processes" than the IT team's definition—and, for that matter, almost everyone else's in the company. In a Sorensen-like moment of inspiration, Tom believed that his media company's processes should resemble the comprehensive approach he recalled from the aerospace plant. All the people in the organization—and all their work activities—should be encompassed within business processes.

He knew his teams were already capable of this: he could simply point to the pocket-sized business process manual that the customer-billing group members had created. After all, *their* definition of "business process" encompassed *everyone in their organization*—their billing "factory." From that starting point, they had proceeded to map out all the sequential work activities that everyone performed. All these workflows were diagrammed in about a half-dozen "business process maps." A half dozen. Not *2,000* . . . or given the IT team's zeal, maybe even *3,000* by now.

And so Tom set to work. Now, "business processes" would include *everyone* on his organization chart. He *mandated* that a manageable number of business process maps be created for all these employees' work activities. He then arbitrarily set a maximum limit on the "size" of each activity. The reason? He wanted *granularity*. No activity was to be more than 15 minutes in duration. Likewise, he arbitrarily capped the total number of maps at 25 to 30 processes, tops. Why? He wanted *manageability*. Next, he directed Larry and the IT team to subsume their thousands of transaction-process maps into these larger, more realistic business processes. He also asked the IT team to look more broadly—from end to end—at the new maps for additional activities that could be automated.

Tom knew that the team would struggle mightily with his specifications, particularly the starting point of the business processes. He'd already seen the IT team define its processes too narrowly. (Recall that Cast Iron Charlie perceived the start of the auto-assembly process much earlier than everyone else in the Ford plant. He began with materials-wrangling at the elevators.)

But Tom wanted this to work. He wanted simple instructions for his team. So he reached back into his memory again, racking his recollection of operations at the aerospace factory. He *had to* rely on his memory, because, on the plant floor, businesses guard the design of these tasks closely: no sketches or photos allowed. They rightly view them as valuable opportunities to gain strategic advantage.

But as Tom closed his eyes, he remembered: At the aerospace plant, *they had designed plant-floor manufacturing processes by starting with the end product's bill of materials,* just like in that (brief, ~30-word) Wikipedia definition. From there, they were able to reverse-engineer almost all the work steps needed for fabrication.

And so Tom directed the people on his team to do the same. But he had them do it from the *customer's* point of view. For example, the customer-billing group's "product" would be "a paid bill from a customer." But they should think of the process from the customer's viewpoint. The process name should reflect that perspective: "Pay my bill." This way of thinking would define an earlier starting point for the processes. It would help them document, improve, and automate the processes to get a significant business benefit: an improved customer experience.

Tom was a realist. He knew that he would need help. He recalled a new hire in his organization: Rosa. She'd be perfect!

### Rosa's Taxonomy

"I want you to graphically lay out all of our business processes," Tom explained to Rosa. "There are about 25 or 30, total." And just like he used to do at the aerospace plant, Tom illustrated the workflow and connections between every business process for Rosa.

After Tom left her office, Rosa quickly came up with a hierarchical naming and numbering scheme. It included all of the processes and subprocesses (like the IT currency conversions), and even the individual work activities *within* processes (which Chapter 10 will cover in detail).

It was a "taxonomy," but Rosa didn't use that term. See how she carved it all up in the sidebar.

---

## Processes: Predictable Patterns and Hierarchies

This is how Rosa divided up the entire organization:

1. **Organizational versus individual processes.** "Organizational processes" were large and involved multiple employees (the new customer onboarding process was an example); "individual processes" were short and involved only one person (contact center reps performed many short, individual processes).

2. **Intraorganizational versus interorganizational processes.** "Intraorganizational processes" were confined within a single organizational group; "interorganizational processes" spanned more than one organizational group.

3. **Geographic, country, and regional processes.** Rosa kept track of examples in each of these categories. She documented the variance in the process characteristics. Typically, it was minimal, less than 10 percent—far less than most people expected. It was helpful—and expeditious—to have data for these process differences in hand, as it eliminated the need to create multiple maps in every region.

4. **Channel-based processes.** Perceptions often clashed with reality in this category. So-called "automated" channels often turned out to include extensive manual and semiautomated process subsegments.

---

*(continued on next page)*

> 5. **Size-based variance.** Rosa discovered that organization size influenced business processes. Although the basic DNA of each process was similar, very small organizations often had processes that tended to resemble the "individual" processes described in "organizational versus individual processes," above.

Rosa's numbered taxonomy, combined with the organization chart, enabled her to compile a simple database of the thousands of work activities and routines documented on the business process map diagrams. This paid off in immediate benefits:

- For example, she could tell the IT team which currency conversions affected the greatest number of transactions and customers, and she could point out which had the greatest number of errors. This helped the team prioritize its automation efforts.
- Rosa could also tell which types of ad contracts and customer types experienced the greatest number of billing errors. Tom used this information to focus his billing and sales teams on preempting these errors before they occurred.

### Rosa "Pulls the Rope": The Demo

Rosa and her team of six other employees (including some from IT) began with a roll of three-foot-wide, heavyweight brown wrapping paper that they'd "requisitioned" from the mail room. They then printed out large-format PowerPoint screenshots for each step of the new process. Finally, they pasted these on the brown paper and drew connections and scribbled notes with colored markers.

Then, on a quiet Saturday in the nearly empty office, Rosa and her team walked Tom through a rough simulation of a self-service, end-to-end order-management capability for the company's advertising customers. "You need to understand," explained Rosa, by way of caveat, "that this is only a makeshift hack."

They had Tom sit at the middle of the giant conference table in the boardroom. Then they slowly pulled the map, from right to left, in front of him to simulate the user experience, all the while providing a voice-over description of what he was seeing: Processes with names like "Place my ad," "Confirm my price," and "Pay my bill."

It was like pulling a Model T along by a rope. Like Sorensen's demo, this helped Tom visualize what the customers would see in this "to-be" world—and the ease of use made possible with new, economical technologies.

"It'll take a couple of years to get all the related processes fully integrated," explained Rosa to a delighted Tom. "But in the meantime, we can probably get to best-in-class performance by continuing to slug away at our business process improvements."

## *The 15-Step Knowledge Work Factory*

At lunch with Rosa and her team afterward, Tom was still brimming with excitement: "You nailed the basic skeleton or schematic of the 'assembly line' to service our customers. I think your work could be a backbone that we can connect to everything else: all the IT apps, the data tables, the service-level targets, our operating performance measures . . . everything. How were you able to do all this—and so quickly? Everyone else in the business has struggled for a year and a half just to get a technology work plan in place."

Rosa replied, "It was actually pretty simple, once we began to think of everything as a *factory*. We made a universal process design template." She reached into her binder and pulled out a single handwritten index card. It read, "Work comes in. It is processed sequentially, more or less, and work goes out."

"That's it?" asked Tom.

"That was the germ of it," replied Rosa. "Two of the six people on our team have worked in manufacturing. So we did some brainstorming and sketched out a sort of 'universal' process flow. It reflects a beginning-to-end movement—something that you might find on a plant floor. We didn't try to design the activities. Instead, we thought through everything that could go wrong—process failures—at each step."

"Let me get this straight," interrupted Tom. "You figured out *how to make things* by starting with *how they might mess up*?"

"Sure," said Rosa. "We created a bill of materials (BOM) for business process errors. It actually simplified things a ton. That's because all these 'errors' are more universal than the work activities. And they're familiar to the people doing the work. Everyone can relate to the errors that they encounter."

"We found," continued Rosa, "that it was really difficult—almost impossible—to get people to describe what they do. Painful. Way too many definitions for the same thing. It just seems infinite. But when we asked them what possibly goes *wrong*, in a start-to-finish sequence, then they described it almost perfectly. They really related to the errors. It's counterintuitive, but it simplified their thinking. From there, we quizzed them, and they easily described the related steps. So we sort of reverse-engineered, based on generic errors."

She concluded: "Overall, we generated a sequential checklist of only 15 of these generic errors. We even sketched it up in a factory-style format, which also seemed to help during interviews. This gave us a process work-flow in an hour or so. Then we could layer on successive detailed steps later, often with others who were involved in the process."

Tom thought to himself, "They're building a knowledge work factory!"

## You Can Do This, Too

A genericized version of Rosa's "factory flow plan" is provided in Figure 9-1. Draw inspiration from it. As with Rosa, it can help you to quickly wrangle thousands of discrete and disparate transactions into the vital few, end-to-end business processes that really matter for your knowledge work factory.

---

## CHAPTER 9: **TAKEAWAYS**

1. Absent breakthrough technology, the limits of knowledge work improvement are conventionally—and falsely—perceived to be current "best practices."

2. Manufacturers routinely shatter this barrier to achieve "better-than-best practice" without breakthrough technology:

   • They consistently challenge conventional perceptions with direct observations by diverse executives and managers, e.g., Gemba walks.

   • They define—and redefine—business processes more broadly to encompass more end-to-end, cause-and-effect improvement opportunities.

   • They formally document business processes and the relationships between them to create comprehensive taxonomies or hierarchies.

   • They focus on improving activities through standardization, specialization, and division of labor—industrialization.

3. All these methods can be adopted by knowledge work organizations, once the numerous definitional "disconnects" are reconciled—particularly between IT and business operations.

---

# The Knowledge Work Factory

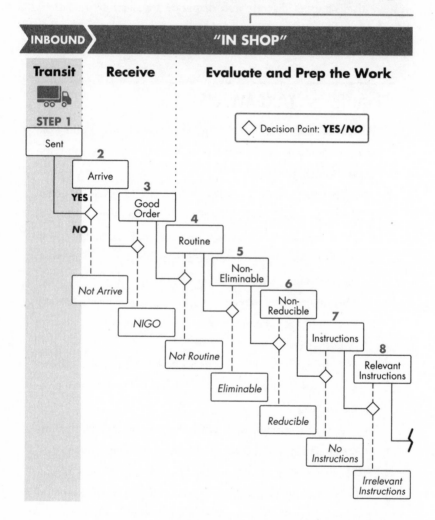

**INBOUND** > **"IN SHOP"**

**Transit**  **Receive**  **Evaluate and Prep the Work**

STEP 1

◇ Decision Point: **YES/NO**

Sent

**2**

Arrive

**YES**

**NO**

**3**

Good Order

**4**

Routine

**5**

Non-Eliminable

**6**

Non-Reducible

**7**

Instructions

**8**

Relevant Instructions

Not Arrive

NIGO

Not Routine

Eliminable

Reducible

No Instructions

Irrelevant Instructions

**FIGURE 9-1**  This standard "factory flow plan" will help organize thousands of discrete and disparate transactions into the vital few, end-to-end business processes that really matter to your knowledge work factory.

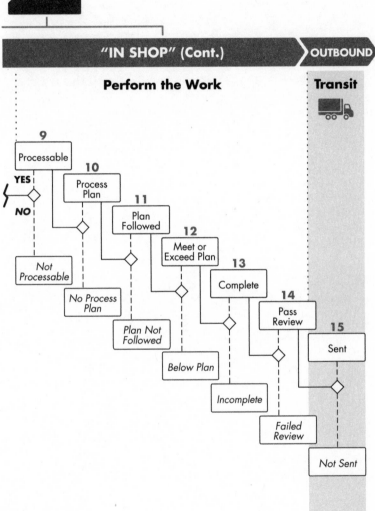

## "IN SHOP" (Cont.) OUTBOUND

### Perform the Work

**Transit**

**9** Processable

YES

NO

Not Processable

**10** Process Plan

No Process Plan

**11** Plan Followed

Plan Not Followed

**12** Meet or Exceed Plan

Below Plan

**13** Complete

Incomplete

**14** Pass Review

Failed Review

**15** Sent

Not Sent

# CHAPTER 10

# ANALYZING AND SIMPLIFYING KNOWLEDGE WORK ACTIVITIES

Now that we've conquered concepts like organizational capacity and learned to "pull the rope" like Sorensen, it's time to analyze and simplify knowledge work activities. This is the final missing piece needed to complete our fully integrated, Ford-style knowledge work factory.

As usual, this task seems overwhelming.

But by now, those qualms can be quelled: despite the initially daunting prospect, there are always simple answers. In this chapter, we're going straight to those answers first—replete with three big plot spoilers. That's because we'll need all the time available to dig into the conceptually and technically challenging aspects of activity-level knowledge work standardization.

Additionally, we need to address three potent organizational challenges to our activity-based efforts:

- **The deathly data void.** Despite the century-long, explosive growth in knowledge work jobs, there has been minimal "nuts-and-bolts" documentation and research into the characteristics of knowledge workers' daily work activities. These operations represent a vast, unexplored void in knowledge work organizations. *Beware:* Creatively fantastic misperceptions abound.
- **Decision-rights danger.** As we learned in Chapter 2, most executives believe that "our most valuable assets (i.e., our knowledge workers) go down the elevator every night." Consequently, *most knowledge workers covet the autonomy that accompanies this perception. Another caveat:* Our expeditions into the furthest reaches of knowledge work activities will be perceived as a direct threat to these decision rights.

- **Cost-accounting failures.** For a century, accountants and engineers have pointed out the significant distortions that the ever-growing share of indirect costs—primarily knowledge work—creates for management decision making and financial performance. Their solutions, in the form of ever-more-sophisticated cost-accounting methods, have routinely met with failure or indifference. This history can negatively influence the perception of any activity-based effort you attempt to undertake.

Steve Jobs famously said, "Simple can be harder than complex: You have to work hard to get your thinking clean to make it simple. But it's worth it in the end because once you get there, you can move mountains."[1]

So in Jobs-like fashion, now that we've identified our mountain range, let's start the hard work required to get our thinking clean.

## How Do You Define "Unique"?

Let's start our journey with one simple word. It's used ubiquitously—and often misunderstood. That word, which you've seen since Chapter 1, is "unique."

Ah, "unique." This one single term causes untold confusion in the efforts to manage knowledge work activities. But let's have some fun here. Let's use its definition to systematically dismantle a longstanding, near-universal misperception regarding the diversity of knowledge work activities.

Try this brief quiz. Read the statements below, which are commonly used by knowledge workers to describe their operations. And then ask yourself which statement is correct.

A. "You've seen businesses in our industry, but we're different. Our operations are *very unique*."

B. "You have heard this before, but for us it's actually true. We are *very, very unique*."

C. "We are *ridiculously unique*. But the thing is, that's our strategic advantage."

D. All of the above.

E. None of the above.

Here's a hint. The *Oxford English Dictionary* defines "unique" as "being the only one of its kind; unlike anything else."[2]

Taken literally, this definition means that choices A and B cannot be true. "Unique" is an absolute; therefore, nothing can be "very" unique. Either something is unique, or it's not. It can't be "more" or "less" unique. That still leaves C as a possibility. But can you think of a business with a "ridiculously unique" product or service? Perhaps Cirque du Soleil might qualify.

OK, this is grammatical hairsplitting. It's unfair.

Let's take a less literal approach. Toss out all the adverbs—*very; very, very; ridiculously*—and reconsider the *intent* of these statements. That would mean that although the three knowledge workers all claim their business operations are unique, they probably mean "different," which is defined as "not the same as another."[3] That's an important distinction.

And as each pondered the perceived complexity of their knowledge work operations, they might have concluded that the word "different" wasn't strong enough. It doesn't support their self-image, which they've strived hard to build and project: "I'm the indispensable, human glue that holds this place together." Therefore, they chose the seemingly stronger "unique." But even *that* word was insufficient. It needed qualifiers; it needed amplification. And so they searched for adverbs; thus "very unique," "very, very unique," and "ridiculously unique."

So let's return to our quiz. Based on the intent of the knowledge workers, what is the correct multiple-choice answer? In this chapter, we'll see that the answer is not so clear-cut. Maybe it falls midway between D, "All of the above," and E, "None of the above." This sounds like hairsplitting again, but on a more cosmic level. It is not.

**Spoiler Number 1:** Contemporary scholarly research, conducted by multiple, independent teams, has identified somewhere between *18 and 34* basic, *unique* knowledge work activities.[4] Between 18 and 34. How can that be?

Of course, this figure sounds implausibly low. The longstanding perception among knowledge workers is that they perform an almost unfathomable number of *very, very unique* activities. How, then, can this perception be explained?

## Conquering the Data Void: The False-Complexity Misperception

A second, simple quiz can shed light on the widespread misperception of the number of knowledge work activities—and the data void that causes it. (*Safety tip:* Choose a new set of workers for each quiz.)

Ask these knowledge workers if they are aware of any analysis or documentation that could provide data on work activities: quantities, frequencies, anything. Be sure to clarify the definition of "activities": tasks that each take between 2 and 15 minutes to complete (just as Tom defined them in Chapter 9).

No documentation? That's typical. Next, ask them to estimate how many unique work activities they believe exist in their operations. Often, you'll get no meaningful answer: "I have nooo i-de-a!" Try it yourself. It's difficult to answer.

So simplify the question. Ask them to guess how many total, unique work activities they perform in a typical day—or even in an hour. They'll *still* struggle. "Too many! You don't want to know," they'll chuckle.

Obviously, these questions are stressful. As we know by now, when the brain confronts difficult queries, it prefers to answer an easier, substitute question. "I don't perform *activities*. I *manage*." Or they might narrow the definition to meaningless, summary-level generalities: "I deliver results. I perform services. I solve problems. There! That's *three* activities."

However, if you persist in your questioning and somehow manage to coax any quantified guesses, knowledge workers will respond tentatively, with staggeringly large estimates. The numbers will range from "thousands" to "tens of thousands," and even "millions." Now we see why they're inclined to say, "very unique," "very, very unique," or "ridiculously unique." Their answers project their longstanding, unshakable misperception: *Knowledge work consists of too many unique activities to manage in a disciplined way. So just give up. Heck, there are so many activities it's not even worth counting them. It can't be done. We should know. We're closest to the work. We're the experts.*

Once again, the brain has misapplied the principle of least effort. It is compensating for their company's—for the business world's—data void. As far as activity-level knowledge work operations go, *nobody knows anything.* These work-activity estimates are frighteningly, surrealistically large . . . and that's partially the intent: to scare you, and your disciplined management methods, away from their knowledge work operations. These imagined numbers also feed the brain's confirmation bias and reinforce the status quo. Later in this chapter, however, we'll learn some simple ways to understand and unravel this misperception in knowledge work.

For the brain, unexplored voids are ideal candidates for creatively surreal, explanatory rationalizations. Remember those maps of the world before Christopher Columbus? The voids of unexplored seas were filled with meticulously imagined sea monsters and other fantastic creatures (see Figure 10-1). The source? They were claimed to have been sighted by sailors. And why not? These seafarers were closest to the work. They were the autonomous oceanic experts of the day.

Note the date on the map in Figure 10-1: it was made in 1585, nearly a century after Columbus's maiden voyage. And by that point, the Magellan expedition had also circumnavigated the globe. Nobody found any of these sea monsters, yet the most distinguished cartographers continued to populate their maps with them. Perceptions and misperceptions, once established, are difficult to change. So it's not surprising that the 40-year

**FIGURE 10-1** Unexplored voids are ideal candidates for creatively surreal, explanatory rationalizations. Cartographers filled maps with fantastic sea monsters, based on sightings reported by sailors—the ocean experts of their day.

Image source: Wikimedia Commons, public domain copy of a 1585 post-Columbus map of Iceland by Abraham Ortelius.

migration of business asset value—from tangible to intangible—remains relatively unnoticed by management.

Columbus and his crew pressed on into the void anyway, past their predicted doom. So did Cast Iron Charlie and his engineers at the Ford plant. Recall: "That way of building cars would ruin the company!"[5] Both Columbus and Sorensen made unexpectedly valuable, world-changing discoveries. Columbus discovered *tangible* assets: continents. Sorensen discovered *intangible* assets: work methods, or competencies. And these intangible assets helped to solve the productivity paradox that plagued the dawn of the twentieth century. By the period 1919 to 1939, American manufacturing productivity per man-hour had doubled. And within the automobile sector, it tripled.[6]

These exploration-era sea-monster maps provide a painfully humorous analogy of the current, widespread misperceptions about the complexity of knowledge work that reinforce the status quo. Check out my latter-day version in Figure 10-2.

**FIGURE 10-2** As you begin to industrialize your knowledge work operations, beware of the "sea monsters" of perceptual bias!

The fact is, almost no one considers the possibility of a vastly simpler, more mundane reality—and one that could be more easily automated to solve today's productivity paradox. Why can't there be a *limited, finite set of knowledge work activities*—or lean operational improvements? Why can't there even be a limited number of *root causes* that generate these improvements? Of course, there is.

**Spoiler Number 2:** Knowledge work activities and the related operations improvements are deceptively simple, easily defined, and finite in number. The list below is based on two-and-a-half decades of analysis and improvement experience by my company, The Lab. Our engagements include a broad range of industries, countries, and knowledge work organizations large and small (project scope has ranged from hundreds of employees to tens of thousands of employees).

1. **There are only 20 universal activities.** Our findings regarding the quantity of unique knowledge work activities are consistent with the scholarly research findings referenced earlier (i.e., 18 to 34 activities). Consequently, we defined a set of 20 standardized, or "universal," knowledge work activities, grouped into 5 categories.
2. **There are only 25 root causes for improvements.** Most knowledge work operations, regardless of size, will exhibit a majority (if not all) of these root causes. However, roughly 80 percent of improvement opportunities and benefits are concentrated in a handful of root causes, typically fewer than 10: "the usual suspects."
3. **There are no more than 500 improvements.** These are defined as activity-level, lean operational improvements that require no new technology. Although quantities vary, most knowledge work organizations with fewer than 2,000 employees will contain 250 or fewer of these improvements. Larger, more diverse organizations will exhibit more, or all, of these 500.

The more you talk to knowledge workers about their work activities, the clearer it becomes that they, and their managers, have devoted almost no thought to this topic. The result? Every organization, often every individual, defines these "atomic-level" universal work activities inadvertently, randomly, and—of course—differently. After all, knowledge workers enjoy the autonomy to define almost every aspect of their work as they see fit. And that is how the definitions of activities become needlessly, *ridiculously, very, very unique.* The data void is born. Misperceptions of false complexity rush in to explain it away. Almost no one even imagines the possibility of similarities. No investment is made to research or analyze these activities.

The potential for activity-level productivity improvement of knowledge work remains unexplored and untapped for three familiar, perceptual reasons:

1. **False complexity.** The misperception of knowledge work's seeming (albeit false) complexity creates a modern-day data void as intimidating and persistent as the sea-monster map seemed to sailors in the fifteenth century and later.

2. **Oversight.** Even those bold enough to press on into the data void are likely to overlook the improvement opportunities. That's because they're not accustomed to searching for improvements that hide, unexpectedly, in plain sight. This bias for overlooking the obvious is not limited to knowledge work. Think of the costly, raw materials wranglers that only Cast Iron Charlie noticed idling at the elevator in Ford's 1908 Piquette Plant (Chapter 9). Noticing is an acquired perceptual skill.

3. **Rationalization.** Finally, even when improvements are discovered and successful solutions are demonstrated, these are easily and prematurely dismissed by the brain's stubborn biases: the virtuous waste perception, the better-mousetrap dogma, the big-rock bias, and on and on. *Remember:* Even Henry Ford and his managers initially and immediately scoffed at Sorensen's first assembly-line demonstration (only Ford reconsidered).

**Spoiler Number 3:** Manufacturers can teach us several best practices for managing knowledge work activities; they crossed the data void a century ago.

## Work Activity Rule: The Shorter the Better

In the early days of the assembly line at Ford, engineers intentionally designed jobs around the repetition of tasks, often a single task, which lasted a minute or so. By 1952, the typical job on the typical assembly line consisted of small tasks of roughly two minutes. Longer tasks stretched up to eight minutes in duration.[7]

By comparison, in 2011, most factories maintained tasks at slightly less than one minute.[8] Henry Ford asserted in his autobiography that "the greater the subdivision of industry, the more likely it was that there would be work for everyone."[9] Here's what he meant in practical terms:

- **Training.** Workers can learn jobs quickly and be useful almost immediately.
- **Simplicity.** Short tasks enable more precise matching with workers' skills.
- **Interchangeability.** Management can move workers easily, based on needs.

In modern production operations, brief, consistently timed activities deliver advantages:

- **Line balancing.** Continuous-flow production is easier to achieve and maintain.
- **Outsourcing.** Unbundling work activities increases opportunities.
- **Automation.** Simple, brief tasks are easier for machines, robots.

## The Periodic Table of (Unique) Knowledge Work Activities

Remember first seeing the periodic table in chemistry class? Today, it includes a total of 118 elements. These few building blocks combine in countless ways to create the physical world. The human body? Sure, every individual is unique. On the other hand, a mere six chemical elements make up 99 percent of every human's body mass. By comparison, it seems that categorizing and standardizing knowledge work activities should be simple.

Manufacturers, construction contractors, distributors, retailers, restaurants, and even casinos have done it. They maintain standard schedules of work activities and related estimates of labor for workforce management. Manufacturers call these "engineered standards." But developing these requires a considerable investment of time and effort. It is inconvenient and counterintuitive. Complex routines have to be deconstructed into standard, granular activities. Taxonomies are required, along with organization charts and business processes.

Just like the periodic table of chemical elements, a small number of standard, "universal" work activities can serve as building blocks. Managers can combine these reusable blocks to efficiently define a seemingly infinite range of complex work tasks. Without sacrificing descriptive detail, these universal knowledge work activities greatly reduce the number of activities perceived as "unique," making it much easier to:

- Manage organizational capacity
- Measure productivity at almost any level: activities, business processes, products
- Identify human work activities that can be automated

Over the course of two decades, The Lab has developed and implemented a Periodic Table of Knowledge Work Activities (see Figure 10-3).

Its mere 20 activities are arranged in a basic, five-category taxonomy that can easily be augmented with descriptive metadata tags (more about these "meta tags" later). Each activity includes engineered standards for estimated work times, based on millions of observations. Almost 90 percent of these standards have durations of 15 minutes or less.

## Knowledge Work
### 20 Universal Activities • 5 Categories

**Receive:**
1. Electronic File
2. E-mail
3. Phone Call
4. Physical Copy

**Review:**
5. Prepare
6. Preview
7. Validate
8. Decide
9. Terminate

**Perform:**
10. Update
11. Correct
12. Create
13. Enter
14. Move

**Attend:**
15. Meeting
16. Communication

**Send:**
17. Electronic File
18. E-mail
19. Phone Call
20. Physical Copy

**FIGURE 10-3**   These 20 "universal" activities help to eliminate the perception that knowledge work is unique.

## The Activity-Level Periodic Table in the Tire Plant

Remember Raylene, our beleaguered (re)scheduling heroine from the tire manufacturing plant in Chapter 1? As we rejoin her, she's sitting in a meeting room at the plant with Michelle, an ultra-bright corporate intern who aspired to rescue Raylene—and the company—from the rescheduling treadmill.

Raylene dumped a huge stack of binders on the table. "Here's all the stuff," she explained, paging through the printouts. "This is a floor plan of the plant. You can see that there are sections for the eight major work areas for production. Each one is assigned a three-digit number and a name, like 'Compounding 300' or 'Tire Making 600.'"

"Next," Raylene said, reaching for another binder, "let's move to raw materials."

"Actually, I'd rather jump to labor, if you don't mind," interrupted Michelle. "I want to understand how this eight-work-area numbering scheme flanges up with the production labor activities."

"Here you go!" said Raylene, opening yet another bound printout book. "Each labor activity is connected to other descriptors that ultimately roll up to the production-area code."

"For example," Raylene continued, "at the very lowest, most detailed level, activities have generic names, like 'Clean,' 'Align,' 'Change,' or 'Test.'"

"They're all verbs," observed Michelle.

"Yes," nodded Raylene. "The next level adds descriptors, such as 'Spacer,' 'Conveyor,' or 'Heater.'"

"And those are nouns. So you can form sentences—like 'Align Spacer.' Right?"

"Very good," nodded Raylene. "But then it gets a little more complex. After the descriptors come sequential codes that designate a ton of extra details—like specific machines, time of day, operator designation, product being produced, maintenance categories, planned versus unplanned . . . There are lots of these 'meta tags.'"

"Y'know, it's just amazing," added Raylene, "just *how many activities* are required to make something as basic as a tire. I mean, there are *thousands*. So I can certainly understand if you want to take this book home with you for a week or two and—"

"Actually," said Michelle, "this looks pretty simple—if you just boil it down."

Raylene blinked.

"Look," said Michelle, pointing to the printout. "If I just take the first column, the one with all the verbs in it, there aren't very many. At a quick glance, I'd say it's somewhere between 50 and 100. Sound about right?"

"Pretty close," nodded Raylene. "There are actually 83. I know because I use them a lot. My spreadsheet has 83 rows. These 83 'verbs' are at the level where we look up and enter the standard times for each activity—the engineered standards. Meaning the estimates of labor required for each activity."

"And how long are those standard times?" Michelle asked.

"Just a few minutes, typically," continued Raylene. "The scheduling software adds them all up to calculate the production schedule cycle time and the plant workforce plan."

"So again, when you boil it down," observed Michelle, smiling, "there are only 83 truly *unique* work activities in the entire plant network—worldwide. Everything else is just additional description."

"Actually, it's less than 83," admitted Raylene. "A number of these are redundant. They describe the exact same activity; they just assign a slightly different time value to it, based on where it's performed."

Michelle's smile broadened. "Even better!" She plopped the book onto the table and spread it open before them. "And if you look at it closely, there are only two types of additional description. That makes it *look like* a lot, but they're not directly related to the labor."

"See all these meta tags?" Michelle went on, running her fingers down the columns for Raylene to see. "There are a couple of dozen here, describing things like 'Location,' 'Account,' 'Shift Operator,' and so on. So I don't really call that 'labor.' I'd call that 'demographic detail that shows where the work is performed and expensed.' Does that make it easier for you to wrap your mind around it all?"

Raylene's jaw dropped as she realized: "Wait, wait! Only the terms in the second column—"

"You mean the nouns."

"Yes, the nouns," said Raylene. "Only those terms—like 'Conveyor,' 'Spacer,' et cetera—actually provide additional detail that relates to direct labor productivity. They help describe the actual work performance."

"Exactly!"

Raylene was amazed. *Why hadn't she seen this before?*

"Do you realize where this is all going?" asked Michelle excitedly. "All we have to do is combine the first two columns—the verbs and the nouns—to a get a feel for the worst-case scenario: that is, the largest possible quantity of unique work activities. For the whole plant! I wonder how big that number is . . ."

"Or how *small*," grinned Raylene. She was catching on.

"Betcha never thought of a *schedule* as an 'inventory of labor activities,' did you?" asked Michelle.

Now Raylene was riffling through the pages in a blur. The ones she didn't want went flying. "Ah—here. This is what I'm looking for." She held up a single long sheet, which unfolded like an accordion.

"What's that?" Michelle asked.

"It's a list," said Raylene, "of combinations for both columns. It's listed on the pages for each of the areas." She frowned. "But for some reason, we just never total it."

Michelle stifled a grin. *Thought so!*

Raylene squinted at the document. "But I'm seeing it now. It's still not that many activities—and you can tell that lots of them are similar. All the production areas come to fewer than 150 activities total. But most of these areas are *way* under—maybe 50 to 75 activities at most. There's just one major outlier among the engineered standards for these activities— but it's a big one."

"I have two questions," said Michelle.

Raylene: "Go ahead. Shoot."

Michelle: "Question one: How old are these engineered standards? When were the labor estimates last updated?"

Raylene: "That's two questions."

Michelle chuckled. "Touché."

"Actually," began Raylene, "I have no idea when these were last updated."

Michelle: "None?"

Raylene: "Put it this way: I've been here 12 years, and—"

Michelle: "And you've never seen it happen?"

Raylene: "Bingo."

They exchanged glances. They both knew they were onto something big here.

"So, what's question two?" asked Raylene.

Michelle: "What's that 'big outlier' you mentioned?"

Raylene: "The compounding area. It provides the feedstock to the rest of the plant. Take a look." She held out the appropriate part of the "accordion" for Michelle to see.

Michelle pored over the information. "Interesting. All this info is buried. It's not in the top sheet; it's not in the summary. It's like its own little super-detailed, subschedule report."

Raylene: "Exactly."

Michelle: "It shows each line item that goes into the schedule—but the top-sheet totals don't reflect them all."

Raylene replied by whistling the spooky music from *The Twilight Zone*. "Why aren't they all shown? Where did they go?" she asked under arched brows.

Michelle ran her finger down the printed list. "Look at this: the line items that are actual engineered standards add up to just a small percentage of the total labor in the area. Your standards may be out of date, but at least they're grounded in fact: they're documented, objective observations. All this other stuff, on the other hand . . ."

"Fluff," said Raylene, flatly (see Figure 10-4).

"Yup. Fluff," Michelle agreed.

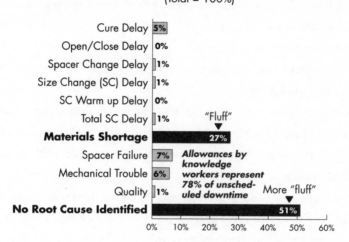

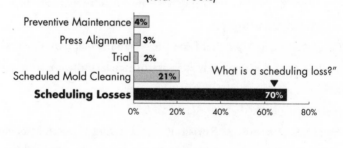

**FIGURE 10-4** Michelle saw that the major root causes of machine downtime were "allowances" that knowledge workers added to the schedule—"fluff" that enabled the adjustments necessary to make the plant's ticket.

Raylene nodded slowly. "I see what you mean. The schedulers can just add 'fluff' line items to build in downtime schedule slack. They do it all the time. Everyone knows that the plant won't be able to meet the real schedule—the one that's based only on the engineered standards."

"Which means," translated Michelle, "that all these numbers are completely subjective. They're *guesses*. And look at how big they are. They eclipse everything else—all of the engineered items." And they're buried on the back sheets.

"But this isn't the entire plant," said Raylene, feeling a tad defensive. "It's just a few work areas."

Michelle continued to page through the other documents. Again, she sighed. "I love these terms they use. 'Scheduling Loss.'" She laughed. "What on earth is that supposed to mean? What kind of 'loss' are they scheduling? Looks to me like they're scheduling an *earnings* loss."

"It's obvious," she concluded, "that nobody ever audits these schedules."

"That *is* odd," noted Raylene, pausing. "I mean, the lack of schedule audits—considering that they audit everything *else* around here: physical inventory, quality, instrumentation calibration . . ."

"Still," Raylene continued, "these scheduling snafus in the compounding department affect everything else in the downstream production flow—through the whole plant."

"Of course," said Michelle. Then she posed the elephant-in-the-living-room question: "Are there any key performance indicators for schedule quality?"

Raylene just looked at her. Vacant.

"You know, timeliness? Revisions . . .? *Anything*?" asked Michelle.

Raylene broke into a sardonic smile. "Oh, come *on*, Michelle. As if you even need to *ask*. KPIs? Around *here*? Of course not."

As they walked back to Raylene's office, Michelle mentioned, casually, "I have an idea. For the scheduling group."

This stopped Raylene in her tracks. "You mean, you want to update the plant labor standards?"

Michelle waved away her fears with a smile. "Oh no. No way. That's a huge waste of time—if you're looking for the biggest, quickest improvements."

"Okay, then," said Raylene. "What do you suggest?"

Michelle: "I want to apply factory-floor 'engineering standards' discipline to the labor in the scheduling department. I want to track the labor activities used to develop the schedule itself. I want to audit it. I want to treat the schedule like a product—a tire—track schedule errors and standardize instructions. I want to manage this *scheduling factory* even more rigorously than the manufacturing plant."

Raylene: "Why?"

"Because," smiled Michelle, "that is the tip of the iceberg. The labor—the work activities—of the small team in the scheduling department inadvertently conspires to create underutilization across the entire factory! What I want to do is to quantify it. And we could pilot it in your section of the schedule."

Raylene smiled in amazement and fear.

But Michelle was just getting started. "Of course, if you don't want to do the schedule, I have other ideas for sifting and sorting the meta tags assigned to the plant-floor labor activities. I think I can link activities to some of the reasons, the root causes, of machine downtime in the plant. If I'm right," she continued contentedly, "we can make some really cool charts that quantify downtime improvement opportunities—even without the schedule improvements. When I go to corporate at the end of my internship, maybe you can come too, and we can show some of them."

"Uh . . . sure," said Raylene, a little overwhelmed. "Say, where did you learn all this? Did you pick all this up from your previous jobs?"

"Some of it. But I learned most of it from this consultant that one of them brought on. I'll have to introduce you someday. His name is Nick Clearsight." (Figures 10-5 and 10-6 demonstrate how work activities can be organized and standardized into a manageable set of "universal" activities, which can then be augmented with additional metadata as necessary.)

# Knowledge Work Activities
Creating Engineered Standards

## Business Process Maps: Document Activities

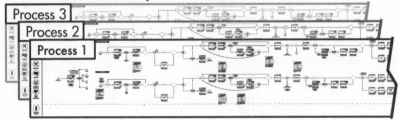

Process 3
Process 2
Process 1

### Informal Definitions Imply "Unique" Activities

*Same activity—multiple definitions*
**"Verify If Existing Customer"** – –

2,700 Activities:
**Employee Defined—Unstandardized**
• Initiate Account Opening Request
• Verify if Existing Customer
• Clear Courier Bag
• Review Documents
• Validate Customer Information
Search & Print Per...

### Define Standard Activities for Employees

200 Activities:
**Agreed Upon**
• New Account Initiation
• New Account Processing
• New Account Verification
• AML Verification
• Enrollment Application
• Enrollment Processing
• Investment Opening
• Account Maintenance
• Amend Account

*One activity—one definition*
**"New Account Verification"**

### Create Engineered Standards for Models and Schedules

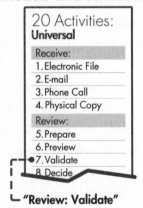

20 Activities:
**Universal**

Receive:
1. Electronic File
2. E-mail
3. Phone Call
4. Physical Copy

Review:
5. Prepare
6. Preview
7. Validate
8. Decide

**"Review: Validate"**

**FIGURE 10-5** Knowledge workers typically perceive that they perform thousands of unique activities. But redefining these into "universal" activities allows for the creation of engineered standards for knowledge work—just like the standards for factory work.

## Business Process Maps

Label each activity with meta tags

### Meta Tags for Business Process Activities

Each activity is labeled with standard meta tags

| **Activity Characteristics:** | **Automation:** | **Operational:** |
|---|---|---|
| 1. Process/Subprocess | **Current** | 1. Frequency |
| 2. Department | 1. Manual | 2. Volume |
| 3. Function | 2. Semiautomated | 3. Duration |
| 4. Job Title | 3. Automated (Now) | • |
| 5. Location | | • |
| 6. Region | **Potential** | • |
| • | 4. RPA—Robotics | 8. Cause |
| • | 5. System—Existing | |
| 11. Priority | 6. System—Future | |

*Custom meta tags can be added*

**FIGURE 10-6**   Each activity can be labeled with meta tags—process, location, frequency, volume, and others—to provide the "GPS coordinates" of activities and improvements.

## Stand Back! Those Are My Decisions

When you ask knowledge workers about their activities, expect pushback. They'll be annoyed. They consider it an intrusion. After all, they *own* their activities. Remember, they, and their managers, perceive that knowledge workers possess the "decision rights" to structure their activities and their workdays as they see fit (Chapter 3). Recall, too, that the repercussions of challenging these decision rights can get downright dangerous—as in the case of that nineteenth-century craftsman in Harpers Ferry back in Chapter 3 who murdered his plant manager. But as long as they make their deadlines—or more to the point, don't run too far *over* deadline, especially on those pesky, unimportant items—knowledge workers expect to enjoy high levels of autonomy.

Put another way, categorizing knowledge work activities in any sort of structured, quantified context represents an affront to these workers' organizational and social status. Why? "Activities" are time-measurement units. And salaried knowledge workers don't think of their time as being measured in units: "That's for hourly workers!" Knowledge workers instead are conditioned to measure their time in terms of *completion*: "When do you need it? Let me see what I can do." Ideally, they want a "nice-to-have" deadline, along with a "must-have" deadline. They revel in the status that negotiation implicitly confers. Many enjoy the glory of their after-hours roles as rework heroes. "Activity-based time measurement? Productivity metrics? Effectiveness? Key performance indicators? No thanks, we're knowledge workers." (*Translation:* "We're exempt.")

We should not be surprised by their misperception of uniqueness and false complexity. Throughout this book we've seen the brain consistently and overconfidently misapply the principle of least effort to develop short-cut explanations that save lots of hard work for itself—while squandering incalculable business value in the process. But now, by industrializing (read: "devaluing") their work activities, we're upping the ante. Improving productivity and business value will be seen as *undermining their status*—a kill shot to the ego. There will be resistance. It will be passive. But Chapter 12 will explain how to preemptively minimize its effects.

This resistance is not new. Structured, quantified descriptions of work activities are nothing more than highly manageable extensions of organization charts: those visual inventories of intangible assets. As we saw in Chapter 6, knowledge workers have successfully resisted the imposition of standardized, quantified, well-labeled organization charts since 1855.

But when traversing the void, all explorers face resistance. On his first journey, Columbus was continually worried about the threat of mutiny. The tension began on day three, once the crew could no longer see familiar navigational landmarks—the status quo. Over the next two months, Columbus cajoled the crew members, understated distances, and falsely argued that they'd passed the point of no return. And Ford's CFO threatened to end all assembly-line experiments when worker injuries increased. Most of the pilot experiments were carried out below the radar of senior management.

## The Costing Couch

Businesses haven't completely ignored the management challenges of knowledge work activities. For a century, many of their efforts concentrated on upgrades to management accounting, or cost accounting. Proponents might point out the technical validity and theoretical usefulness of these efforts. However, most managers reject cost accounting for knowledge work productivity. It's not worth the effort. And they resent the lack of clarity produced by confusing, unclear, and, above all, what they perceive to be "unfair" allocations, over which they exert no influence. For example, they might point out that these allocations could include the costs of corporate jets and the executive gym. How can they "manage" those? On top of everything, they will also tell you that cost accounting is terminally boring.

Nonetheless, these exact same managers may use these activity-based cost-accounting efforts to thwart the development of your knowledge work factory. "We've tried it and it doesn't work." You can't ignore it. So let's try to understand its pros and cons as simply and quickly as possible.

Remember how, in 1908, Cast Iron Charlie Sorensen began every day in the Ford plant? He visited the shipping room and analyzed the documents there to identify problems, because those gave him a good idea of where he should visit on his yet-to-be-named Gemba walk. In the twenty-first century, Tom, our global media guy, did the same when he visited the customer-billing department, searching for errors that could guide his own Gemba walk through sales and IT. But now, *try to imagine what would happen if both of those executives had stopped there.* Instead of going on Gemba walks, what if they chose to become analytical "couch potatoes" and retreated to their offices with either slide rule or laptop in hand, depending on the century?

In 1908, at the same time that Sorensen was performing his Gemba walks at Ford, Alexander Hamilton Church, an English electrical engineer turned consultant, published his first book describing his ideas for a more scientific approach to allocating costs and improving management decision making. In particular, Church pointed out the absurdity of using simple averages and percentages to allocate the costs of knowledge work to diverse products. Church focused instead on two categories of "indirect" costs.[10] The first was shop overhead, which included the costs of maintaining and managing the conventional factory. The second was the SG&A (selling, general, and administrative) costs for the enterprise, the same ones that Nick Clearsight and Toby, the CFO, debated a century later in their tire factory discussion. And notably, these are the same costs that Amazon is now successfully targeting, as Nick pointed out (Chapter 4).

Church's book, *The Proper Distribution of Expense Burden,* helped launch a century of intellectually intriguing activity-cost analysis that delivered few benefits. The trend culminated in 2007 with another book, *Time-Driven Activity-Based Costing,* that advocated combining time estimates with work activities. Unfortunately, these pundits are still stuck on the costing couch, no Gemba walking needed, as illustrated by this passage:

> In this chapter, we focus on developing equations that estimate
> the demands for time on capacity resources. But the approach generalizes readily to other resources . . . whose capacity is measured
> in units other than time.[11]

Confused yet?

As you might expect from that quote, advocates of activity-based costing (ABC) are fiercely proud of their engineering chops and intellectual horsepower. They will provide lots of theories and equations, but precious few direct observations of knowledge work activities—which simply leads to a more rigorously precise data void. And that is exactly what we have today.

# Tales of Terror: Real-World Examples of Hidden Waste (with Happy Endings)

## Tale 1: Activity-Based Waste

Nick Clearsight looked up as a youthful-sounding woman interrupted his thoughts. "Hey, I finally got this printout: a data dump from their ABC system. Think it might provide something useful . . . ?"

Nick was running out of time. His analytical team was jammed, finalizing the due diligence for their PE investment firm's bid. They were competing with similar investment firms to acquire a target company. But he and his team were struggling. They couldn't document enough airtight evidence of savings to convince their risk-averse investment partners that the (seemingly too high) bid for the target company could be profitably recouped. Nick knew from experience that his team could easily reduce the target company's SG&A expense by 25 percent or more. That would handily support their bid and even leave a bit of room to sweeten it if needed. But Nick's experience-based estimates wouldn't cut it with this super-cautious team of investors.

Compounding this problem, existing management at the target company was touting its "lean" organization to Nick's investment partners—building their credibility and undermining his. In the privacy of his deal team, Nick had started to cynically refer to the target company as "LeanCo"—and LeanCo (I'll also use this name, for convenience) clearly favored another acquirer over Nick's firm—irrespective of price. LeanCo supported its efficiency claim by pointing proudly to its brand-new, leading-edge ABC system as incontrovertible evidence that the company was already rigorously managed. "There's nothing left; you can't get blood from a stone," the LeanCo folks told Nick's skittish investors.

Nick pored over the printout with Michelle, the newest member of his team. She had recently completed her MBA after a summer internship at a global tire manufacturer, where she had catalyzed an impressive labor-saving turnaround.

"Well, this is sure embarrassing for our executive friends at LeanCo," said Michelle, pointing to the printout. "Their ABC system overstates the work performed by the SG&A organizations. And it's not a trivial amount: it's about 2.5 times larger than the existing capacity—the total employee headcounts—of these organizations. That's because their ABC system doesn't automatically reconcile its activity-based capacity figures with reality—as in the actual number of SG&A employees on the payroll. And no one at LeanCo sanity checks these data manually, so their efficiency stats are fantasy figures; the arithmetic is wrong."

"Great catch," Nick smiled, "but it's not enough to close the deal. We need unambiguous evidence of near-term savings, not just sloppy record-keeping—that's everywhere in business." He suddenly perked up.

"Whatcha thinking, Boss?" asked Michelle.

"I have an idea," said Nick, almost to himself, "of how we might use these ABC data, *especially* since those executives are so confident in the activities. Think of all that time they spent telling us how they were so certain that the activity definitions and time estimates were accurate, based on direct observations. They probably *are* accurate, and we can build our case on that. Let's meet with the team in the LeanCo lunchroom, and I'll tell you what I have in mind. But I have to warn you, this'll be an all-nighter."

Nick's nocturnal scheduling forecast proved accurate, but Michelle enjoyed leading the all-hands blitz analysis. The team already had a rich set of headcount benchmarks for all the major SG&A organizations: finance, customer service, engineering, sales, and more. LeanCo was significantly overstaffed compared with almost all of its peers, but of course management disputed this hotly with their ABC data and discussions had stalled quickly.

But LeanCo had also turned over business process maps, and operating statistics, with comprehensive descriptions, to all bidders. As usual, Nick's team had augmented this information with extensive interviews. Consequently, they were able to identify most of the transactions and processes that represented error corrections, rework, and avoidable customer service, i.e., virtuous waste. Now, Nick planned to use the data dump from LeanCo's ABC system to quantify the time spent on these individual virtuous waste activities.

These activities could be matched with the ABC costs to document the SG&A savings opportunity at LeanCo—unambiguously. Of course, the team had to build this estimate from scratch with a time-consuming, activity-by-activity approach. The resulting all-night exercise was tedious beyond belief but satisfying because it would deliver inarguable findings. Michelle called the closest Starbucks and ordered a couple of boxes of coffee for pickup right before it closed at 11 p.m.

The next morning, Michelle opened the presentation to LeanCo management and the investor team. "So are we all still agreed that the ABC data accurately reflect the time intervals that the organization spends on individual work activities? These were validated through direct observations, correct?" she asked.

LeanCo's CEO enthusiastically agreed. "Those ABC data provide the most detailed time estimates of our work activities."

Michelle began by pointing out the arithmetic error, carefully explaining the breathtaking 2.5x overage resulting from the lack of reconciliation between the ABC-generated data and the actual organizational capacity. That insight alone won back the credibility of the skittish investors. Next, the reconfigured ABC data provided quantified estimates of the virtuous waste that Nick's team had documented overnight using LeanCo's business process maps and operating stats.

"So," concluded Michelle, "No matter how you cut the ABC data, this reconfigured analysis shows that LeanCo can achieve savings of 25 to 40 percent, across its SG&A organizations. These figures are also consistent with those external benchmark comparisons that we originally presented. And we've reconciled our figures with the employee headcounts. Are there questions? Can we tentatively agree on these figures? The savings targets?" You could hear a pin drop in the boardroom.

The CEO nodded reluctantly, "It's possible that you may be on to something. Of course, we'll have to check the data."

As the meeting began to slowly break up, Nick could sense his investors' sudden, quiet enthusiasm. This deal was back on track, he thought, or at least until the next surprise.

## Tale 2: The Linguistics of Shared Services

Remember Julie, Bert, and the self-reported list of Shared Service Initiative (SSI) activities from Chapter 7? The healthcare organization surveyed employees with a standard form to determine which activities could be moved to the new SSI facility. However, the results were anything but standard. The analyst had only entered about half of the returned survey forms, but the database of reportedly "unique" activities already exceeded 10,000.

The tabulation of the survey forms was halted. A new analyst, Kendra—with a graduate degree, oddly enough, in English—had joined the team at the SSI facility. Now it was her turn to try to compile, quantify, and make sense of the survey returns.

The first thing that Kendra noticed as she scrolled through the answers to the survey questions was how many different ways the respondents could say the same thing. This reminded Kendra of her classes in linguistics: She remembered that the average person had a vocabulary of somewhere between 11,000 and 14,000 words.[12] And most people use only a small minority of their total vocabulary in day-to-day conversation. Text-crazed teens often use less than 1,000 words a day. Paradoxically, if you attempted to create a dictionary, these figures exploded. The complete 20 volumes of the *Oxford English Dictionary* include over 170,000 defined words. Nouns outnumber verbs by a factor of 3.5 to 1.[13] She began to view the SSI activity survey as an unintended dictionary-development effort.

Kendra studied the survey returns from her English major, linguistic-oriented background and quickly saw ways to simplify the database. For example, she noticed that, absent any instructions, employees tended to describe similar tasks an average of five different ways. For example: "verify a charge," "check a charge," "charge verification," "charge reviews," "review of charge," "make sure charge is correct," etc. This single insight of hers allowed her to collapse the database of 10,000 "unique" activities to roughly 2,000 terms. Next, she "standardized" these by requiring that each description begin with a verb and be followed by a noun. Suddenly, the total was consolidated and streamlined to just around 500 "unique" activities. And bear in mind that this list was strictly preliminary. It still had not been reviewed by anyone with a finance or accounting background.

Over the course of a week, Julie, Bert, and a few other knowledgeable accountants reviewed Kendra's list. They agreed on roughly 350 standardized terms. They jointly decided which could be performed centrally in the new SSI facility (about 40 percent of the total) and which activities should remain behind in their original location.

The SSI team was finally moving forward again.

## Tale 3: Robotics Update—All Forest, No Trees in Sight

The word came down from corporate: robotics was the wave of the future. Everyone in the boardroom agreed on that. Over the last year, they'd seen astonishing demos from robotics salespeople. They'd chatted with their business friends on the golf course and received the confirmation they needed to dispel their persistent "better mousetrap" doubts. Now it was confidently decided. All that remained was for the company's executives to mandate that the organization adopt this new way of working: robotic process automation, or RPA.

But how to get started? The CEO consulted with the IT department, and a list of RPA opportunity identification criteria was promptly distributed throughout the business. Promising processes for robotic automation were "simply" those that exhibited three characteristics.

The best processes for RPA technology:

- Are primarily "rules-based"—although "rules-based" was undefined. (And that's no small task. Google it.)
- Consume a significant amount of time. (Even though knowledge workers are not measured for "time.")

- Are performed at frequent intervals. (Again, these are not typically measured in knowledge work. But if they were, what would constitute an "interval"? Five minutes? Five hours? What is "frequent"?)

How well did the board's mandate work?

The RPA delays began with the IT opportunity identification criteria. "Process" was never defined. (As we saw in Chapter 9, this definitional ambiguity has been the cause of costly confusion in knowledge work automation long before RPA arrived.) Definition-wise, things went downhill from there. No one was able to clarify, document, or quantify the terms "rules-based," "time-consuming," and "high-frequency." Consequently, the list of criteria from IT was not just unhelpful, it was confusingly counterproductive. It seemed as if "nobody knew anything."

Initially, no one saw this as a major problem. Management simply delegated the job of identifying robotics opportunities to their frontline workers. After all, they were closest to the work—the experts. At first, this approach seemed to make perfect sense. But after nearly a year, virtually no processes had been identified as RPA candidates. No RPA "use cases" were developed. Almost no RPA technology was implemented—just a few pilot apps. Pressure from the board and senior executives escalated sharply.

Desperate managers abandoned the list of opportunity identification criteria from IT along with their suggested new RPA technology providers. Instead, the managers contacted familiar vendors who offered existing technologies, recently rebranded as "robotics" applications. For example, an accounts receivable application, developed long before RPA was invented, was suddenly a "cloud-based robotics and artificial intelligence tool." The same was true for a customer relationship management (CRM) system. These were purchased and implemented. However, the economics of these applications—the return on investment—remained unchanged by the rebranding: unfavorable.

The board's mandate, along with the transformative promise of breakthrough new RPA technology, remained unfulfilled. The reason? Nobody wanted to do the difficult work of documenting and standardizing the work activities to "feed" the robots. That task seemed impossibly complex. The principle of least effort was quickly invoked and misapplied. The RPA efforts stalled. The scope of "automatable activities" remained overly limited and widely overlooked. It was trapped in the void of misperception and anti-standardization bias. The century-old productivity paradox was back on the job, quietly and effectively extinguishing this new threat of massive gains in knowledge work productivity from the latest technology for office work: RPA.

How to overcome this? Let's see how Nick's team back at LeanCo handled RPA.

## Activity-Based Robotic Process Automation

Nick's PE firm ultimately prevailed in their acquisition attempt. The LeanCo CEO happily cashed out his shares and moved on to the next opportunity. Meanwhile, Michelle was busy leading the improvement efforts at the company. RPA was part of their plan, and they were succeeding wildly. Although they didn't realize it, they were automating exactly like Cast Iron Charlie Sorensen did it in 1908 at Ford. And their approach did not even remotely resemble the bullet point mandates from IT listed above.

Rules-based? Michelle's team simply assumed that "nobody knows anything," and they were correct. Consequently, they defined, and documented, their own new rules as they went. They got out of the office and went down to the knowledge work "plant floor." They did the Gemba walk. They defined "processes" as comprehensively as Charlie did: wall to wall, every employee and every work activity found in the plant. They documented these, building from the existing LeanCo process maps and stats from the acquisition's due diligence effort. They eliminated as many of these activities as possible—roughly 30 percent—*before* they started their standardization and automation efforts. By beginning with nontechnology improvement and targeting virtuous waste reduction, they cut the subsequent automation scope in half, focusing it exclusively on value-added activities.

Time-consuming, high-frequency candidates for RPA? Michelle knew that there were few stats on these activity characteristics. However, a quick review of the existing ABC data pointed the team toward promising areas where they conducted brief observations. It soon became apparent that the most relevant activities for RPA involved employees working with technologies: entering data, downloading files, accessing systems and moving data from one to another. These "semiautomated" tasks represented 60 percent of all knowledge work activities across the organization. They were similar and repetitive. They did not take much effort to further standardize. So these semiautomated tasks became their first priority for RPA. For each activity, they documented keystroke-level instructions to configure—and "feed"—the robots ("robot food").

Michelle's team decided to walk before they ran. They kept their initial RPA goals modest, automating an average of 1 to 3 work activities per bot. Each activity involved about 8 to 15 keystrokes of human work activity. These were robots with basic functionality. They required humans to launch and oversee their work. In RPA terms, these are called "attended" bots. Later, Michelle would have her team connect many of these basic bots into more complex, more automated configurations. They would design "unattended" bots to launch and manage many of the original attended bots.

By first targeting nontechnology reduction of virtuous waste, prior to RPA, Michelle's team reduced knowledge work labor by 20 percent within weeks. These nontechnology savings funded over 75 percent of the subsequent robotics investment. And this was *before* the bots started to generate their own savings—another 20 percent. All of this was achieved within seven months.

By the way, robots aren't nearly as new as you think. Nor are the robotics opportunity perception challenges—they date back over 100 years; see the sidebar.

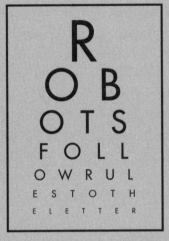

**FIGURE 10-7** Roughly two-thirds of knowledge workers' activities are ideal for standardization—and, subsequently, automation.

## Robotics Perception Struggles: 1916 Versus 2018

Most executives don't realize that robots have been successfully deployed for a century. Over that period, the challenge of identifying—perceiving—valuable robotics opportunities has changed fundamentally, but it has not become any easier.

### Yesterday's Success

In 1916, a Wisconsin auto parts maker, A. O. Smith Corporation, struggled to perceive a valuable robotics opportunity. The company's engineers knew that they could design robots to perform the repetitious activities involved with fabricating automobile frames (chassis). A massive investment, mandated standardization, and a five-year construction effort could deliver a start-to-finish robotic chassis fabrication plant—no direct human labor required. But economic feasibility required a minimum annual production of 1 million chassis to

*(continued on next page)*

"feed" the robots. The entire auto industry then produced roughly 1.5 million vehicles each year.[14]

### The 1916 Robotics Challenge: See the Future

The A. O. Smith board of directors faced a daunting challenge. They had to perceive a vast, emerging market—an "ocean" of near-term future demand for auto chassis—to economically justify a bet-the-company investment in robotic process technology. In this case, management confidently perceived (or maybe it wished?) correctly. Over the course of the 1920s, Americans bought 25 million cars (and chassis).[15] The company's robotics strategy succeeded wildly.[16]

### Today's Failure

In 2003, the U.S. division of a global manufacturer adopted user-friendly robotic process automation technology for knowledge work. It was first introduced in the customer service organization. Over the next 15 years, numerous other RPA technologies were introduced at the company and successfully demonstrated to various organizations comprising 28,000 knowledge workers. These employees perform a total of 500 million human work activities annually (on average, each activity is five minutes in duration).

The catch? Standard activities—just like the auto chassis plant—are needed to feed the robots in customer service operations. But management has not mandated that these activities be standardized. Consequently, these continue to be misperceived as "unique." Robotics technology is currently used on less than 1 percent of these activities. Company executives struggle to perceive valuable new robotics opportunities within their business.[17]

### The 2018 Robotics Challenge: See the Present

The management of the global manufacturer faces a daunting challenge. They have to perceive a vast, existing market and an embar-

(continued on next page)

rassing oversight—an "ocean" of under-standardized, robot-ready, manual knowledge work activities—that penalizes business productivity and profits. In this case, management confidently perceives incorrectly. They believe that few significant robotics opportunities remain unaddressed. ("Somebody would notice that!" Maybe management is wishing again?) The company's customer service satisfaction levels are among the lowest in the industry.

What can we learn from 1916? What can we learn from 2018?

The lessons from 1916 and 2018 are similar. Robotics success depends on management's capabilities of perception:

- Identify the opportunity—emerging or underfoot.
- Understand that standardization must be mandated.
- Recognize the strategic risks—early adopter, laggard.

## What's Next?

In any conventional factory, the sum of the total times of work activities must reconcile with the available organizational capacity. And it will, in the Ford-style knowledge work factory that we're now building. We'll keep on building—in Chapter 11, we will complete it.

## CHAPTER 10: **TAKEAWAYS**

1. Three potent organizational challenges impede the efforts of knowledge work organizations to identify, analyze, and manage their operational work activities:
    - Lack of data—few characteristics, such as definitions, volumes, and locations, are routinely recorded.
    - Decentralized decision rights—individual employees can design their own work activities.

- Cost-accounting failures—prior activity-based costing efforts can undermine new efforts to manage activities.

2. Contrary to widely held misperceptions, knowledge work activities are not unmanageably unique. Similar to manufacturing, these tasks and related improvements can be concisely defined with:

- Roughly 18 to 34 unique activities
- Approximately 25 root causes of improvement
- No more than 500 total operational improvements

3. Best practices from manufacturing can be easily adapted for knowledge work activity management:

- Standardized hierarchies for universal descriptions
- Normalization protocols for verb-noun descriptions
- Reconciliation of activity-time intervals with relevant organizational capacity

# CHAPTER 11

# TURBOCHARGING YOUR KNOWLEDGE WORK FACTORY

Remember Alex, the data dude? When we last left him, back in the Introduction, he'd abandoned Josh and all those drop-everything management reports for the greener pastures of Seattle in a bid to reboot his career. He'd thrown in his bet with a hot tech start-up, and his wager had paid off well.

Alex's new company had been carving out a niche in the nascent robotic process automation, or RPA, market. The company had been in business for nearly a decade—struggling mostly—when Alex arrived.

But now, suddenly, robotics was hot. Red hot. The company was valued north of a billion dollars, as were several of its peers. It recently secured second-round venture financing of $150 million. It was a story that made the business news—and caught the eye of Nick Clearsight.

Nick personally knew people involved with making this investment, but that wasn't unusual. What *was* unusual: Nick respected their insights. Clearly, something was afoot in robotics, and Nick resolved to learn more. He requested more information, and Alex's company dispatched a rep to Nick's office.

That visit didn't last long. By the third time that Nick heard the rep proclaim, "Our technology can do anything," he ended the meeting.

Normally, the robotics company would simply move on; demand for its product was strong. In this case, however, the company was determined to win over Nick. After all, the private equity firm where Nick worked was worth the sales effort: it maintained a large number of marquee companies in its buyout portfolio. Each of these businesses had been purchased at a premium price and required a radical increase in value to enable a profitable resale. Thus, the RPA start-up resolved to persuade Nick of the inevitable, rapid, and valuable rise of robotics. And so the company sent one of its most senior managers to meet with him: Alex, the former data wrangler.

## The Activity Cube

Nick opened his meeting with Alex candidly. "Let me save you a little breath. And time," he said. "All robotics sales reps—like those from virtually *all* technology providers—make the same promise: 'Our stuff can do anything.' That's not exactly helpful."

"Furthermore," he added, "they all want *us* to give *them* work activities for their robots to perform."

"They want *you* to 'feed' the machines," offered Alex.

"Yes," nodded Nick. "And not only that, they request—to borrow your metaphor—a fairly restricted diet. All the work activities must adhere to a very limited short list of characteristics. They have to be 'similar,' 'repetitive,' and 'rules-based.' I understand the first two—although these could describe two-thirds of knowledge work activities."

"But . . . ?" interjected Alex.

"But," chimed in Nick, "what does 'rules-based' really mean? Who makes the rules? For that matter, who talks like that in business? 'Here are your rules-based tasks for the day.'"

"Point well taken," conceded Alex. "Sounds like a sales pitch written by a coder."

Nick chuckled. "Look. I know all about similar and repetitive work activities. These characteristics are codependent. The more you standardize—make similar work activities identical—the more repetition you get. Similar and repetitive work activities are easy to *request*; any fool can do that. But the challenge is *recognizing* them. They're not obvious. But why am I explaining this to you? Why don't I just show you?"

He called up a slide on the projection screen; see Figure 11-1. "This," Nick explained, "is a simple operations model that we've developed. We have the most sophisticated work-activity-level management capability in

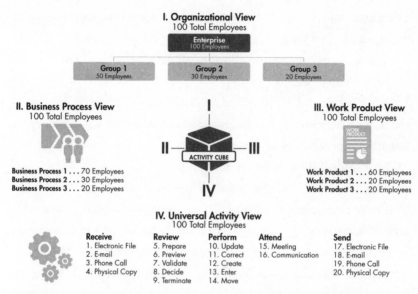

**FIGURE 11-1** The knowledge work factory overview that Nick showed Alex looked like this. The Activity Cube reconciles net organizational capacity with business processes, work products, and work activities.

business today. I think that the two of us reviewing it would be a good prerequisite to discussing your new robotics technology."

Alex: "What are you using? Big data? AI—I mean, artificial intelligence?"

"Nope," smiled Nick. "Just good old-fashioned off-the-rack databases and spreadsheets."

Nick explained, "This is an overview of the model. We call it our 'knowledge work factory.' It shows how we manage every aspect of each business that we own. We can operate each business just as you would do in a factory; hence the name. The capacity model, what we call the Activity Cube, is in the middle. We use that to generate and reconcile four different views of operations. Let me walk you through them."

He began: "First, there's the Organizational View. We can calculate this net available capacity by adding up the employees and making deductions for vacations, lunch breaks, holidays . . . this gives us our maximum factory capacity, what we call the 'nameplate' capacity. Next, we can jump to the Work Product View of capacity. It shows the—"

"Ah, yes," interrupted Alex. "Fudge-less data."

Nick: "'Fudge-less'?"

"Sure," nodded Alex. "Once you quantify the organizational capacity, the way you're showing me, then no one can argue with it. No one can fudge the numbers. Hence: 'fudge-less.'"

Nick smiled. He liked that term.

Alex continued. "It's the same for the work products: the outputs. They're easy to quantify and track." Then, thinking, he added, "So all this means that you can get some pretty accurate, unit-based measurements on productivity performance from just those two data sets. You divide net capacity by the relevant work products. I'm impressed. That's pretty unusual for knowledge work."

Nick: "Oh, I'm just getting started."

"At my old job," said Alex, "these two reconciled views of yours would've delivered fudge-less unit costs and put me out of work. I was a full-time data wrangler. I spent days—heck, my entire *job*—calculating unit costs and margins based on frantic one-off requests from managers."

"Well," said Nick, "those two views constitute only half of the four-way match in the Activity Cube. Next," he said, "we map all the work processes. This identifies and defines every single work activity."

"Wow," said Alex, "That seems incredibly tedious."

"Hey," countered Nick, "tedious is valuable. And it actually doesn't take that long—several weeks at most, in the largest organizations—to build out the business process maps. You just have to avoid the false precision. Organizations love to drag this out for months.

"The maps give us two things," Nick said. "First, they define the work activities—using employees' terms. Second, they provide flowcharts for connecting those activities. This helps us understand the cause-and-effect relationships across operations. Your robotics company is looking for 'rules-based' activities? Here they are: summary-level rules."

"Okay, I see it," said Alex. "These process maps are like roads for the activities. And the activities are like cars moving over the roads." But he was thinking ahead to himself: *"We have recording technology that could totally capture the frequency of these activities. And we could also record the employees' actual keystrokes involved with each activity to configure the bots."*

"Next," said Nick, "we standardize all the diverse activity definitions. Employees will—predictably—define an identical work activity using a seemingly unlimited number of terms. And even when the terms are *identical*, they'll be in a different order. Here's a chart showing how we standardize these." Nick then showed him the slide in Figure 11-2.

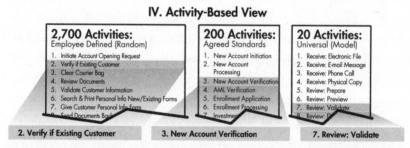

**IV. Activity-Based View**

**2,700 Activities:**
Employee Defined (Random)
1. Initiate Account Opening Request
2. Verify if Existing Customer
3. Clear Courier Bag
4. Review Documents
5. Validate Customer Information
6. Search & Print Personal Info New/Existing Forms
7. Give Customer Personal Info Form

**2. Verify if Existing Customer**

**200 Activities:**
Agreed Standards
1. New Account Initiation
2. New Account Processing
3. New Account Verification
4. AML Verification
5. Enrollment Application
6. Enrollment Processing
7. Investment

**3. New Account Verification**

**20 Activities:**
Universal (Model)
1. Receive: Electronic File
2. Receive: E-mail Message
3. Receive: Phone Call
4. Receive: Physical Copy
5. Review: Prepare
6. Review: Preview
7. Review: Validate
8. Review:

**7. Review: Validate**

**FIGURE 11-2** The Activity Cube standardizes knowledge work activities into 20 "universal" activities to create a standard vocabulary of knowledge work.

Alex's eyes bugged out. "This example has 2,700 activities?!"

"No," replied Nick, calmly. "It has just 20 'universal' activities, but they're defined 2,700 different ways, almost randomly, by employees. There are no controls for definitions."

Alex: "So why the list of 200 in the middle?"

"Well," replied Nick, "the 20 universal activity definitions don't work for day-to-day, human communication; they're just for the model. They're like computer code. Spreadsheets and databases love them, but people need about a 200- to 400-term standardized vocabulary."

Alex: "That number seems too low."

"Not really. For example, today's teenagers need as few as 240 words, *total*, to communicate with their friends through text messages.[1] With all their texting, their vocabulary gets incredibly streamlined. So it's certainly feasible to have 400 standard names—or 200—simply for describing an organization's 'work activities.' It's kind of crazy when you think about it: Teenagers accidentally developed the best practices for lean, standardized communication in business today. That's not trivial, considering the price these businesses pay for their runaway verbosity, especially when it undermines technology and prevents automation."

"Tell me about it!" nodded Alex. "My former company had multiple systems with conflicting fields for something as no-brainer as customers' names. One system would be first name first, the next would be last name first. Or one system could only hold *short* names, like 'John Smith.' Try using that system when your customers are from India or Malaysia. And so someone—me—had to wrangle these into a single, reconciled format."

"But then it would be fixed . . . ? For good, right?" Nick asked slyly. He was intentionally baiting him.

"The heck it was!" complained Alex. "They'd do it all over again for the next one-off report. It was great for my job security, but not for my sanity."

Nick pressed on. "So. We can whittle down the initial list of 2,700 'employee-defined' activities to, say, 200 standard activities that everyone agrees on and uses. And then we can further reduce those to just 20 universal activities, which we use in our Activity Cube capacity model: a *spreadsheet.*"

"My bots would love that," said Alex.

"But you have to be vigilant," warned Nick. "If you don't maintain control and limit the options, the employees will grow these definitions back into the thousands again."

Alex nodded. He was thinking aloud now, and Nick could see the wheels turning in his head. "The bots could keep all of this under control," Alex said. "The definitions, the sequence of activities . . . There wouldn't be random, unbridled growth. I could build a standard bot—probably based on one or two templates—for each of those 20 universal activities. Then

I could string them together, as needed, just like they're sketched out on those process maps."

Alex continued. "I see where you're going with this. You've built a standardized grid, like the Manhattan street grid, for work activities. It's a grid that could work nicely for methodically digitizing the operations and managing the installed bots."

"A bot grid. Intriguing," said Nick. "We call it a cube. The Activity Cube. And once we have the total work activities reconciled against the organizational capacity, we can make some interesting cuts or pivots using the activity data. Here's a look at a typical company, when we first acquire it. This is an insurance company we recently bought; it's very similar to most knowledge work businesses." And then he brought up a new graphic on the screen; see Figure 11-3.

Alex let out a low whistle. "A *third* of the organization—35 percent, actually—is doing corrections and validations? . . . Honestly, it's not too surprising, once I think about my own experience."

Nick: "Now do you see why your sales rep's specs were so annoying?"

"You mean our request for 'similar, repetitive, rules-based activities' for the robots?" chuckled Alex. "Sure, but I had no idea of what's involved—and what's possible."

Nick zoomed in on the graphic. "Notice that we have *actively standardized* the work activities. Similar activities are not obvious; they don't just happen. In fact, just the opposite happens. All these crazy definitions make similar activities seem unique at first glance. We start with thousands. We reduce them to 20. *Now* they're standardized.

"Also notice that we have *documented the frequency* of these standardized activities. We know what is repetitive—exactly where, when, and how much."

"That's pretty cool," Alex admitted. "I've only seen this kind of stuff in factories before."

"Just look at the meetings," Nick explained. "Everyone complains about these. Journalists publish entire articles bemoaning the time wasted in business meetings. But that's nothing compared with the time wasted on

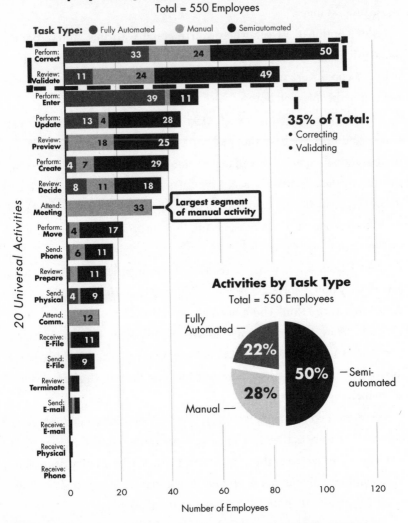

**FIGURE 11-3** Standardizing activities uncovers massive improvement opportunity. One-third of organizational capacity is typically devoted to corrections and validations.

rework. You can see the activity data right there in front of you. Inarguable ... Or should I say 'fudge-less'?"

Alex smiled, vaguely flattered. "Meetings are the largest category of manual activity, by far. They're visible. They're about the only visible 'scrap piles' in your knowledge work factory."

Nick nodded. "But as long as you're wasting time on rework in front of a computer, the keystrokes and mouse clicks all look alike. No visible scrap pile for those wasted tasks. Everything looks identical: rework *and* value-added activity. On the surface, they appear the same."

Alex: "But why is it so important to reconcile everything?"

"Two reasons," said Nick. "The first is political or perceptual. We do it to eliminate excuses, denials, and false trade-offs—make it 'fudge-less.' When we can quantify and reconcile every activity with the organizational capacity, the value becomes clear, and the math is inarguable. We've accounted for everything. Nobody can dismiss improvements by saying, 'Oh, it's not that much lost time. It'll cost more to fix it.'"

"The second reason," Nick explained, "is technical. We have to know how much waste is available, and we have to track its removal—and then we have to keep on tracking so that it doesn't creep back in."

"That's one of the beauties of bots," offered Alex. "They're once and done. Sure, there's maintenance. But once you set them up, data-wrangling hell goes away. The bots always follow the rules. They won't redefine activities."

Nick nodded slowly, thinking to himself, *"Done properly—if you 'feed' the bots the proper restricted 'diet'—you could put the experience curve into practice. You could codify it for knowledge work operations. You'd build the know-how directly into the factory, activity by activity, like the jigs and machine tools that all manufacturers use."* Then he noticed that Alex was speaking again—

"There's so much waste there," Alex was saying, "I can sure see how people would be skeptical. But it looks like you're only targeting capacity savings. As they always say, 'You can't *cost-cut* your way to greatness.'"

"I love these false trade-offs," replied Nick. "We've built our entire investment business on these misbeliefs. But I want to go way beyond conventional 5 to 15 percent cost-cuts. I want to scale—just like manufacturers do. I want double, triple increases in total productivity—50 to 75 percent labor reduction. What can you do with your bots?"

## Roads for Robots

Alex thought for a moment before responding. "Look at your process maps. They're divided into swim lanes, like a highway system, or a road network. So think about how to go about improving *that*. I mean, our two companies would have to work together on simultaneously improving everything."

Nick: "It's doable. As owners, we'd have to improve the 'highway' network, the business processes—shorten wasteful routes and cut out detours. We already do lots of that without technology."

"Yes!" Alex chimed in, excitedly. "And next, think of the work activities as people and vehicles moving and operating along these roads. Some are people only walking—those are the manual activities. Others are in puttering cars—like Model Ts—semiautomated activities."

Nick: "Then I guess you and I are walking right now . . . manual activity? . . .along the improvement process road?"

Alex shrugged. "Maybe. Or maybe we're looking down on all kinds of operations traffic. And those lanes on the process maps aren't only highways for cars. Think of major IT systems as railroads. These are the fully automated activities. They require massive investments in fixed infrastructure: bridges, tracks, and most importantly, acquisition of right of way. That's why major IT systems are so slow and costly to deploy: it's like railroad construction. You have to work with all the users to agree on the routes and secure the right of way."

"I don't have time to build any more railroads," chuckled Nick. "I just want better routes, straighter highways, and faster cars—how about self-driving cars? Isn't that what robots are?"

"Sure," replied Alex. "We have those. They're called 'unattended' robots. But for your current operations, that's like Star Wars—not the place to start. Let's walk first, run later. Not only are your existing roads crooked; they're jammed with Model Ts: slow, short-range, low-power, labor-intensive technology. Think of them as the 'semiautomated' work activities performed today by your employees. Not quite manual, but not fully automated."

Nick bristled slightly. "I already said I'd straighten the roads. What do you have in mind for my 'Model T' work activities?"

Alex grinned. "We turn 'em into hot rods. We turbocharge 'em into hot bots." (Figure 11-4 provides an example of what Alex was thinking.)

"How long would that take?"

Alex shrugged it off. "Given the rich detail in your existing process maps, we could get some of them going in a matter of days. We'll start out

**FIGURE 11-4** Robotic process automation can turbocharge operations, just like a hot rod. But business processes and work activities must be standardized first.

Image sources: Shutterstock and Alamy

with simple robots—what we call 'attended' robots. Think of these as adding power-assisted options to your existing cars . . . er, work activities. For example, lots of your 'cars' currently need hand cranks to get started. We'll take care of that and even add some more sophisticated powered options."

Nick: "You mean, like power steering? Power windows?"

"Yes," replied Alex, "except think of power windows that open and close in a nanosecond. We just have to comb through all your activities, decide which ones we'll turbocharge first, and break those down further into keystrokes—what I'll call 'digital-grade operations documentation.'"

"That seems tedious."

"Hey," countered Alex, "tedious is valuable."

Nick shot him a sideways glance. "I'm swamped. I've got a dozen companies in my portfolio where I could use this—not to mention other companies I've got my sights on. What you're describing sounds like it requires both time and patient capital."

Alex burst out laughing. "'Patient capital'? Very funny—just like 'jumbo shrimp.'" Then he grew serious. "I know the feeling. Our investors are relentless. So I've got to move fast, too. But we can scale easily—we can reuse templates to design the bots."

Alex then said, "The first order of business for me is to introduce you to robotics—get some hands-on examples from your business in front of you and operational. You can't understand it by talking or reading about it. Can I get a copy of that model, the Activity Cube? And is there someone we can work with to do some prototyping? On real business operations?"

"Yes, Michelle, from my team," said Nick. Then he shot Alex a warning glance. "This isn't simply 20 drag-and-drop activities. They're similar, and that's a good start, but they are not identical. And they never will be. We won't deliver digital-grade operational detail to you. In other words, no keystrokes. Can you and your bots handle that?"

"Sure," said Alex, albeit nervously. He'd find a way. With templates.

## Doubling and Redoubling Productivity, One Wrench Turn at a Time

Let's take a step back for a moment and examine how manufacturers approach industrialization improvement—how they set aggressive goals . . . how they "scale."

It was the 2016 Lunar New Year holiday in an industrial center in China's Pearl River Delta, north of Hong Kong. Most workers were home celebrating, but not at a local telecom equipment maker. Executives and administrative employees abandoned their desks to help on the production floor, working late to ship products on time.

Fast-forward two years to 2018. The production-floor operation, which used to employ 300 workers, is now down to 100; two-thirds were replaced by automation. Down the road, a manufacturer of smartphone parts now employs 16 workers on a shift that used to require 103, an 85 percent reduction due to automation.[2]

Are these "labor-cost reductions?" Or are they "productivity investments?" The answer to both is yes. And this type of thinking, and improvement, is simply business as usual in the manufacturing industry. The manufacturers in these stories were not responding to an explosion in growth. Their stunning gains did not depend on a breakthrough development like the moving assembly line. But then, initially, neither did Ford's. (More about that shortly.) Manufacturers simply hunker down and relentlessly improve productivity by standardizing and automating, one wrench turn at a time. Industrialization is just business as usual.

But try asking knowledge work operations managers to achieve a fraction of this improvement in a similar time frame. They will groan, insisting that cutting labor costs or improving productivity by 15 to 25 percent within a year or 18 months is simply impossible. They'll respond with warnings in the form of false trade-offs: "You will be cutting muscle, not just fat."

But can they tell muscle from fat? And if so, why have they been tolerating the fat? Does that also mean they know how to build the muscle? To "scale" productivity?

People in knowledge work will say that the Ford example, or any other manufacturing example, for that matter, when applied to *their* work, is irrelevant: "These are from the past century; don't bother me with those . . ." And yet, here these examples are today, alive and well and quietly delivering massive competitive gains, day in, day out, even in low-cost labor markets like China. It's a topic that rarely makes the headlines because it's simply no big deal in manufacturing.

Which industrialization elements will we need to master in order to scale knowledge work operations? Again, let's look at Ford. Manufacturing historian David Nye highlighted these for the early, pre-assembly-line days at Ford:

> The majority of the cost savings achieved at Ford's Highland Park factory were not due to the introduction of the moving assembly line itself; rather they resulted from efficiencies realized through
>
> - subdivision of labor,
> - improved accuracy in making interchangeable parts,
> - rearrangement of machinery,
> - and better workflow layouts.[3]

On the one hand, in manufacturing, this can be described very simply: "Design for manufacturability and machinability." There are costly physical assets involved, so that limits the options, especially in the near term.

For knowledge work, however, it's both fiendishly simpler and infinitely more complex—all you need to do is design for *digital* manufacturability and machinability (simple). But maybe that's the problem: too many options—the "paradox of choice," where "more is less" (complex). Basic standardization becomes more conceptually challenging: "*Our technology can do anything.*" And that's the problem, not the solution.

To achieve these same industrialization goals, Ford increased its investment in tools and factory equipment more than tenfold between 1909 and 1914.[4] Relatively new machines were constantly being discarded as these rapidly became underproductive. Yet modern-day knowledge work, performed in a manual and digital environment, faces virtually *no similar capital or technology constraints*. Look back at the same list that Professor Nye compiled from Ford, but now view it through the lens of our knowledge work factory:

- Subdivide labor? Document operations at the work-activity level (5- to 15-minute increments).
- Improve accuracy of interchangeable parts? Standardize and improve the quality of data elements.
- Rearrange machinery? *Move it digitally.*
- Improve workflow layouts? Document and upgrade business processes.

What is your productivity growth target for next year? What will you do on your "production floor"? Why can't you plan to quickly increase your knowledge workers' productivity by half? Or double it? How many hard facts do you have on the feasibility of this objective? Compared with manufacturing's tangible-asset constraints, doubling and redoubling productivity in the intangible-asset world of knowledge work is a walk in the park. Let's take a quick tour of the past century in auto manufacturing productivity, since data and documented facts are available:

- Ford initially didn't have productivity targets, either—other than meeting the overwhelming demand for its cars. Total autos produced increased eighteenfold over the five-year period from 1909 to 1914.[5]
- Over the five-year period ending in 1914, Ford scaled its existing methods to achieve a productivity gain that delivered nearly eight times more Model T cars per assembly worker.[6] And this was *before* the assembly line made its most significant contribution—in the 1914–1923 period.

- By 1923, the assembly line helped Ford further *quadruple* productivity.[7] This drove a crippling wedge of performance capability between Ford and its competitors. As you'll recall from Chapter 8, Ford was more than 30 times more productive than one competitor, the Packard Motor Company, which operated a Taylor-designed production plant.[8] Taylor's methods favor savers, not scalers.
- Over the next 50 years, ending in 1973, Ford's productivity was doubled again in small, steady increments.[9]
- During the 1970–1985 period, Japanese automakers further scaled the industry's existing assembly-line methods, largely without new technology. They created lean techniques to eliminate waste that was hiding in plain sight. And they became roughly 2.5 times as productive as their U.S. competitors.[10]

Knowledge workers will overconfidently reject these examples. What will they tell you? The usual:

- "That's not comparable."
- "It's a century old."
- "That's based on the one-time implementation of a breakthrough innovation for the industry: the moving assembly line."

But as usual, these perceptions are false.

## Doubling Productivity: The Anticlimax

Alex was back at Nick's office. In the two weeks since their first meeting, Alex had mastered the Activity Cube. He was a convert. The thing was astonishingly useful. It seemed that there wasn't a single operational question it couldn't answer for him in a matter of minutes.

Now, however, it was time to get to work. And thus he'd arrived to make a presentation on how his company's robots could deliver massive, immediate-term (as in "six months") improvement—to double productivity for several of Nick's portfolio companies.

Minutes later, he and Michelle—whom he had been e-mailing since his meeting with Nick—were heading to a conference room together. "You'll be presenting to both Nick and his partner, Ray," explained Michelle.

"Ray . . .?"

"Raymond Dash. Of Clearsight–Dash. They were originally going to call it 'Clearsight & Dash,' with an ampersand, but given Ray's predilection for speed, he said, 'Why not dash twice?' Hence the punctuation: Clearsight–Dash."

Next thing Alex knew, he and Michelle were in a conference room in front of Nick and Ray, tag-teaming the remote control to their PowerPoint presentation.

"I believe," said Michelle, "that we can quickly dispense with the basics. Everyone in this room is familiar with our knowledge work factory concept, the underlying Activity Cube, and its four-way reconciliation."

Nods all around.

"Today," continued Michelle, "we're going to review our plan for doubling productivity at one of our portfolio companies. We chose it because it's a pretty good proxy for plenty of the others."

Alex looked across at Ray. Sitting beside Nick on one of the couches, Ray said nothing.

"I know that 'doubling' sounds like a tall order," continued Michelle, "but it's not too far of a stretch. We'll just pretend we're working with a manufacturer. Manufacturers do this routinely, day in, day out. And if it works for us—even halfway—we'll roll it out to every business in our portfolio."

She brought up her first slide; see Figure 11-5.

"As usual," said Michelle, "we mapped all the business processes and entered the work activities into the Activity Cube. Obviously, for robotics automation, we are going to focus on the human work activities. However, we do not want the robots to automate the low-value activities that we typically remove with our nontechnology, lean improvements. So we had to isolate these for Alex and his team."

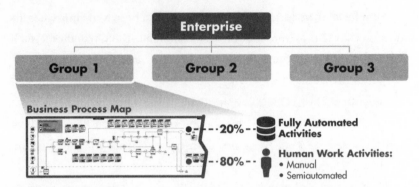

**FIGURE 11-5** Work activities from business process maps are loaded into the Activity Cube. From there, they can be divided into fully automated activities and human work activities (manual and semiautomated).

And then she explained, "We began by using the Activity Cube to sort all of the human work activities into two sets of familiar categories, as you can see here." And then she brought up the next slide; see Figure 11-6.

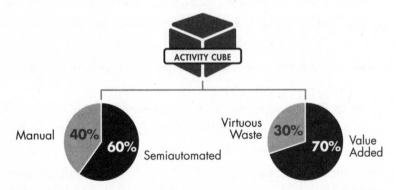

**FIGURE 11-6** The Activity Cube enables segmentation of human work activities into multiple categories based on current automation levels and value categories.

"First," Michelle continued, "we separate 'manual' versus 'semiautomated' activities; remember, we define any activity that involves any automation—even a spreadsheet—as 'semiautomated.' And next we can sort activities based on whether they are 'value added' or 'virtuous waste.'"

"But then," she said, with excitement rising in her voice, "we took it a bit further than usual. We combined these categories to create a simple matrix—a quad. This will focus our activity-level improvement strategies."

She exchanged a quick glance with Alex and then clicked up the next slide, the one they'd both been waiting to show off; see Figure 11-7.

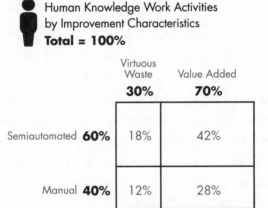

**FIGURE 11-7**   Here's a typical distribution of human knowledge work activities.

She took a moment to let everyone absorb the input. Nick rubbed his chin and nodded slowly. Ray displayed no emotion.

Michelle continued. "This matrix lets us identify the value-added activities that are not targeted for removal by our lean, nontechnology improvement efforts. This is necessary, because Alex is going to provide some estimates of how we can further standardize and automate these with robotics."

"This matrix," continued Michelle, "provides a generic way to target the activities worthy of robotic investment. Obviously, you'd want to first target those in the upper-right quadrant. These are value-added activities that won't be eliminated by our lean improvement efforts. These are also semiautomated."

Nick interrupted. "Wouldn't that mean that they're already optimized? I mean, some sort of technology is already in use."

Michelle shook her head. "Just the opposite, usually. For example, most of these activities are often simple, repetitive transcription. There might be a decision or a review interspersed, but employees are typically just moving data from one document or system to the next. These are ideal candidates for robotics. But first we'll have to prioritize the activities and then invest in keystroke-level 'digital-grade operations documentation'—turn them into 'food' for robots."

"Now," she continued, "at the risk of overcommunicating, I'll breeze through a summary of our current improvement efforts. Just to be clear with everyone, we have not changed our time-tested Clearsight–Dash mode of nontechnology operation improvement for the left-hand side of this matrix. We've started by targeting the virtuous waste, the 30 percent of total human work activity in the business—and we're well under way removing this wasted effort, as we speak. Let me double-click on the left-hand side of the matrix. Here's how that 30 percent of virtuous waste breaks down by subsegment."

She brought up a new slide; see Figure 11-8.

"No surprises here," she continued. "As you can see, there are two major subsegments of roughly equal value: undermanaged performance and rework activities. And these line up directly with our traditional improvement strategies. We immediately install our management dashboards, divide organizational capacity by work products, identify the key performance indicators (KPIs), and begin daily productivity reporting, all the way down to the individual-employee level."

Alex thought to himself, "Fudge-less, daily productivity reports. I can use bots to automate that reporting process—simple and fast."

Michelle continued, "Our field teams have also identified about 250 activity-level business process improvements, and more than half of these have already been implemented over the past four months. You should see the improvements we're making in claims."

**FIGURE 11-8** Virtuous waste activities can be further divided into two major subsegments: undermanaged performance and rework activities.

That's when Nick perked up. "Claims?" he said. "You didn't tell me this was one of our insurance companies."

Michelle blushed. "Sorry, Nick," she said. "Guess I was going too fast. It's InsureCo."

"InsureCo!" said Nick cheerfully. "How could I forget? How's my friend Laura doing over there?"

Michelle: "She's a true believer now. The KPI management dashboards have been in place for several months. She's often out on the floor, with her copy in hand, working with the frontline managers. They've been able to bring the low-performing quartile up much closer to best-practice levels; they cut the productivity shortfall in half."

Nick smiled, gratified. "And how about those claims overpayments? Still trending down?"

"Ohhh yeah," said Michelle, smiling right back at him. "It's amazing what a gain-sharing plan can do to change an executive's lifelong misperceptions.

"And now, with no further ado," she added, "let me turn things over to our new robotics partner, Alex. He's going to take you through some uncharted improvement territory for us: the right side of the matrix."

"You mean the 70 percent of total human work activities that will not be eliminated by our lean efforts?" asked Nick.

"Absolutely," said Alex. "But of course, these will rise to 100 percent of human work activities, once your lean improvements are complete and the 30 percent of virtuous waste is gone."

"Well, then, robotics will be even more valuable," said Nick. "Regale us."

Alex took the remote control from Michelle and stepped to the front of the room. "It was pretty simple," he began, "for us to sort these work activities into candidates that offered high potential for robotic process automation. The standardized activity names in the Activity Cube pointed us in the general direction. But we also did some hands-on, sanity-check observations on-site with your field teams. The idea is to make it as simple as a children's picture book."

"What I think Alex is saying here," interjected Nick, "is that you can never oversimplify anything for our investors. They have the attention span of a movie producer: you need a 10-second pitch."

"And it's even shorter for some of our portfolio company execs," offered Michelle. "But that's only because some don't *want* to understand. It means change."

Ray nodded. Alex then clicked up the next slide in the deck; see Figure 11-9.

Alex gave the others a moment to review it, and then he continued. "We sorted and prioritized the value-added activities into two broad categories: those with higher potential as RPA candidates and those with lower potential. This first-pass list targets similar, repetitive activities that deliver major labor savings: entering, updating, moving, etc. For this first wave of RPA, we're keeping everything very simple. Later, after we have

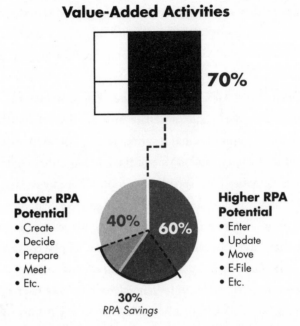

**FIGURE 11-9**   Robotic process automation can reduce or eliminate the human work effort for about 30 percent of value-added activities.

some bots up and running, we'll circle back and focus on activities that deliver other types of benefits: cycle time and error reduction, risk mitigation, and customer-experience upgrades."

A deep voice arose from the darkness. "Let me make sure I'm reading this chart correctly."

Alex blinked. It was *Ray*. The Sphinx was finally speaking!

Ray sat forward on the couch. "Hold on here. This 30 percent labor reduction that you're showing me . . . This comes out of a base of 70 percent? We can always get 30 percent reduction from the starting point with no technology. Are you saying you can give us 20 percent more than we already get? This is *in addition* to the 30 percent reduction in the 'Virtuous Waste' column?"

Alex: "That's correct, sir."

Michelle said, "We're aiming to double productivity. Recoup 50 percent of all labor."

Ray squinted at the numbers, then turned to Alex. "That would be astonishing. How does it work?"

"Let me show you," said Alex, bringing another graphic up on the screen; see Figure 11-10.

"This chart," said Alex, "shows one of 22 RPA candidates in this business process. This particular candidate includes five universal activities documented on the process maps, summarized in the Activity Cube, and categorized in the value-added side of the quadrant. Remember that the 20 universal activities have spreadsheet-model-friendly names. This one is termed 'Perform: Enter,' and it involves the entry of customer data from a request, or order, into an IT system. An activity description like "enter customer data" might be adequate for a human employee who's familiar with the work. But not for bots. They need deeper detail."

Alex continued to explain. "In general, each activity requires an average of about 10 to 15 keystroke-level details to get it into robot-ready form—what we've been calling 'digital-grade operations documentation.' We can use our digital recording technology to capture many of these keystrokes. However, we'll need humans to sanity check them and configure the bot to perform the keystrokes. Once it's in place, however, the bot performs the keystrokes so fast you can hardly follow its actions onscreen."

"That looks tedious," said Ray.

"Tedious is valuable," replied Alex, hoping it would score him some points.

Ray grunted, unconvinced. "With technology, it's usually slow and costly," he said.

Alex smiled. He was prepared for this. "The cost of the core robotics technology is negligible," he said, seeing if it would chink Ray's armor; it did. "Most of your investment," Alex continued, "is involved with finding the RPA candidates and documenting the keystroke-level tasks. That's way more than half of the challenge. But the Activity Cube helps you find and evaluate these quickly. It's like a GPS capability for each of the work activities in your operations. Next, we simply record existing keystrokes, as I'd mentioned before. Then we'll use your process maps to understand the

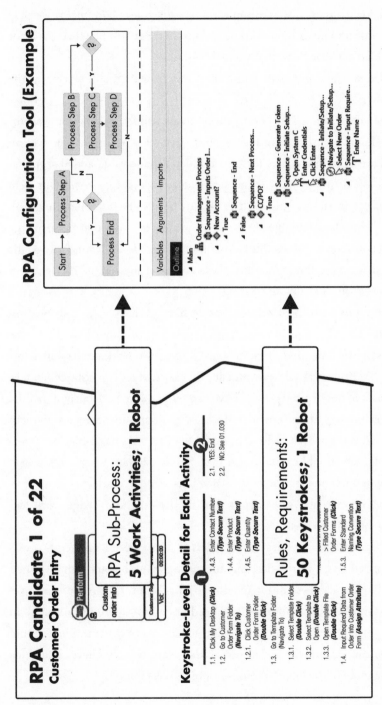

**FIGURE 11-10** Recording all the keystrokes required to implement RPA might be tedious, but it's also extremely valuable.

workflow connections and implications—the rules. And finally, we plug all of this into my company's bots and install them. Just like that, the labor for those activities is virtually gone!"

There was a pregnant pause. Ray was frowning, still staring at the numbers.

Michelle jumped in. "Our process maps will let us lay out a wall-to-wall design for a bot farm for the entire InsureCo business. Then we can incrementally install RPA for the candidates in the value-added segment. We'll avoid the virtuous waste segments, as we always have. Our field teams can learn this quickly; they already have some bots operating. And they're building reusable shells, or templates, for bots that perform the most common activities. Stuff as painfully mundane as downloading a file from a network. But in quantity, these savings really add up. It's a game of minutes—just like manufacturing."

Ray turned to Nick, sitting beside him. "What's your take on this, partner?"

Nick was sanguine. "I'm on board. I've seen it working. It's super-low risk. It's throwaway cheap. And I see that it provides two complementary avenues of opportunities, which we can pursue simultaneously: First, the nontechnology improvement that we always do includes a huge amount of standardization. This is directly useful for RPA—it's hand-in-glove compatible. We should capitalize on that. Second, I want to connect everything in operations more tightly using bots—end to end."

Alex spoke up. "But doesn't your model—the knowledge work factory—already do this?"

Nick nodded. "Yes. It's connected. It's a factory. But it's not end-to-end optimized, like a world-class manufacturing plant. It could still be leaned out, like the Japanese did with auto production in the '80s. For example, the InsureCo policy underwriters need to be more tightly connected, in real time, to these claims losses—and see the overpayments. They should be 'hardwired,' and they aren't now. If they were, we could have algorithms doing more of the underwriting—more of everything."

"The same holds true for the sales force," Nick went on. "Similar data could be recycled back to the individual salespeople for every one of their customers—again, algorithms could optimize their targeting efforts and track the effectiveness of the company's marketing campaigns. And the CFO should be connected directly with margin reports and financial statement impact. Robots could do all of this—no IT mega-system needed."

Ray perked up. "What about the competitive implications? We could make more acquisitions."

Nick smiled. "You read my mind. That was my next priority."

Ray scoffed. "That's the *first* priority, in my mind. But I guess that's why you're the *operations* partner, and I'm the *deal* partner, at this firm."

Nick laughed, then gestured expansively. "Yes," he said, "you could buy the company outright. *Or* I could acquire it competitively, stealing one policyholder at a time."

Michelle interjected. "Sounds to me like another false trade-off."

Alex saw a glint of insight in Ray's eyes. Ray leaned forward. "She's right, of course. We could do *both*. Start sequentially. One policyholder at a time . . . And then—*then!*—after the target company's execs are totally bewildered, and the stock price is maybe lower, but long before they figure out how to do this themselves, we make an offer for the whole company. Boom."

He sat back on the couch and, for the first time in the meeting, smiled.

Michelle saw the parallel: "It's competitive digitization, just like Amazon or Uber, only for the insurance business."

Ray corrected her. "No. It's like Amazon or Uber for *any* business. Let's get started."

## Leverage What You've Learned

As this chapter has detailed, the knowledge work factory concept can succeed without new technology. But that doesn't mean it can't *leverage* technology—new or existing—to overcome the productivity paradox. RPA is simply the latest shining example. It offers the advantage of minimal investment and involvement from conventional IT resources. But like any technology, process robots are no magic bullet. They're only as good as the lean, standardized processes and digital-grade operations documentation that you feed them.

The next and final chapter looks at the three strategic milestones that stand in the way of implementing a knowledge work factory.

## CHAPTER 11: **TAKEAWAYS**

1. The management capabilities delivered by the knowledge work factory (Chapter 8) can be enhanced—turbocharged—by using the work activities from the business process maps.

2. The Activity Cube provides a simple way to inventory, reconcile, measure—and automate—the four basic operational elements of the turbocharged knowledge work factory:
   - Organizational capacity
   - Work products
   - Business processes
   - Work activities

3. Knowledge work operations can achieve similar breakthrough gains in productivity as manufacturers, by using similar industrialization methods—but without similar capital investment.

4. The Productivity Quad is a simple matrix for categorizing work activities for two fundamentally different improvement strategies:
   - Eliminate. Virtuous waste activities
   - Automate. Value-added activities (semiautomated, manual)

# CHAPTER 12

# MANAGING INDUSTRIALIZATION

Want a little sugar rush of self-indulgent fun? Read the compilation shown in Figure 12-1, what I call "Insanely Great Business Idea Dismissals (IGBIDs) Throughout History." Why is it so much fun to read this list? Because it is smugly satisfying junk food for the brain's deepest, most biased cravings: hindsight and overconfidence.

Hindsight bias helps to conjure a dramatic moment: there, right in front of each decision maker, lies a Steve Jobs–worthy, "insanely great" proposition—a big rock. And it's all so painfully obvious. The decision involves a simple, clearly framed choice: seize this once-in-a-lifetime opportunity—or dismiss it and be a loser. It's clear-cut. Obvious.

And then, as if to underscore the drama—the *tragedy*—of the moment, each dismissal cited in the figure seems to snatch failure from the jaws of success. The disappointment of these historic dismisses is almost palpable. Then the brain's overconfident inner voice provides reassurance: "*I* would never have made such a boneheaded error. *I* would have noticed, clearly, the obvious value that all these others overlooked!"

> I used to think that the brain was the most wonderful organ in my body. Then I realized who was telling me this.
>
> —Emo Philips

In part, this book has attempted to demonstrate the ways in which the brain's powerful biases triumph over rational perception and decision making. And understanding that relationship is critical for successfully implementing a knowledge work factory (KWF). That's because the KWF appears just as unconventional as anything on this historic failures list.

# Insanely Great Business Idea
# Dismissals (IGBIDs) Throughout History

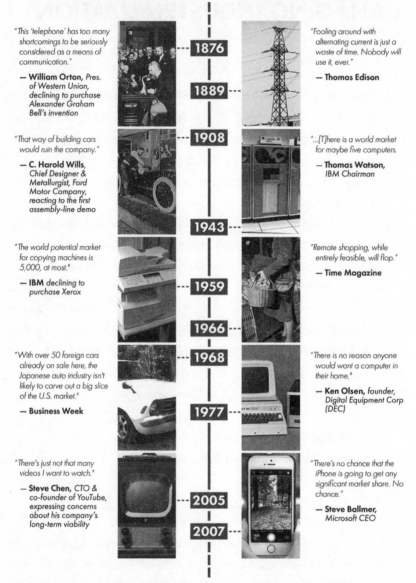

*"This 'telephone' has too many shortcomings to be seriously considered as a means of communication."*

— **William Orton,** Pres. of Western Union, declining to purchase Alexander Graham Bell's invention

**1876**

*"Fooling around with alternating current is just a waste of time. Nobody will use it, ever."*

— **Thomas Edison**

**1889**

**1908**

*"That way of building cars would ruin the company."*

— **C. Harold Wills,** Chief Designer & Metallurgist, Ford Motor Company, reacting to the first assembly-line demo

*"...[T]here is a world market for maybe five computers.*

— **Thomas Watson,** IBM Chairman

**1943**

*"The world potential market for copying machines is 5,000, at most."*

— **IBM** declining to purchase Xerox

**1959**

*"Remote shopping, while entirely feasible, will flop."*

— **Time Magazine**

**1966**

**1968**

*"With over 50 foreign cars already on sale here, the Japanese auto industry isn't likely to carve out a big slice of the U.S. market."*

— **Business Week**

*"There is no reason anyone would want a computer in their home."*

— **Ken Olsen,** founder, Digital Equipment Corp (DEC)

**1977**

*"There's just not that many videos I want to watch."*

— **Steve Chen,** CTO & co-founder of YouTube, expressing concerns about his company's long-term viability

**2005**

*"There's no chance that the iPhone is going to get any significant market share. No chance."*

— **Steve Ballmer,** Microsoft CEO

**2007**

**FIGURE 12-1** In retrospect, these business ideas are no-brainers. At the time, however, even the most savvy executives dismissed these "insanely great business ideas" as impractical.

All images from Wikimedia Commons, public domain.

And it will be similarly, overconfidently dismissed—by both your competitors and, initially, people in your own organization.

This chapter therefore provides useful, time-tested techniques to overcome these dismissals. Compared with conventional management methods, these techniques will be more preemptive and proactive. They describe how to avoid, rather than remediate, these implementation management issues. Adopting these methods will initially feel as counterintuitive as mastering the perceptual biases covered in the earlier chapters. But the conceptual discomfort will pay off.

## Crossing the Void: Three Strategic Milestones

Implementing a KWF requires changing the *organization's* conventional, intuitively biased perception—crossing the void. Here, a successful journey is not described by a direct, obvious route. It requires navigating around the hazards (the sea monsters) of perceptual bias.

Think of a video game. The route will be similarly counterintuitive, circuitous, and rife with restarts. Impatient, first-time voyagers are usually eager to save time and get results quickly. Intuition, along with the misapplication of the principle of least effort, will send them powering through their organizations with a conventional, head-on, bluntly rational approach. They are playing to win, using a conventional strategy.

And how do these go-getters fare? They could save even *more* time by fast-forwarding directly to the dismissals list above—and adding their own names as losers.

Therefore, go in the *other* direction. In the void, you win by *playing not to lose*. Yes, this violates every cheesy motivational poster (see Figure 12-2). Manage everything counterintuitively. For example, to accelerate progress, don't push harder. Instead, work on reducing the organization's objections and delays—just as Columbus first cajoled his crew across the Atlantic.

**FIGURE 12-2** Despite all the motivational posters, you can best succeed with your knowledge work factory (KWF) implementation effort by *playing not to lose.*

Image source: Shutterstock.

This chapter outlines a counterintuitive, void-crossing strategy for your KWF initiative that targets three milestones:

1. **Avoid dismissals.** First, it begins by *managing the organization's dismissal biases*—anxieties—when the initiative is launched. *A forewarning:* Don't expect these biased-based challenges to ever recede entirely.
2. **Reconcile perceptions.** Next, and most importantly, it *reconciles organizational perceptions.* It achieves the formidable task of resolving everyone's individual, diverse, biased, and passionately held perceptions of operations. This is surprisingly simpler than it sounds.
3. **Preempt objections.** And finally, it *anticipates the most common objections* that organizations routinely employ to neutralize change and shows how to navigate past them.

The most effective KWF management approach addresses these three milestones in the sequence in which they appear, just like in any journey.

## First: Avoid Dismissals—or the Frog-and-Camel Strategy

Look back at the list of insanely great dismissals in Figure 12-1. All the ideas therein eventually succeeded wildly. Of course, that's the only reason that the list is stunning and satisfying. But these ideas have something else in common: *They all represent untested, disruptive products and services. Each is a revolution;* these are decidedly *not* transfers of proven, existing technology and time-tested methods to new applications inside an existing business.

Now think of the decision makers/"dismissers" on that list. None of them could have looked elsewhere for a working precedent for success or failure. Each decision on that list was a gamble at the time: a coin-toss that offered success or failure. Each proposal generated unprecedented risk for the business. This characteristic of "unprecedented risk" is important because dismissers will invariably portray KWF industrialization initiatives as if they resemble the untested, high-risk investments on the list.

But that's flat-out wrong. Such a comparison implies a false equivalency. Industrialization is *not* a speculative new technology like the telephone, the photocopier, or the iPhone. The executive sponsoring a KWF initiative is *not* faced with an all-or-nothing decision that depends on successfully predicting technology feasibility or the size of future markets (e.g., the robotics–automobile-chassis decision in Chapter 10). Industrialization is instead a low-risk methodology that has drastically improved productivity and enabled automation, century after century. It's a time-tested "product" that already works. Compared with the risks inherent in the dismissals listed above, industrialization enjoys three advantages:

1. **No new-market-development risk.** A sponsoring executive already has the captive demand within the organization to make this "product" extremely profitable.
2. **Minimal adoption and start-up risk.** Industrialization can be adopted and tested incrementally, adjusting the scope and pace as implementation proceeds.

3. **No technology risk.** Standardization, specialization, and division of labor require no new technology for 70 percent of the improvement opportunities available in knowledge work.

(Surprisingly, a KWF initiative turns out to be a highly effective way to mitigate the significant, unperceived risks inherent in knowledge work assets: loss and underproductivity. More about this in the discussion of the second milestone, below.)

The industrialization examples in this book will help to deflect—or, the hope is, convince—naysayers. You can point out the anti-standardization bias that has existed for centuries—even at the birth of Ford's first assembly line. Recall that the dismissals list above includes C. H. Wills's overconfident prediction, upon witnessing the first demonstration of the Ford assembly-line concept in 1908: "That way of building cars would ruin the company." Fast-forward just 13 years later, to 1921. In that year, Wills's own car company produced the Wills Sainte Claire, legendary for its high standards of quality and durability. That's when the first auto rolled off Wills's very own—you guessed it—assembly line.

But this isn't about proving people wrong—Pyrrhic victories. The first objective of an effective nondismissal strategy is *not* organizational acceptance of the KWF idea. That's just too much for an organization to absorb. It will simply elicit waves of passionately expressed, overconfident dismissals. And once people go on the record with overconfident positions, they are loath to retract them.

*The first goal of the nondismissal plan,* then, *is to hold this counterproductive organizational overconfidence at bay.* Buy time to let the frog-and-camel strategy do its incremental work of building credibility (see Figure 12-3).

Frog-and-camel strategy? Let me explain.

How do you boil a frog? Put him in tepid water and raise the temperature gradually; he won't notice the change. And if a camel is allowed to get his nose in your tent, his body will slowly follow. These parables are intended to convey the power of incrementalism—the most effective way

**FIGURE 12-3** You can implement your own KWF with an incremental approach. Think of two common adages:

1. You can boil a frog by slowly raising the temperature of the water.
2. Once the camel's nose is under the tent, his body will slowly follow.

Image sources: Wikimedia Commons, public domain images posted by the Biodiversity Heritage Library.

---

to overcome organizational dismissal. It's the same strategy employed by Cast Iron Charlie after his disappointing 1908 demo at the Ford plant. He went to work achieving and delivering inarguable and stunning improvement gains . . . step by step. He began with small operations that involved 10 to 20 employees.

As vague as this frog-and-camel strategy may sound, it involves rock-solid, tactical implications. For example, use communications that position the KWF effort as a beta test from a new idea incubator. Frame the early efforts as fact-gathering and documentation exercises—because that's exactly what they are.

Next, keep the scope of pilot tests small. Employ a lather-rinse-repeat approach. Avoid a big-bang implementation. The goal is to preempt as much on-the-record, early rejection as possible. Try to maintain a state of delayed judgment, a temporary moratorium on rejection throughout the organization. This will buy time for the initiative to succeed decisively with a pilot test or two. The goal is to demonstrate undeniable success and put the brain's hindsight bias to work in a positive fashion. You'll know this strategy is working when you begin to hear, "I always knew it would work."

Success has many fathers.

## Second: Reconcile Perceptions—the Map Fair

Here's the biggest management challenge confronting KWF efforts: *everyone is right*. And most of their perceptions are correct, at least partially. This fact seems mind-boggling, because it is.

But there is an easy way to understand how these disparate views are created—and a simple method for reconciling them.

All employees and managers effectively conduct their own informal Gemba walks every day. They don't use that name, but they personally observe the work *where it is happening*. That is the very definition of the Japanese term "Gemba." It translates as "the actual place."[1] Based on their Gemba walks, the employees each casually maintain an informal, undocumented, and biased database of work activities—in their memory. These are intangible assets known as "competencies." (Remember these from Chapter 2?) These incredibly important and valuable assets are stored, organization-wide in the collective memory of employees, as tribal knowledge. That's irresponsible and risky. It's also extraordinarily inefficient. And all of this is ordinarily overlooked.

But while each employee's perceptions are *right*, they are also *incomplete*. Think about that. People view organizations and operating processes through the keyhole of their own perception, as well as from their own vantage point. And together, these incomplete perceptions create conflicting, biased beliefs that employees defend with rock-jawed certainty. And why shouldn't they? After all, they have personally observed these activities. They know what they see. They know what they know.

Thus, each person's memory of operations represents only part of a giant, partially assembled, undocumented jigsaw puzzle of perceived work activities (2 to 15 minutes each, as defined in Chapter 10). Of course, these puzzle pieces don't mesh perfectly. The individual perceptions of employees are not completely reconciled. And so, people disagree about what exactly happens in operations. Sure, that means that your KWF initiative will be bogged down. But it's a much more costly, day-to-day problem for the business overall.

The operational details of know-how (i.e., competencies) represent the strategic high ground for owning and managing intangible assets. And yet the business is not in direct possession of this critical operational detail. Instead, possession of this high ground has been casually delegated to individual employees. In turn, they casually maintain these assets as undocumented, collective, tribal knowledge. Consequently, these assets can only be casually managed and secured—by employees or management.

So what do you do? Implementing a KWF initiative helps solve the problem of documenting and managing competencies. It mitigates the risks of asset loss and the costs of underproductivity. (Point this out to the dismissers who argue that a KWF initiative poses an unacceptable "new" risk to the existing operations.)

Risk mitigation aside, the immediate challenge is to *get the KWF effort, or any improvement, moving.* Yet the organization's disparate Gemba perceptions have everything gridlocked. Here's how this chicken-and-egg dilemma unfolds: Whenever someone proposes an improvement, employees spring forth to describe their own Gemba perceptions. That's when the unreconciled operational details gush forth. The jigsaw puzzle pieces of operations details don't fit together. No one has the complete, reconciled map of the as-is operations. Nothing is inarguable. Debates and disagreements about improvement follow. And since it's almost impossible to sort out, a standoff ensues.

How, then, do you break this stalemate? Three steps:

1. **Document** these valuable, activity-level assets to secure ownership for the business.
2. **Reconcile** the organization's disparate Gemba perceptions of as-is operations to the point of inarguability.
3. **Maintain** these assets in a highly manageable form that ensures continual reconciliation.

Codifying business process maps (Chapter 9) solves this documentation problem. And the Activity Cube capacity model (Chapter 11) provides ongoing, fully reconciled maintenance and management capabilities. But first, we need to reconcile everyone's perceptions. One simple management trick can quickly and unambiguously accomplish this goal: it's called the "Process Map Fair" (see Figure 12-4).

**FIGURE 12-4**  A Process Map Fair gives employees the opportunity to review and validate the graphical depictions of business processes. This establishes an unambiguous, common understanding of the work performed in the organization.

Image source: Lab Consulting Partnership, Inc.

Here's how to do it:

Simply post the business process maps in a meeting room or auditorium for a day. Invite everyone in the relevant organizations to stop by and review the detail on the maps. Have sticky notes available. Let people mark directly on the maps, too. The goal is to get an accurate representation of the work as it is performed in "the actual place." The maps effectively become the reconciled, activity-level-detailed, formal documentation of the employees' Gemba walks. Repeat the process as needed over the course of a couple of days, until employees cease to argue or dispute the details.

This map fair accomplishes several critical objectives:

- Achieve an *unambiguous definition* of the current-state operations.
- *Reconcile everything*: employee perceptions, operational detail, and definitions.

- Reclaim ownership of the company's *competencies*.
- Provide a *fact base* to propel and navigate the KWF initiative across the void.

After avoiding dismissal of your KWF initiative, and reconciling disparate perceptions into an inarguable fact base, only one milestone remains.

## Third: Preempt Objections—or How to Navigate the Predictable

Organizational resistance is one of executives' biggest fears as they embark on a KWF initiative. It's a legitimate concern, but it usually manifests itself in an unexpected way. Employees don't simply say, "No, I won't do that." Instead, they raise a predictable array of reasonable-sounding, ostensibly earnest concerns. These provide politically acceptable, and often familiar, forms of passive resistance:

- They delay.
- They insist on additional, more detailed analysis.
- They request excessive pilot testing.
- They make numerous changes that blunt the effectiveness of the improvements.
- They negotiate (downward) the estimates of improvement benefits.

In sum, it's a battle of attrition. Ideally—for those protesting—the KWF will recede into the background, joining the scrap heap of previous failed initiatives.

An experienced executive will undoubtedly find all of these passive-resistance maneuvers familiar. But what's different this time is the inarguable, activity-level fact base created from the business process maps, the Activity Cube, and the Map Fair. This means that a more buttoned-down approach to the KWF initiative is possible. As sponsor, you can set expectations (both yours and your organization's) and take steps to preempt many of the organizational misperceptions and maneuvers that will impede progress. Design the program to include the following characteristics, which will help to overcome or simply avoid the vast majority of the organization's concerns:

- **Phased approach.** Separating the initial, fact-gathering phase from subsequent implementation phases is most effective (see Figure 12-5). This enables the development of the indisputable fact base—and helps preempt the requests for false precision—details that lead to analysis paralysis. Subsequent phases should begin implementation immediately upon completion of the Phase I analysis.

## Two-Phased Approach

| Phase I: Analysis and Design Objectives | Phase II: Implementation Objectives |
|---|---|
| *Document operations and improvements; develop an implementation work plan* | *Implement improvements and document ongoing performance* |
| **Duration: 6 to 10 Weeks** | **Duration: 6 to 8 Months** |
| • Document/reconcile operations<br>• Draft an implementation work plan<br>• Develop an improvement business case | • Launch immediate action improvements<br>• Install nontechnology improvements<br>• Optimize future-state operations |

**FIGURE 12-5** A two-phased approach to KWF initiatives begins with a fact-gathering phase to develop an indisputable view of operations. A six- to eight-month Phase II implementation should begin immediately after the six- to ten-week Phase I.

- **Time (i.e., speed) guidelines.** The entire Phase I analysis can be completed in just six to ten weeks. That's right; that's all it should take. At that point, any additional analysis will simply deliver diminishing returns. Regardless of the size of the organization in scope, the KWF initiative must move quickly. Subsequent implementation should not take longer than six to eight months. The longer the initiative, the less successful.
- **Scope.** Select target organizations first; then map the processes within them. Make certain that 80 to 90 percent of the human work activities are documented at the activity level of detail. Expect—and largely

ignore—the following objections that typically arise from long-held, intuitive misperceptions during scope discussions.

*Objection.* "All our errors and problems originate upstream in processes and organizations that are out of our control."

*Fact.* This is never true. Only about 15 to 30 percent of inbound work arrives not-in-good-order (NIGO). And often a majority of this NIGO is self-inflicted by the recipients, e.g., a lack of instructions for the senders of NIGO.

*Objection.* "Regulations prevent us from changing operations."

*Fact.* At least 70 percent (and often 100 percent) of KWF improvements involve no regulatory activities.

*Objection.* "We have different systems. We have to key data from one to the next."

*Fact.* These represent ideal nontechnology industrialization opportunities. After standardization, these are perfect candidates for robotic process automation.

- **Announcement.** It's essential that the Phase I initiative be announced via a memo or e-mail. This should be issued by the executive sponsor of the initiative—the person to whom the employees within the scope of the effort report. It's impossible to make progress otherwise. For example, you cannot sponsor an initiative in your colleague's organization, no matter how much you may want to.

The memo is critical (see Figure 12-6 for an example). It should address six major questions that the organization will likely ask:

1. **Source.** Who is sending this message? This requires no further explanation.
2. **Rationale.** Why are we doing this?
   *Sample verbiage:* "We constantly strive to improve the performance of our company's operating processes and related organizations."

**The Knowledge Work Factory (KWF)
Initiative Announcement Memo**

We constantly strive to improve the performance of
our company's operating processes and related
organizations. Consequently, our internal
improvement team has launched an effort to identify
process improvements and best practices.

Over the next few weeks, team members will meet
with many of you to discuss the sources and scope of
improvement opportunities. I strongly encourage
your complete openness and candor.

I want to thank all employees in advance for their
help and valuable input on this important initiative.
We will keep you informed about the progress
of the initiative.

**FIGURE 12-6**   KWF initiatives should be launched with an announcement
memo to briefly explain the objectives and set expectations.

3. **Objectives.** What do we hope to accomplish?
   *Sample verbiage:* "Consequently, our internal improvement team
   has launched an effort to identify process improvements and best
   practices."
4. **Approach.** How will we conduct this assessment?
   *Sample verbiage:* "Over the next few weeks, team members will meet
   with many of you to discuss the sources and scope of improvement
   opportunities."
5. **The recipient's role, i.e., "What do you need from me?"** Here,
   the memo will address a predictable employee question and preempt
   employee concerns.

*Sample verbiage:* "I strongly encourage your complete openness and candor. I want to thank all employees in advance for their help and valuable input on this important initiative."

6. **Communication.** How will you (the reader) learn more?
   *Sample verbiage:* "We will continue to keep you informed about the progress of the initiative."

## Avoid the Demons of the Deep

As you cross the void, be on the lookout for the following traps and "sea monsters." Avoid and neutralize them as necessary.

- **Consensus.** Avoid this term and approach. Nothing valuable will come from it. It didn't work for Columbus or Ford, and it won't work for a KWF initiative. This is not to recommend the tyrannical approach—or suggest that it works. Instead, find the middle ground. *But remember:* The project sponsor always, ultimately, calls the shots and sets the course.

- **Change management.** Another term to avoid. "Change management" implies that analysis and improvement design will be separate from implementation. In other words, it suggests that improvement decisions and design will occur in a "back room" and will be trotted out and forced down the throats of frontline "experts"—those closest to the work. It's far easier to work everything out in the open—just like the Process Map Fair. Build change management into the daily activities of the KWF and lose the term.

- **False trade-offs.** These are familiar, widely accepted misperceptions of decision options that oversimplify and devalue decision making. They oversimplify the thinking required for difficult, fact-based decisions by replacing them with easier, belief-based judgment calls. False trade-offs implicitly assume that listeners tacitly agree with the speaker's framing of an "either-or" relationship between only two possible choices. These choices typically involve zero-sum logic, with gains in one choice coming at the expense of losses in the other. Typically, these are clumsy attempts to reframe decisions in an obvious, no-brainer "good-versus-bad" context and bias the outcome. Common examples include:

1. Operational versus strategic
2. Near term versus long term
3. Cost improvement versus service improvement
4. Efficient versus effective
5. Cost reduction (save) versus revenue increase (grow)
6. . . . and many others

Just think of Laura, from Chapter 8, who insisted (wrongly) to Nick Clearsight that he could only have speed "or" overpayment of claims.

- **The false ceiling of benefits targets.** Knowledge workers will often object to the total estimated benefits of KWF improvements. They'll feel acutely uncomfortable with quantification—to the point that they might perceive that falling even $1 short of a quantified goal will be perceived as a failure. Consequently, they'll attempt to negotiate a "ceiling" on the benefits estimate. Sponsors might hear the executive responsible for the organization say such things as, "I don't agree that there's a $10 million savings opportunity in my organization. However, I'm willing to agree to half that amount."

Think about the absurdity of the underlying illogic of this statement—and its implications for the business. Is this not simply another *partial dismissal* of a valuable business idea? Just a smaller-scale version of the IGBIDs listed at the beginning of the chapter? Put another way, why wouldn't everyone attempt to deliver the *maximum* improvement for the business? Why does this executive perceive that he or she "owns" the decision rights for establishing a benefits ceiling? In reality, either the executive wants to implement less improvement than is available, or the plan is to underpromise and overdeliver. This seems like a lose-lose proposition for the business.

It would be almost impossible to find similar thinking among executives and managers in a conventional manufacturing plant. For example, they might have an aspirational goal of zero defects for a particular part produced. This goal may represent a ceiling that is impossible to achieve. However, they will continually pursue improvement after improvement to relentlessly narrow the gap, often surprising themselves with their progress.

As an improvement sponsor of a KWF initiative, you can take a similar continuous approach. The goals, however, must be reoriented. Here's how this can easily be accomplished, using the first example of $10 million in benefits: When a manager proposes a "ceiling" of $5 million, convert that agreed-upon figure to a "floor." Something like this: "Well then, we both agree that there is at least a $5 million benefit available over the period discussed. Let's make that a minimum, a 'floor.' And then let's see how well your team can do toward exceeding it. Maybe you can even blow past the $10 million goal! There shouldn't be any benefits 'ceiling' here."

- **Too much change.** The simple response to this pushback is, "Why? Compared with what? How do you know? Any facts?"
- **Now is not the right time.** Laugh this off. When is it ever the right time? Why would you ever want to delay improvement? Of course, now is the right time.

## Time to Begin Your Journey

By this point—here, at the end of the book—you are armed. You know that knowledge work waste is hiding. You know it's hiding in plain sight, but you also know where and how to look for it. It's not just an abstract concept anymore.

We've covered how to build a KWF. How to gauge its capacity and catalog its products. Drawing inspiration from historical figures like Adam Smith and Cast Iron Charlie Sorensen, and even our fictional superhero Nick Clearsight, we've examined the vital separation between the *manage-*

*ment* of knowledge work and the *performance* thereof. We've reviewed org charts, taxonomies, and BOMs, and explored the power of these proven tools and how they apply to knowledge work—just as they do to manufacturing. We've uncovered the secrets of the process map, the Map Fair, and the Activity Cube.

You're now ready to put your newfound skills to work. You can set sail, like Columbus, even amid the doubts and pushback of the crew. Unlike Columbus, however, you know exactly where you're going. The rewards are rich, and they're yours for the taking.

## CHAPTER 12: **TAKEAWAYS**

1. Implementing a KWF requires changing the organization's conventional, intuitively biased perception. Plan a strategy well suited for initial dismissal and persistent skepticism of the notion.

2. A successful implementation management strategy can use counter-intuitive methods to most effectively achieve three major milestones:

   • Avoid dismissals—Playing "not to lose" is the best way to navigate around the inherent dismissal bias typical of most organizations and achieve success incrementally.

   • Reconcile perceptions—Diverse, passionately held perceptions of existing operations can be reconciled promptly and efficiently with a simultaneous group review of highly detailed current-state maps, i.e., the Process Map Fair.

   • Preempt objections—Almost all organizational objections are highly predictable and can be preemptively minimized with simple tools and techniques.

3. The most costly management mistake is agreeing to a "false ceiling" of benefits targets. Instead, agree to a "minimum floor" for benefits and leave the upside potential unconstrained.

# ENDNOTES

## Chapter 1

1. Rani Molla, "In Just Five Years, Facebook, Apple, Amazon, Netflix and Google Have Doubled Their Effect on the S&P 500," Recode.net, accessed March 30, 2018, https://www.recode.net/2018/3/30/17180932/facebook-apple-amazon-netflix-google-doubled-sp500-index.
2. This figure, based on The Lab's experience, analysis, and benchmarks, excludes service workers (e.g., food, retail, transportation, hospitality).
3. Ibid.
4. Ibid.
5. Based on $60,000 annual compensation and benefits per knowledge worker.
6. "Fortune 500 List," Fortune.com, accessed July 8, 2018, http://fortune.com/fortune500/.
7. Based on a Fortune 500 price-to-earnings ratio of 16.
8. "Knowledge Worker," Wikipedia, last modified April 14, 2018, https://en.wikipedia.org/wiki/Knowledge_worker.

## Chapter 2

1. Richard Brealey, Stewart Myers, and Franklin Allen, *Principles of Corporate Finance*, 12th ed. (New York: McGraw-Hill/Irwin, 2017).
2. For the dollar value of intangible assets among U.S. publicly traded companies, see Kevin Hassett and Robert Shapiro, "What Ideas Are Worth: The Value of Intellectual Capital and Intangible Assets in the American Economy" (Sonecon, White Paper, 2011), iv.
3. For the two types of competencies, see Carol Corrado, Jonathan Haskel, Cecilia Jona-Lasinio, and Massimiliano Iommi, "Intangible Capital in Advanced Economies: Measurement Methods and Comparative Results" (Institute for the Study of Labor, Discussion Paper No. 6733, July 2012), 13. These data are confirmed by The Lab's experience and analysis.
4. Peter Drucker, "The New Productivity Challenge," *Harvard Business Review* (November–December 1991), accessed January 26, 2018, https://hbr.org/1991/11/the-new-productivity-challenge.
5. For the common perception that knowledge workers "solve non-routine problems . . . that require creative thinking," see Wolfgang Reinhardt,

Benedikt Schmidt, Peter Sloep, and Hendrik Drachsler, "Knowledge Worker Roles and Actions—Results of Two Empirical Studies," *Knowledge and Process Management*, Vol. 18, No. 3 (July/September 2011), 150.

6. For the two-thirds of knowledge work that is similar and repetitive, see Ian Brinkley, Rebecca Fauth, Michelle Mahdon, and Sotiria Theodoropoulou, "Knowledge Workers and Knowledge Work" (The Work Foundation, June 2009), 52. This is confirmed by The Lab's database of work activities and analysis.

## Chapter 3

1. Think of this as roughly the equivalent of the modern-day gross domestic product.

2. Nicholas Crafts, "Productivity Growth in the Industrial Revolution: A New Growth Accounting Perspective," *Journal of Economic History*, Vol. 64, No. 2 (June 2004): 522.

3. Robert Gordon, *The Rise and Fall of American Growth: The U.S. Standard of Living Since the Civil War* (Princeton, NJ, and Oxford: Princeton University Press, 2016), 16.

4. William Easterly and Ross Levine, "It's Not Factor Accumulation: Stylized Facts and Growth Models," *World Bank Economic Review*, Vol. 15, No. 2 (2001): 185.

5. Robert Solow, "We'd Better Watch Out," *New York Times*, July 22, 1987.

6. Gordon, 16 (for the 1960s); 575 (for the 1990s).

7. Thomas Haigh, "Technology, Information and Power: Managerial Technicians in Corporate America, 1917–2000" (PhD diss., University of Pennsylvania, 2003), 75.

8. Ibid., 78.

9. Crafts, 531–532.

10. Chad Syverson, "Will History Repeat Itself? Comments on 'Is the Information Technology Revolution Over?'" *International Productivity Monitor*, No. 25 (2013): 37–40.

11. Alan Blinder, "The Mystery of Declining Productivity Growth," *Wall Street Journal*, May 14, 2015, accessed January 1, 2018, https://www.wsj.com/articles/the-mystery-of-declining-productivity-growth-1431645038.

12. Mark Raskino and Jorge Lopez, "CEO and Senior Executive Survey 2013: As Uncertainty Recedes, the Digital Future Emerges" (Gartner, 2013), 23.

13. Ola Svenson, "Are We All Less Risky and More Skillful Than Our Fellow Drivers?" *Acta Psychologica*, Vol. 47, No. 2 (1981): 143–148.

14. Erik Brynjolfsson and Andrew McAfee, *The Second Machine Age: Work, Progress, and Prosperity in a Time of Brilliant Technologies* (New York:

W. W. Norton & Company, Inc., 2014), 7. Erik Brynjolfsson and Andrew McAfee used a graph developed by Ian Morris in *Why the West Rules— for Now: The Patterns of History, and What They Reveal About the Future* (New York: Farrar, Straus, and Giroux, 2010), 73.

15. Brynjolfsson and McAfee, 5.
16. Scott Plous, *The Psychology of Judgment and Decision Making* (New York: McGraw-Hill, 1993), 233.
17. David Anthony, *The Horse, the Wheel, and Language: How Bronze-Age Riders from the Eurasian Steppes Shaped the Modern World* (Princeton, NJ: Princeton University Press, 2007), 67.
18. David Hounshell, *From the American System to Mass Production, 1800–1932* (Baltimore: Johns Hopkins University Press, 1984), 272.
19. Ibid., 241.
20. Richard Donkin, *The History of Work* (New York: Palgrave, 2010), 2.
21. Ibid., 5.
22. Ibid., 1.
23. Ibid., 7.
24. Walter Isaacson, *Leonardo Da Vinci* (New York: Simon & Schuster, 2017), 193.
25. Adam Smith, *An Inquiry into the Nature and Causes of the Wealth of Nations* (1776), accessed January 11, 2011, http://geolib.com/smith. adam/won1-01.html.
26. Gordon, 561–562.
27. Ibid., 549.
28. Vincent Curcio, *Chrysler: The Life and Times of an Automotive Genius* (Oxford: Oxford University Press, 2000), 206.
29. Richard Langlois, "Cognitive Comparative Advantage and the Organization of Work: Lessons from Herbert Simon's Vision of the Future," University of Connecticut Economics Working Papers, Paper 200220 (2002), 5.
30. Andrew Lee, "The U.S. Armory at Harpers Ferry: Historic Resource Study" (Harpers Ferry National Historical Park Archeology Program, 2006), 43.
31. Charles Babbage, *On the Economy of Machinery and Manufactures* (London: Charles Knight, 1832), 162.

## Chapter 4

1. Ezra Zuckerman and John Jost, "What Makes You Think You're So Popular? Self-Evaluation Maintenance and the Subjective Side of the 'Friendship Paradox,'" *Social Psychology Quarterly*, Vol. 64, No. 3 (2001), 208.

2. K. Patricia Cross, "Not Can But Will College Teachers Be Improved?," *New Directions for Higher Education*, 17 (Spring 1977): 1–15.
3. Mark Alicke and Olesya Govorun, "The Better-Than-Average Effect," in Mark Alicke, David Dunning, and Joachim I. Krueger, eds., *The Self in Social Judgment* (New York: Psychology Press, 2005): 85–106.
4. Ibid.
5. Ibid.
6. Emily Pronin, Daniel Lin, and Lee Ross, "The Bias Blind Spot: Perceptions of Bias in Self Versus Others," *Personality and Social Psychology Bulletin*, Vol. 28, No. 3 (2002), 317.
7. George Kingsley Zipf, *Human Behaviour and the Principle of Least Effort: An Introduction to Human Ecology* (New York: Addison-Wesley Publishing, 1949), 1.
8. Ibid.
9. Ibid.
10. Christopher Chabris and Daniel Simons, *The Invisible Gorilla and Other Ways Our Intuitions Deceive Us* (New York: Crown Publishers, 2010), 7.
11. Ibid., 7, note 10.
12. Pronin, Lin, and Ross, 369–381.
13. Daniel Kahneman, "We're Blind to Our Blindness. We Have Very Little Idea of How Little We Know. We're Not Designed To," Independent .co.uk, accessed November 24, 2017, http://www.independent.co.uk/arts -entertainment/books/features/were-blind-to-our-blindness-we-have -very-little-idea-of-how-little-we-know-were-not-designed-to-6267089 .html.
14. Kathryn Schulz, *Being Wrong: Adventures in the Margin of Error* (New York: HarperCollins Publishers, 2010), 82.

## Chapter 5

1. David Nye, *America's Assembly Line* (Cambridge, MA: MIT Press, 2013), 3.
2. Ted Friedman and Michael Smith, "Measuring the Business Value of Data Quality," Gartner (October 10, 2011), accessed March 20, 2018, https:// www.gartner.com/doc/1819214/measuring-business-value-data-quality.
3. "DTCC Data Quality Survey: Industry Report," DTCC (November 2013), accessed January 16, 2018, https://www.edmcouncil.org/downloads/ DTCC_DQ_Survey.pdf, 6.
4. Bert Hölldobler and Edward Wilson, *The Ants* (Cambridge, MA: Harvard University Press, 1990), 29.

## Chapter 6

1. William Goldman, *Adventures in the Screen Trade* (New York: Warner Books, 1989), 39.
2. Caitlin Rosenthal, "Big Data in the Age of the Telegraph," McKinsey & Company, accessed January 27, 2018, https://www.mckinsey.com/business-functions/organization/our-insights/big-data-in-the-age-of-the-telegraph.
3. Ibid.
4. Peter Drucker, *Management Challenges of the 21st Century* (New York: HarperBusiness, 1999), 142.
5. Claudia Schoonhoven and Mariann Jelinek, "Dynamic Tension in Innovative, High Technology Firms: Managing Rapid Technological Change Through Organizational Structure," in M. A. Von Glinow and S. A. Mohrman, eds., *Managing Complexity in High Technology Organizations* (New York: Oxford University Press, 1990), 90–118.
6. See the data for men's occupations in Theodore Caplow, Louis Hicks, and Ben Wattenberg, *The First Measured Century: An Illustrated Guide to Trends in America, 1900-2000* (Washington, D.C.: AEI Press, 2001), 25.
7. Willard Brinton, *Graphic Methods for Presenting Facts* (New York: The Engineering Magazine Company, 1919), 15.
8. David Nye, *America's Assembly Line* (Cambridge, MA: MIT Press, 2013), 37.
9. Carl Parsons, *Office Organization and Management* (Chicago: LaSalle Extension University, 1917), 2.
10. Ibid., 16.
11. Thomas Haigh, "Technology, Information and Power: Managerial Technicians in Corporate America, 1917–2000" (PhD diss., University of Pennsylvania, 2003), 59–60.
12. Stewart Clegg and James Russell Bailey, *International Encyclopedia of Organization Studies* (Los Angeles: Sage Publications, 2008), xliii.
13. Dwight Waldo, "Organization Theory: Revisiting the Elephant," *Public Administration Review*, Vol. 38, No. 6 (November/December 1978): 589–597.
14. Chris Argyris, *Overcoming Organizational Defenses: Facilitating Organizational Learning* (Wellesley, MA: Allyn and Bacon, 1990), 10.

## Chapter 7

1. George Plossl, "MRP Yesterday, Today and Tomorrow," *Production and Inventory Control*, Vol. 21, No. 3 (Q3/1980): 1–10.

2. Lynn Ellis, *Data on Advertising Department Records* (New York: A. W. Shaw Company, 1917), 10.
3. Ibid.

## Chapter 8

1. Daniel Raff, "Productivity Growth at Ford in the Coming of Mass Production: A Preliminary Analysis," *Business and Economic History*, Vol. 25, No. 1 (Fall 1996): 183.
2. Robert Gordon, *The Rise and Fall of American Growth* (Princeton, NJ: Princeton University Press, 2016), 16.
3. A postcard issued by the Ford Motor Company circa 1917 indicates that the company's automobile production for 1911 totaled 34,528 cars. In 1912 the number had increased to 78,440 cars.
4. David Nye, *America's Assembly Line* (Cambridge, MA: MIT Press, 2013), 250.
5. Raff, 183.
6. Frederick Taylor, *The Principles of Scientific Management* (New York: Harper & Brothers, 1915), 36.

## Chapter 9

1. "2015 Management and Organizational Practices Survey Responses," U.S. Census Bureau, Massachusetts Institute of Technology, National Bureau of Economic Research, and Stanford University (2016), Table 6.
2. Mark Raskino and Jorge Lopez, "CEO and Senior Executive Survey 2013: As Uncertainty Recedes, the Digital Future Emerges," Gartner (March 25, 2013), 23.
3. Taiichi Ohno, *Toyota Production System: Beyond Large-Scale Production* (New York: Productivity Press, 1988), 57.
4. Charles Sorensen, *My Forty Years with Ford* (Detroit, MI: Wayne State University Press, 2006), 116. (The 2006 edition is a reprint of Sorenson's original 1956 memoir.)
5. Ibid., 117.
6. Ibid., 118–119.
7. Ibid., 118.
8. Lindsay Brooke, *Ford Model T: The Car That Put the World on Wheels* (Minneapolis, MN: Motorbooks, 2008), 47.
9. Fred H. Colvin, "Building an Automobile Every 40 Seconds," *American Machinist*, Vol. 38, No. 19 (May 8, 1913): 757–762.
10. David Hounshell, *From the American System to Mass Production, 1800–1932* (Baltimore: Johns Hopkins University Press, 1984), 224.

11. Ibid.
12. "U.S. Automobile Production Figures," Wikipedia, accessed June 8, 2018, https://en.wikipedia.org/wiki/U.S._Automobile_Production_Figures.
13. Sorensen, 128.
14. Ibid., 131.
15. Superscript numbers in brackets are the footnotes that accompany the text in the Wikipedia entry and are included here for illustrative purposes only. "Business Process," Wikipedia, accessed June 8, 2018, https://en.wikipedia.org/wiki/Business_process.
16. "Manufacturing," Wikipedia, accessed June 8, 2018, https://en.wikipedia.org/wiki/Manufacturing.

## Chapter 10

1. "Steve Jobs: There's Sanity Returning," *BusinessWeek* (May 25, 1998), accessed May 4, 2018, https://www.bloomberg.com/news/articles/1998-05-25/steve-jobs-theres-sanity-returning.
2. *Oxford English Dictionary*, s.v. "Unique," https://en.oxforddictionaries.com/definition/unique.
3. Ibid., s.v. "Different," https://en.oxforddictionaries.com/definition/different.
4. Wolfgang Reinhardt, Benedikt Schmidt, Peter Sloep, and Hendrik Drachsler, "Knowledge Worker Roles and Actions—Results of Two Empirical Studies," *Knowledge and Process Management*, Vol. 18, No. 3 (July/September 2011): 150–174.
5. Charles Sorensen, *My Forty Years with Ford* (Detroit, MI: Wayne State University Press, 2006), 118. (The 2006 edition is a reprint of Sorenson's original 1956 memoir.)
6. Charles Walker and Robert Guest, *The Man on the Assembly Line* (Cambridge, MA: Harvard University Press, 1952), 2.
7. Ibid., 12.
8. David Nye, *America's Assembly Line* (Cambridge, MA: MIT Press, 2013), 23.
9. Ibid., 24.
10. Alexander Church, *The Proper Distribution of Expense Burden* (New York: The Engineering Magazine Co., 1916), 47–53.
11. Robert Kaplan and Steven Anderson, *Time-Driven Activity-Based Costing: A Simpler and More Powerful Path to Higher Profits* (Boston: Harvard Business School Press, 2007), 23.
12. Marc Brysbaert, Michael Stevens, Pawel Mandera, and Emmanuel Keuleers, "How Many Words Do We Know? Practical Estimates of Vocabulary Size Dependent on Word Definition, the Degree of Language

Input and the Participant's Age," *Frontiers in Psychology*, Vol. 7, Article 1116 (July 29, 2016): 1–11.

13. "How Many Words Are There in the English Language?" *Oxford English Dictionary* (online), accessed June 10, 2018, https://en.oxforddictionaries .com/explore/how-many-words-are-there-in-the-english-language/.

14. Sigfried Giedion, *Mechanization Takes Command: A Contribution to Anonymous History* (New York: Oxford University Press, 1948), 118–120.

15. "1920s," *Automotive News*, accessed June 10, 2018, http://www.autonews .com/article/20000828/ANA/8280853/1920s.

16. "Remembering an Era, 1921–1958: 10,000 Automobile Frames a Day" (Milwaukee, WI: A. O. Smith Corporation, 1979): 1–12.

17. Based on The Lab's experience and analysis.

## Chapter 11

1. Carlos Quiles, "How Many Words Do We Use in Daily Speech? A New Study from the Royal Spanish Academy on Language Acquisition," *Indo-European* (November 21, 2008), accessed July 8, 2018, https://indo -european.eu/2008/11/how-many-words-we-use-in-daily-speech-a-new -study-from-the-royal-spanish-academy-on-language-acquisition/.

2. Li Yuan, "Why Made in China 2025 Will Succeed, Despite Trump," *New York Times*, July 4, 2018.

3. David Nye, *America's Assembly Line* (Cambridge, MA: MIT Press, 2013), 38.

4. Daniel Raff, "Productivity Growth at Ford in the Coming of Mass Production: A Preliminary Analysis," *Business and Economic History*, Vol. 25, No. 1 (Fall 1996), 178.

5. "U.S. Automobile Production Figures," Wikipedia, https://en.wikipedia .org/wiki/U.S._Automobile_Production_Figures, accessed, July 8, 2018.

6. Nye, 28.

7. Ibid., 250.

8. Ibid., 34.

9. Ibid., 250.

10. Michael A. Cusumano, "Manufacturing Innovation: Lessons from the Japanese Auto Industry," *MIT Sloan Management Review* (October 15, 1988), accessed July 8, 2018, https://sloanreview.mit.edu/article/ manufacturing-innovation-lessons-from-the-japanese-auto-industry/.

## Chapter 12

1. Masaaki Imai, *Gemba Kaizen: A Commonsense Low-Cost Approach to Management* (New York: McGraw-Hill Professional, 1997), 13.

# INDEX

Page numbers followed by *f* indicate figures; *t* indicate tables.

# ABOUT THE AUTHOR

**William Heitman** is the founder and managing director of The Lab Consulting, a management consulting firm headquartered in Houston, Texas, which has been implementing knowledge work standardization improvements for *Fortune* 500 clients since 1993.

In his 10-year management consulting career prior to creating The Lab, Bill was employed by CapGemini and a predecessor strategy consulting firm named The MAC Group. He has led strategy development and operations improvement efforts for senior management across major supply chain and services businesses. Earlier in his career, he worked in the engineering and construction management industry.

Bill holds an MBA from The Wharton School of the University of Pennsylvania and a BBA from Southern Methodist University.

His views have been published in *Forbes*, *Fast Company*, *Industry Week*, *CFO* magazine, *Journal of Private Equity*, *Strategic Finance*, and *CIO* magazine.